Understanding Pawn Play in Chess

Dražen Marović

First published in the UK by Gambit Publications Ltd 2000
Reprinted 2001

ISBN 1 901983 31 5

DISTRIBUTION:
Worldwide (except USA): Central Books Ltd, 99 Wallis Rd, London E9 5LN.
Tel +44 (0)20 8986 4854 Fax +44 (0)20 8533 5821.
E-mail: orders@Centralbooks.com
USA: BHB International, Inc., 41 Monroe Turnpike, Trumbull, CT 06611, USA.

For all other enquiries (including a full list of all Gambit Chess titles) please contact the publishers, Gambit Publications Ltd, P.O. Box 32640, London W14 0JN.
E-mail Murray@gambitchess.freeserve.co.uk
Or vi   e GAMBIT web site at http://www.gambitbooks.com

Edit   y Graham Burgess
Type: by John Nunn
Printe in Great Britain by The Bath Press, Bath, Somerset.

10 9 8 7 6 5 4 3 2

Gambit Publications Ltd
Managing Director: GM Murray Chandler
Chess Director: GM John Nunn
Editorial Director: FM Graham Burgess
German Editor: WFM Petra Nunn

Contents

Symbols

+	check
++	double check
#	checkmate
!!	brilliant move
!	good move
!?	interesting move
?!	dubious move
?	bad move
??	blunder
Ch	championship
1-0	the game ends in a win for White
½-½	the game ends in a draw
0-1	the game ends in a win for Black
(D)	see next diagram

Introduction

"[Pawns] are the very Life of this Game: They alone form the Attack and the Defence...". Many a contemporary chess enthusiast must have been amazed to read this solemn statement by Philidor, bestowing such honours on the modest pawns, of which Philidor's famous predecessors, Greco and the Italian chess school, thought so little. Philidor's small booklet was published in London in 1749 and is remembered under the title of its first edition – "L'analyze des échecs".

A long time was to pass before the ideas expressed by Philidor were understood properly, but the famous French musician and chess-player saw the role of pawns from an unconventional angle and much ahead of his time. Insisting on harmonious relations between pawns and pieces, Philidor cast new light on development and the centre.

Philidor practised what he preached: pawn-formations were well-known characteristics of his style. Contrary to the Italian school of thought, which enjoyed the play of the pieces, he understood those deeply-hidden relations between pawns and pieces that condition any serious plan on the board. Neither impressive nor elegant, yet above Greco's traps and false analyses, it was a style which, by elevating the standards of defence, announced that elaborate but unjustified attacks lose ground.

As a consequence, owing primarily to the significance of pawns, the game took on new traits – of balance and restraint – those same characteristics that the 18th century valued so much. All the underlying currents of intellectual and artistic life of the century in France were imbued by common sense and restraint. Looking back at the man, his play and his teachings, we can recognize the prevailing tendency of the times towards the clear and simple, the regular and harmonious.

Not many players followed in Philidor's footsteps. One must advance well into the next century to see another great player, Howard Staunton, exploring such niceties as the restrained engagement of pawns, play against doubled pawns or blockade. He broadened Philidor's views of pawn-formations, formulating ideas that Aron Nimzowitsch and Richard Réti were to extend over half a century later. Of course, Philidor's age had its shortcomings too. The philosophy of order and discipline had been developed since the end of the 17th century. It left a deep trace in fine arts and literature, but was essentially as non-dynamic as it was rational. On the chessboard, the period showed a tendency to reduce its interests to static positional values. It does not come as a surprise, therefore, that the period of chess romanticism that followed did not build on these premises.

The epoch of Adolf Anderssen and Paul Morphy nourished some other convictions. Putting it most concisely, theirs was an age marked by a strong movement from an intellectual to a new, emotional culture, in which the aim of art in general was not to teach but to excite, which preferred freedom to discipline, personal taste to stereotypes. The leading chess-players, sharing the spiritual climate, did not try to formulate a frame of general maxims in the good tradition of common sense like Philidor. They relied on their feeling, their intuition. A game of chess was primarily a fruit of personal taste, an individual creation. Since it was not conditioned by severe rules, the chess style of the period was free and dynamic. Chess combination as the symbol of the period was a matter of faith, of optimism, we could say of heart, certainly not of common sense. Pawns lost their meaning and importance in the construction of the game. It was no longer the pawns that shaped attack and defence. The centre often disintegrated, games became an open battle, with pawns cannon-fodder, and the rational build-up of central formations was gone.

It is not difficult to recognize in these traits the hidden relation between chess and other forms in which romanticism expressed itself when it rolled over Europe as an enormous wave. In chess it came with the usual delay, but it came with force and in complete harmony with general tendencies of the movement as they were expressed in literature, arts and above all in music, its most natural expression.

However, the end of the 19th century, not surprisingly, brought a new turn. In the foundations of the 19th century there was a stressed tendency to formulate systematically the mass of existing knowledge and thus to express general laws of development. It is not by chance that Wilhelm Steinitz belongs to that epoch. He came as a lawgiver and the core of his teaching was the law of balance. According to Steinitz, a game of chess runs equal until some blunder, or a series of small errors, disturbs the balance and tips the scale to one or the other side. This general law took the form of practical advice and various maxims. Steinitz insisted on the building of positions, and therefore on the elements on which positional advantages are built. Together with weak squares, open files, the bishop-pair, etc., etc., there was again talk of pawns. Pawns were resurrected. In order to keep the balance one had to fight for the centre, to occupy it, to share it. 1 d4 was met by 1...d5, the strong points in the centre were held as long as normal development was possible behind the central pawn-structure, which became significant. It was firm, symmetrical, sharing influence on the vital central squares. The Queen's Gambit and related systems became the fashion of the day and pawns got a new lease of life.

However, changes started to take place characterizing the play of a group of great players and theoreticians in the first decades of the 20th century. They called themselves 'hypermoderns' and revolted against the dominant dry and somewhat dogmatic style of Steinitz's followers. Aron Nimzowitsch and Richard Réti, the founders of the school, published masterworks of what may be called a chess revolution. The former wrote *My System*, and the latter *New Ideas in Chess*. Rising against rules and routine, the hypermoderns warned, "there are no general, constantly valid rules". "We are interested in exceptions, not rules", declares the motto of the movement. Looking behind the mass of notions and assertions expressed by Nimzowitsch, we find that the core of the new teaching lies in the new concept of the centre and pawn-structures. While classical chess insisted on pawn symmetry, the hypermoderns introduced the concept of control by pieces. The restricted engagement of pawns in the early phase of the game led to a number of new opening systems. Simultaneously, for the first time in the history of chess, all sorts of pawn-formations were studied in all the phases of the game. What we know today we owe in great part to Aron Nimzowitsch. In *My System* pawns lived their days of glory. The new teaching about the centre focused on them and their subtle interrelation with pieces.

However, ironically, Nimzowitsch's philosophy of the centre was the beginning of a marked process in the foundations of modern chess – the disintegration of classical pawn-structures and asymmetry of modern pawn-formations. Typically, and in harmony with general artistic and intellectual trends, the process became stronger towards the middle of the 20th century. After the Second World War, this tendency manifested itself in modern opening systems like the Sicilian and Benoni.

As a matter of fact, as early as the 1940s and 1950s, David Bronstein and Isaak Boleslavsky went further than Nimzowitsch, expressing the conviction that Black should neither seek symmetry in the centre nor try to control it. One should cede the centre, they proclaimed, finish basic development as soon as possible, and then try to fix and undermine the opponent's centre by side-blows.

The key was to fix the centre, which meant to provoke a blockade, and sap the centre of its dynamic potential. They relied on the simple, universal truth that whatever is fixed, immobile, has a tendency to grow weaker. It was exactly on these new propositions that new, modern opening systems were introduced, with the King's Indian Defence conspicuous among them.

So we reach the second part of the 20th century aware of the constant flow and change of two dominant trends, exploring in turn attacking and defensive possibilities. It is interesting in comparison that the history of art follows the same pattern. There is a constant repetition of the typical process from the severe to the free, from the simple to the complex, from the closed to the open, from the static to the dynamic.

In the constant change of chess vogue, of static and dynamic factors, I see the inner logic of chess development. Each of the epochs we analysed in passing bore the germ of the coming period, and each of them was dominated by one style, one understanding. In that sense, however, the 20th century was essentially different. Just like 20th century art, modern chess is characterized by a mixture of different styles. At the same time, in the same place, strong stylistic currents run side by side – a complex tapestry of ideas and attitudes.

The destiny of pawns in chess, their rise and fall, is interwoven into the patterns of change. The periods that discarded them were followed by those in which rational play was based on them. Our time has finally absorbed the experience of previous centuries, understood fully the pawns' intrinsic values and the varied roles they can play in a game of chess. Today we are aware indeed that they form the backbone of opening systems, that it really is the pawns that shape in a unique way attack and defence!

The intention of your author is to explore the nature of pawns and the basic forms in which they appear. My aim is not to dwell on every single aspect of different pawn-formations in innumerable examples of master practice, and so to tell the reader what to do in any single case. There are no rules that would fully define the complex life of a chess pawn, or offer secure, constantly valid advice. Besides, I am afraid that examining too many cases might just mystify things.

What I am trying to do is to reveal the changeable, ambiguous nature of pawns, always depending on the surroundings in which they are called upon to fulfil their duty. Understanding fully that relation will help us to choose the right path in our own games.

We shall learn from games remarkable for their clarity and simplicity of thought. First we shall analyse them, see how the pawns fare in the circumstances and then draw some valuable conclusions. I believe it is indispensable to analyse the phenomenon of pawn-structures, especially those in the centre, on the central files, on the basis of whole games, because only then is the whole process in front of us: we see how the structures are brought about and what becomes of them, and the causes behind the process. The result is inevitably rewarding: we can grasp the general lesson on the subject.

I attach great importance to general understanding. If well understood and stored in our mind, it will always help us to choose the right plan, even when we do not know concrete lines and theoretical novelties, and although we are not conscious of the mental processes behind our decisions. If we are able to formulate general plans relying on general knowledge, calculating concrete possibilities will be easier and more fruitful. We should never forget that only by understanding deeply the general laws which govern the game of chess can we attain that high level of skill and intuition which makes it possible to break the rules and see beyond them.

1 Isolated Pawns

It is proper to start our survey of central pawn-formations with isolated pawns, if for no other reason than because they are such a common feature in modern systems. We find them in a surprising number of important lines and amazingly different move-orders, from the Orthodox Queen's Gambit to the Caro-Kann, from the Queen's Gambit Accepted to the French Defence, from the English Opening to the Nimzo-Indian, from the Sicilian to the Tarrasch, etc., etc. However, in spite of the fact that the positions I mention are reached by various roads and hide some peculiarities, they remain intrinsically determined by the very existence and nature of the central isolated pawns. And that nature is so fickle that it has always represented a specific problem.

Our diagram is the most common case of an isolated pawn in the centre. Each time we are confronted with this type of position there is that latent, unavoidable question: do we have something to worry about or a hidden weapon of attack? I could remark from my own experience that we play such positions with a sense of unease, no matter which side we take. We learn early on in our chess practice what a menace they represent to the opponent, but also how vulnerable they are and what a small step separates a promising situation in the centre from a desperately passive one. The fact that the isolated pawn can move forward at any moment is in itself frightening. On the other side, having no companion on the neighbouring files, isolated pawns, like lonely people, are lonely creatures and therefore vulnerable.

In order to distinguish clearly whether we have an asset in the centre on which to build our play or a reason for an uncertain future, we must learn from the rich existing experience. I shall start our survey with a game that was a turning point in my own education. I had always felt an isolated pawn as an unpleasant burden; to me it was a regular source of anxiety, until one day I saw its other, hidden face in a game by Alexander Alekhine...

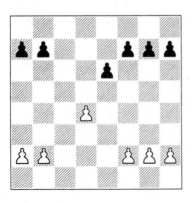

Euwe – Alekhine
World Ch match (game 25),
The Hague 1937
Nimzo-Indian Defence

1 d4 ♘f6 2 c4 e6 3 ♘c3 ♗b4 4 e3 0-0 5 ♘e2

In the Rubinstein Nimzo-Indian, the knight can be somewhat passive on e2, as it offers restricted possibilities. However, it has its positive side too: White looks after his pawn-structure, avoiding doubled pawns on the c-file.

5...d5 6 a3 ♗e7 7 cxd5 exd5 8 ♘g3 c5 9 dxc5 ♗xc5 10 b4 *(D)*

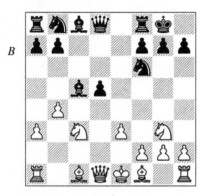

Having isolated Black's pawn in the centre, White's intention was to take full control of the d4-square, which would be possible after the withdrawal of the bishop. Analysing the game years ago, and I still remember it vividly, my reaction was the same: my hand was quicker than my mind and I grabbed the bishop to retreat it. A glance at the text surprised me as much as it must have surprised Dr Euwe during the game...

10...d4!

A splendid tactical blow! Now it is not difficult to conclude that 11 ♘ce4 does not work after 11...♘xe4 12 ♘xe4 ♗b6. If White had relied on 11 ♘a4?, then he had to face rude realities – 11...dxe3 12 ♕xd8? loses quickly to 12...exf2+ 13 ♔e2 ♗g4+. Therefore...

11 bxc5 dxc3 12 ♕c2?!

We witness here a metamorphosis quite common in similar situations: a central thrust has transformed an isolated pawn into a passed pawn, a pawn of higher quality, more mobile and consequently more dangerous. In our game White does not realize how vicious the pawn has become; otherwise he would have followed Alekhine's advice and played 12 ♕xd8 ♖xd8, and then 13 ♘e2 ♘e4 14 f3 ♘xc5 15 ♘xc3, although Black still maintains the advantage. In a more recent game, Agdamus-Ra.Garcia, Buenos Aires 1972, I found 13 a4 ♗d7 14 ♖a3 c2 15 ♗b5 a6, which was again good for Black. However, with the queens on the board it will be more difficult.

12...♕a5 13 ♖b1

In case of direct attack by 13 ♘e2 there is 13...♘d5 14 e4 ♘b4 15 ♕b1 ♘4a6.

13...♗d7

It is not so easy to capture the passed pawn as it may appear. Black threatens 14...♗a4, which can be usefully prevented neither by 14 ♗c4 ♗a4 15 ♗b3 ♗b5 nor by 14 ♖b4 because of 14...♘a6 15 ♗xa6 ♕xa6; in both cases White is prevented from castling. White tries to escape in another way...

14 Rb3 Ba4 15 Wxc3 Wd8

Since the rook cannot move due to mate on d1, an exchange is lost. So the mobility of the isolated pawn was transformed into a passed pawn, which was then transformed into a material advantage. It all happened after a series of tactical strokes, a common result of a breakthrough in the centre. What follows is just the usual technical problem.

16 Bc4 Na6

This is the strongest move. Black evaluates correctly that White's passed pawn on the c-file won't be dangerous and that realizing the material advantage will be easier without White's bishop.

17 Bxa6 bxa6 18 0-0 Bxb3 19 Wxb3 Rb8 20 Wc2 Wd5 21 e4 Wb3 22 We2 Wb5 23 Wf3 Wxc5 24 Nf5 Rb1 25 Wf4

If 25 Wg3, then 25...g6 26 Wg5 Nxe4 27 Ne7+ Kh8.

25...Nxe4 26 h4 Re8 27 Re1 Wc3 28 Rd1 Nd2

A clever move, disrupting the coordination of White's pieces in order to simplify the position.

29 Rxd2 Rxc1+ 30 Kh2 Wc7 31 Rd6 Rc5 32 g3

The last trap, if we can call it so, because after 32...Rxf5 the intended 33 Re6 is not enough in view of 33...fxe6 34 Wxc7 Rxf2+, etc. Alekhine, however, prefers to avoid it, leading his ship in this important game into calmer waters...

32...Rf8 33 g4 f6 34 Kh3 h5 35 Wd2 hxg4+ 36 Kxg4 Wf7 37 h5 Rxf5 38 Kxf5 Wxh5+ 39 Kf4 Wh4+ 40 Kf3

Wh3+ 41 Ke4 Re8+ 42 Kd5 Wb3+ 43 Kd4 Wxa3 0-1

Since I saw this game, each time I faced a position characterized by an isolated pawn in the centre, I asked myself the same question: can the pawn move forward or not? It is the basic, crucial question one should ask on every move.

The second lesson we learn from Alekhine's victory is as simple and important: a successful central thrust may promote isolated pawns into passed pawns, increasing in the process all sorts of tactical threats. The following games will confirm our first impressions...

Kasparov – Short
Brussels 1986
Queen's Gambit

1 d4 e6 2 Nf3 Nf6 3 c4 d5 4 Nc3 Be7 5 Bg5 h6 6 Bxf6 Bxf6 7 e3 0-0 8 Rc1 c6 9 Bd3

The continuation employed by White is a way to avoid the main lines of the Tartakower. White cedes the bishop-pair, but in a closed position in which black bishops can hardly play an important role.

9...Nd7 10 0-0 dxc4 11 Bxc4 e5

In Kasparov-Karpov, World Ch match (game 12), London 1986, Black played 11...c5, trying to open the position and awaken his bishops, but after 12 We2 a6 13 Rfd1 cxd4 14 Nxd4 he did not achieve his aim. The text-move was played with the same idea.

12 h3 exd4 13 exd4 Nb6 14 Bb3 Bf5 15 Re1 Bg5?! *(D)*

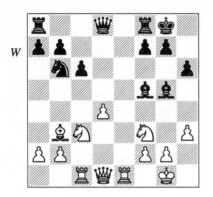

This was meant as an improvement, because the exchange on g5 simplifies the situation on the board. In two world championship games against Kasparov, Karpov defended by opposing his rook on the e-file, which after ♖xe8+ ♕xe8 made possible the manoeuvre ♕d2-f4, which gave White an initiative on the kingside. In both cases, however, note that Black's basic problems remain the same. White's light-squared bishop is a mighty piece on a diagonal on which Black has no means to oppose it. White is, consequently, stronger on the key square d5 and can advance his pawn at any moment. Our isolated pawn is very healthy indeed!

16 ♖a1!

It takes patience to choose this move! Let the queen stay on d8, while ♖e5 is threatened.

16...♘d7

A passive reaction, but sometimes there is no appealing option; at least now the e5-square is controlled. Unfortunately for Black, what was hanging in the air since the early phase of the game now comes by force...

17 d5

The right time to advance in the centre.

17...♖c8?

Since 17...cxd5 is obviously out of the question and 17...♘c5 would be met by 18 ♗c2 ♗xc2 19 ♕xc2 cxd5 20 ♖ad1 with advantage, Black, as often happens in such circumstances, takes the most perilous path.

18 ♘d4 ♗g6 19 ♘e6!

One of the tactical motifs arising after the pawn-thrust is the penetration of the knight in its footsteps. Using the vacated square as a springboard, White forces events to his advantage.

19...fxe6 20 dxe6 ♔h7 21 ♕xd7 ♕b6

The exchange of queens would just make things easier for White. With queens on, there is some dim hope of counterplay. However, nothing can change the crucial fact: like in Alekhine's game, the isolated pawn has turned into a far-advanced passed pawn that will cost Black dearly.

22 e7 ♖fe8

22...♖xf2 loses to 23 ♘a4, while 22...♕xf2+ 23 ♔h1 ♖fe8 24 ♘e4 looks rather desperate.

23 ♕g4!

White finds an excellent tactical solution.

23...♕c5

Kasparov explained he had in mind 23...♖c7 24 h4 ♖cxe7 25 ♖xe7 ♗xe7 26 h5 ♗d3 27 ♖d1 ♗d6 28 ♗f7. However, with a passed pawn on the seventh rank there is always some solution.

24 ♘e4! ♕xe7 *(D)*

25 ♗c2!

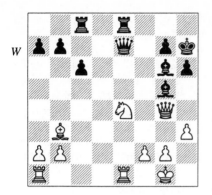

Not everybody would see this hidden possibility, emphasizing that Black is vulnerable on the b1-h7 diagonal and there is little he can do about it.

25...Rf8 26 g3!

26 h4 Bxh4 27 Ng3 Qg5 28 Bxg6+ wins as well but the quiet text-move accentuates Black's helplessness.

26...Qd8 27 Rad1 Qa5 28 h4 Be7 29 Nc3!

The last subtle point: the rooks penetrate to the seventh rank. The game is decided.

29...Bxc2 30 Rxe7 Rg8 31 Rdd7 Bf5 32 Rxg7+ Kh8 33 Qd4 1-0

The same ominous metamorphosis! The vigorous isolated pawn turned into a passed pawn causing havoc on the seventh rank.

Smyslov – Karpov
USSR Ch, Leningrad 1971
English Opening

1 c4 c5 2 Nf3 Nf6 3 Nc3 d5 4 cxd5 Nxd5 5 e3 e6 6 d4 cxd4 7 exd4

This time we have a case of an isolated pawn in the English Opening, which many players would rather avoid by playing 5...Nxc3 followed by ...g6. As a matter of fact, we have transposed into the Caro-Kann, Panov Attack.

7...Be7 8 Bd3 0-0 9 0-0 Nc6 10 Re1 Nf6

A frequent alternative here has been 10...Bf6. There is not much logic in the retreat from the centre, since White's next move thwarts the planned ...Nb4, which would impose full control on the isolated pawn.

11 a3

There is an additional meaning behind this move. It makes possible the standard manoeuvre Bc2 and Qd3, causing difficulties to Black's king.

11...b6 12 Bc2 Bb7 13 Qd3 Rc8? (D)

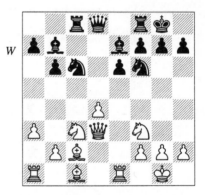

It is somewhat strange that these two great players only noticed the consequences of this error in analysis afterwards. Now, so early in the game, the decisive breakthrough in the centre was possible: 14 d5 when 14...exd5 is punished by 15 Bg5 g6 16 Rxe7, while 14...♘a5 meets with 15 ♗g5 g6 16 d6.

As you see, if not blockaded, an isolated pawn is a Sword of Damocles, ready to strike at any moment. Evidently 13...g6 was indispensable.

14 ♗g5? g6 15 ♖ad1 ♘d5 16 ♗h6 ♖e8 17 ♗a4 a6

17...♘xc3 18 bxc3 ♗xa3 would be highly risky due to 19 c4 ♗f8 20 ♗g5 or 20 ♕e3.

18 ♘xd5 ♕xd5?!

Better is 18...exd5, but wishing to keep the diagonal of his light-squared bishop open, Karpov forgets the danger.

19 ♕e3 ♗f6?

This is a serious mistake. Dr Euwe proposed 19...♕h5, while Korchnoi thought of 19...♖ed8. The punishment comes at once...

20 ♗b3 ♕h5?! *(D)*

20...♕d8 21 ♘e5 is favourable for White.

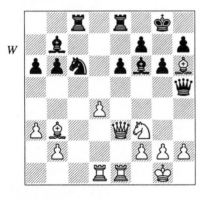

21 d5 ♘d8 22 d6

Again the same metamorphosis with the same brutal consequences.

The appearance of the far-advanced passed pawn represents a victory in itself.

22...♖c5 23 d7 ♖e7 24 ♕f4 ♗g7 25 ♕b8 ♕xh6 26 ♕xd8+ ♗f8 27 ♖e3 ♗c6 28 ♕xf8+ ♕xf8 29 d8♕ 1-0

Such a crushing defeat must have left a strong impression on Karpov. However, a couple of years later he was again to find himself suffering. With the isolated pawn one can never be cautious enough.

Portisch – Karpov
Milan 1975
Nimzo-Indian Defence

1 c4 ♘f6 2 ♘c3 e6 3 d4 ♗b4 4 e3 c5 5 ♗d3 0-0 6 ♘f3 d5 7 0-0 cxd4 8 exd4 dxc4 9 ♗xc4 b6

From another sequence we reach the same pawn-formation in the centre, but with the pieces in different positions. Karpov plans a queen's fianchetto to establish control over the d5-square.

10 ♖e1 ♗b7 11 ♗d3

The bishop is needed on the more important diagonal.

11...♘c6

The experience of recent decades seems to show that Black's defence is sounder if based on ...♘bd7. On c6, the knight is awkward as it blocks its own bishop. Positions with an isolated pawn in the centre are as a rule very sensitive and require full harmony of pieces and pawns. Some seemingly unimportant detail may make a crucial difference.

12 a3 ♗e7 13 ♗c2 ♖e8 14 ♕d3 *(D)*

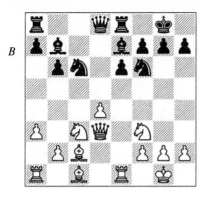

B

14...Rc8?

When the duo of queen on d3 and bishop on c2 have taken their menacing position on the b1-h7 diagonal, extreme caution is necessary. Karpov surprisingly reacts with the same superficiality as we saw in the previous game. 14...g6 was indispensable.

15 d5 exd5

There is no real choice. If 15...Na5 then 16 Bg5 g6 17 d6 wins material.

16 Bg5 Ne4

Now it is too late for 16...g6 because 17 Rxe7 decides at once.

17 Nxe4 dxe4 18 Wxe4 g6 19 Wh4 h5

It is curious that a year earlier, in T.Petrosian-Balashov, Leningrad 1974, 19...Wc7 was played, but Black fell under a devastating attack after 20 Bb3 h5 21 We4 Kg7 22 Bxf7 Kxf7 23 Bh6 Wd6 24 Wc4+. Instead, Karpov weakens his kingside at once. Did he know about Balashov's defeat and could it be possible that he considered the text-move an improvement? Hardly so, because in reply 20 Bb3 would have created unsolvable difficulties.

Instead, Portisch complicates matters and Black manages to save a draw...

20 Rad1? Wc7 21 Bxg6 fxg6 22 Wc4+ Kg7 23 Bf4 Ba6

Was it this move that White missed in his calculations?

24 Wc3+ Bf6 25 Bxc7 Bxc3 26 Rxe8 Rxe8 27 bxc3 Be2 28 Re1 Rc8 29 Rxe2 Rxc7 30 Re6 Nd8 31 Re3 Kf6 32 Kf1 Ne6 33 g3 g5 34 h3 Nc5 35 Nd2 Rd7 36 Ke2 Rd5 37 c4 Rd4 38 Re8 h4 39 Rf8+ Ke7 40 Rh8 hxg3 41 fxg3 Rd3 ½-½

Karpov's failure to parry the threats in the opening broadens our experience about isolated pawns. Their advance in the centre creates direct threats to Black's castled position. Note that in both games the threat arose on the b1-h7 diagonal. The central thrust succeeds in exposing the king to strong attacks. In our example, it came as a result of more or less obvious errors. Sometimes, however, the danger is hidden in a more sophisticated way. Take a game played recently...

Kramnik – Anand
Dos Hermanas 1999
Queen's Gambit Accepted

1 d4 d5 2 c4 dxc4 3 Nf3 e6 4 e3 Nf6 5 Bxc4 c5 6 0-0 a6 7 Bb3

This continuation, resurrected by Kasparov, attracted much attention in the 1990s. It is a quiet manner of thwarting Black's expansion on the queenside, since 7...b5 would be undermined at once by the unpleasant 8 a4.

7...♘c6 8 ♘c3 cxd4 9 exd4 ♗e7 10 ♖e1 0-0 11 a3

In Kasparov-Anand, Wijk aan Zee 1999, Kasparov chose 11 ♗f4 ♘a5 12 ♗c2 b5 13 d5, demonstrating that the central thrust does not need to be supported directly by the bishop, which is more useful on the other diagonal. In case of 13...♘xd5 there is 14 ♘xd5 exd5 15 ♕d3 g6 16 ♗h6 ♖e8 (or 16...♗f5 17 ♕e2 ♗xc2 18 ♕xc2) 17 ♕c3 f6 18 ♘d4 with strong pressure. Anand replied more strongly: 13...exd5 14 ♕d3 ♘c6 (14...g6 asks for trouble after 15 ♗g5), when 15 ♗c7 ♕d7 16 ♘e5 ♘xe5 17 ♗xe5 g6 18 ♗xf6 ♗xf6 19 ♘xd5 ♗g7 led to a balanced position.

11...♘a5

A connoisseur of these positions will remember at once that in case of 11...b5 we have on the board a position from the Nimzo-Indian Defence but with one difference – there the light-squared bishop is on a2 and White can punish Black's expansion by 12 d5 ♘xd5 13 ♘xd5 exd5 14 ♕xd5 ♗b7 15 ♕h5, moving the queen into an aggressive position. In our game, however, the bishop is on b3 and after 11...b5 12 d5 ♘xd5 13 ♘xd5 exd5 14 ♕xd5 Black has at his disposal 14...♘a5 offering White a choice between 15 ♕xa8 ♘xb3 16 ♖a2 ♗e6 17 ♕xd8 ♖xd8 (or perhaps more precise 17...♗xd8) and 15 ♕xd8 ♗xd8 16 ♗a2 ♗b7. The idea occurred to me while analysing the game Kasparov-Anand, in which the quick retreat of the knight to c6 played a crucial role in the defence.

12 ♗c2 b5 13 d5! (D)

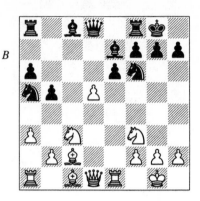

All at once it becomes clear that the move a3 is more useful than Kasparov's ♗f4. It is clear also that the fight against d5 is more difficult.

13...♖e8

An improvement over Kasparov-Ivanchuk, Linares 1999 (to be analysed later), where 13...♘c4?! was played.

Apart from 13...♘xd5, the alternative 13...exd5 had to be examined. 14 ♕d3 g6 (14...♘c6 does not threaten ...♘b4, and so the simple 15 ♗g5 g6 16 ♖xe7 decides the game in White's favour) 15 ♗g5 ♗f5 16 ♕e2 ♗xc2 17 ♕xc2, for instance, creates serious threats (♖xe7).

14 ♗g5 h6

14...♘xd5 15 ♘xd5 ♗xg5 16 ♘xg5 cannot be recommended, and 14...exd5 15 ♕d3 g6 16 ♖xe7 even less. Some commentators proposed 14...♘c4, but then the ill-omened 15 ♘d4 enhances White's pressure.

15 ♗h4 ♘xd5

15...g5 invites repressive measures in the form of 16 ♘xg5 hxg5 17 ♗xg5 with perilous consequences. If 15...♘c4 then 16 ♘d4 again looks strong.

16 ♘xd5 exd5 17 ♕d3 g6 18 ♕e3 ♗e6

18...♘c6 19 ♕xh6 is advantageous to White as well, while 18...g5 19 ♘d4 looks desperate for Black.

19 ♕xh6 ♗xh4 20 ♗xg6 ♕f6 21 ♗h7+ ♔h8 22 ♗g6+ ♔g8 23 ♕h7+ ♔f8 24 ♘xh4 ♕g7

Black could keep the material balance by 24...♕xb2 but then he could not force the exchange of queens. His king is naked and he decides to fight for his life in a difficult endgame rather than expose the king to an all-out attack.

25 ♕xg7+ ♔xg7 26 ♗d3 ♘c4 27 b4

Unnecessary. 27 ♖e2 is the natural move.

27...♘b2 28 ♗f1 d4 29 ♘f3 ♖ad8 30 ♖eb1 ♘c4 31 ♖d1 ♗g4 32 ♖d3 ♘b2 33 ♖xd4 ♗xf3 34 ♖xd8 ♖xd8 35 gxf3 ♖c8 36 ♖a2

Played to invalidate 36...♖c2 by 37 a4.

36...♘a4 37 ♖d2 ♖c6 38 f4 ♘b6 39 ♔g2 ♘c4 40 ♖d3 ♘b2

40...♖g6+ 41 ♔g3 ♘xa3 loses to 42 ♗d3 and the knight cannot come out.

41 ♖g3+ ♔h8 42 ♗e2 ♖c2 43 ♗h5 ♖c7 44 f5?!

A strange move, to put it mildly.

44...♔h7 45 ♗e2 ♔h6 46 h4 ♖c2 47 ♗f3 ♘c4 48 ♗d5 ♘d6 49 ♖d3 ♔g7 50 ♗f3 ♘xf5 51 ♗b7 ♘xh4+ 52 ♔g1 ♖e2 53 ♗xa6 ♖e5 54 ♖c3 ♘f5 55 ♖c5 ♖xc5 56 bxc5 ♘d4 57 c6 ♘xc6 58 ♗xb5 ♘a5 59 ♔g2 ♔f6 60 ♔f3 ♔e5 61 ♔e3 ♘b7 62 ♗c4 f6 63

a4 ♘a5 64 ♗f7 ♘c6 65 ♔d3 ♔d6 66 ♔e4 ♘e7 67 a5 ♔c5 68 a6 ♘c8 69 ♗h5 ♔d6 70 ♗f3 1-0

The endgame play featured some errors, and does not impress, but our interest in this game is of a different nature. Complex and exciting from the early opening, it contains all that such positions can offer: there is the usual suspense about the pawn advance in the centre, a series of tactical threats on the diagonals towards Black's kingside, dubious endgames hanging over Black's head, the strong knight in the centre with additional threats and motifs. An instructive game indeed!

Like Karpov, Anand succumbed to the threats made possible by an unexpected and seemingly insufficiently supported breakthrough in the centre. Unfortunately for Black, the b1-h7 diagonal is not the only route of White's attack. The following games warn that the a2-g8 diagonal plays an equal role in his plans...

Botvinnik – Vidmar
Nottingham 1936
Queen's Gambit

1 c4 e6 2 ♘f3 d5 3 d4 ♘f6 4 ♘c3 ♗e7 5 ♗g5 0-0 6 e3 ♘bd7 7 ♗d3

Although it allows Black an early ...c5, Botvinnik was happy to play this move.

7...c5 8 0-0 cxd4

A good alternative is 8...dxc4 9 ♗xc4 a6.

9 exd4 dxc4 10 ♗xc4 ♘b6

Again 10...a6 seems more precise, provoking a4. Vidmar, however, was so intent on blockading the central pawn that he could not wait.

11 ♗b3 ♗d7?!

We are entering a delicate phase of the game. Black has blockaded the isolated pawn successfully, but is unaware of another threat. It is true that in case of 11...♘bd5 12 ♘e5 White keeps a spatial advantage, but 11...♘fd5, attempting to simplify through exchanges, definitely looks better.

12 ♕d3 ♘bd5?!

Once more 12...♘fd5 was recommended. Vidmar misses his chance to defuse White's pressure. He forgets the golden rule that isolated pawns in general lose their strength when pieces are exchanged.

13 ♘e5 ♗c6 14 ♖ad1 ♘b4

Another attempt at simplification in the form of 14...♘h5 would be met by 15 ♘xc6 bxc6 16 ♗c1. With his queen's rook already developed on d1, the retreat to c1 comes naturally.

15 ♕h3 ♗d5

It was too late for 15...♘fd5, which would now be met by 16 ♗c1. Vidmar, therefore, tries to reduce the pressure by giving up his light-squared bishop.

16 ♘xd5 ♘bxd5 (D)

For the third time in the game, Vidmar plays with the wrong knight. He underrates the oncoming attack.

17 f4 ♖c8

Now that f4 has been played, it is apparent why 16...♘fxd5 would have been better: Black would now be able to meet the pawn advance by 17...f5. We should also note that 17...g6 fails to 18 ♗h6 ♖e8 19 ♗a4. In case of 17...♘e4, Botvinnik demonstrated a

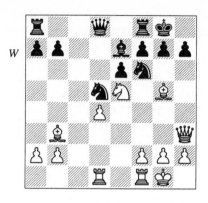

devastating tactical blow – 18 ♘xf7 ♔xf7 19 ♖de1. We begin to feel the strength of the b3-bishop.

18 f5 exf5 19 ♖xf5 ♕d6 (D)

It is worth noting here two lines that emphasize Black's troubles after 19...♖c7 20 ♖df1:

a) 20...a6 21 ♘xf7 ♖xf7 22 ♗xd5 ♘xd5 23 ♖xf7 ♗xg5 24 ♕e6.

b) 20...♘b6 21 ♕h4 ♘bd5 22 ♘xf7 ♖xf7 23 ♗xd5 ♘xd5 24 ♖xf7 ♗xg5 25 ♕xg5, winning. The coordinated pressure on the a2-g8 diagonal and the f-file is more than Black can endure.

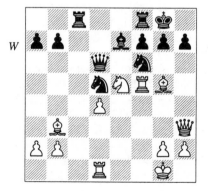

20 ♘xf7! ♖xf7 21 ♗xf6 ♗xf6 22 ♖xd5 ♛c6 23 ♖d6 ♛e8 24 ♖d7 1-0

Vidmar lost because he was completely unaware of the threat on the a2-g8 diagonal. Note another feature of the game: all through the game we never felt the d4-pawn as a weakness. On the contrary, although blocked, its support for the dominant knight on e5 played a key role in Botvinnik's attack.

Botvinnik's win is too well-known, perhaps somewhat worn out by long years of attention paid to it, but it was played with such clarity of purpose that in the topic we tackle no other game can stand instead of it.

The following is a less famous but quite instructive game in which decisive pressure and threats again come along the same treacherous diagonal.

Gligorić – Pomar
Olympiad, Nice 1974
Nimzo-Indian Defence

1 d4 ♘f6 2 c4 e6 3 ♘c3 ♗b4 4 e3 0-0 5 ♗d3 d5 6 ♘f3 c5 7 0-0 dxc4 8 ♗xc4 ♘c6

In later years, other lines gained favour. Black usually fianchettoed his queen's bishop before developing the knight, or opted for 8...♗d7.

9 ♗d3 ♗d7 10 a3 cxd4 11 exd4 ♗e7 12 ♖e1 ♖c8 (D)

A glance at the position will be sufficient for an experienced observer to conclude that Black's queenside pieces are unnaturally placed against the menacing central thrust. The bishop is passively posted on d7, and the c6-knight

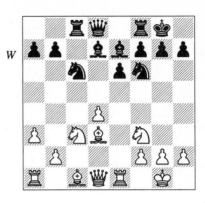

is exposed to d5, and no serious steps have been taken against the basic threat.

13 ♗b1!

This introduces the standard procedure of forcing a weakening of Black's kingside by ♛d3. However, this is not the only idea behind Gligorić's excellent move.

13...♖e8 14 ♛d3 g6

With the d5 advance hanging in the air, Black has to close the b1-h7 diagonal, but the light-squared bishop switches to a more active position.

15 ♗a2

Pomar's passive position is not prepared for the obvious breakthrough in the centre, which is about to become reality. His next useless move (15...♛a5 at least should have been played at once) just adds oil to the fire.

15...a6 16 ♗h6 ♛a5 (D)

Against White's clear-cut plan, the black pieces are grouped in the centre with no sense of imminent danger. Even Pomar's last move comes a step too late.

17 d5 exd5 18 ♘xd5 ♗f5

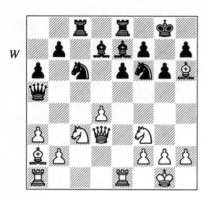

After 18...♘xd5 19 ♗xd5, the f7-pawn would become a target, but the text-move leads to a quick debacle...

19 ♖xe7 ♖xe7

Or the obvious 19...♗xd3 20 ♘xf6+ ♔h8 21 ♖xf7, etc.

20 ♘xf6+ ♔h8 21 ♕d2 ♗e6 22 ♘d5 ♕xd2 23 ♗xd2 ♗xd5 24 ♗c3+ ♔g8 25 ♗xd5 ♖d7 26 ♗xc6 bxc6 27 ♘e5 ♖dd8 28 ♔f1 h5 29 ♖e1 ♖d5 30 ♘xc6 1-0

The lesson is simple: when facing an isolated pawn in the centre, you cannot ignore the vital issue of its potential advance. You must either prevent it for good or be ready for it. Grandmaster Pomar did neither.

However, the threat of a central thrust and its consequences are not always so dramatic. What the advance in the centre often brings is a better endgame or a dominant centralized piece at the end of exchanges, positional advantages one should learn to fear as much as the violent attacks we have seen. A couple of instructive games will help the reader to stay aware of it.

Gligorić – Eliskases
Buenos Aires 1960
Caro-Kann Defence

1 e4 c6 2 d4 d5 3 exd5 cxd5 4 c4 ♘f6 5 ♘c3 e6 6 ♘f3 ♗e7 7 cxd5 ♘xd5 8 ♗d3 ♘c6 9 0-0 0-0

This time we reach our pawn-structure from the Caro-Kann, Panov Attack; numerous roads lead to the same place.

10 ♖e1 ♗f6

It is not in vain to repeat that in case of 10...♘f6, with the idea of establishing a firm blockade on d5 by a subsequent ...♘b4, White's best reaction is 11 a3, which prevents the manoeuvre and at the same time makes possible ♗c2 and ♕d3, building pressure on Black's kingside.

11 ♗e4 ♘ce7

We see now the idea behind the move ...♗f6: Black holds firm in the centre.

12 ♘e5

Probably the most unpleasant for Black. Supported by White's d4-pawn, the dominant knight squeezes Black, whose further development is rather limited. In such a situation ♕d3, with threats on the b1-h7 diagonal, as well as the possible ♘g4, may be quite annoying for Black.

12...♗d7?!

Note that after 12...♘xc3 followed by ...♗xe5 Black remains weak on the dark squares, but the text-move is also considered inferior. Several theoreticians proposed 12...g6.

13 ♕d3 g6 14 ♗h6 ♗g7 15 ♗xg7 ♔xg7 16 ♘xd5 ♘xd5?!

On 16...exd5 White must have had in mind 17 ♘xd7 ♛xd7 (17...dxe4 fails to 18 ♛b5) 18 ♗f3 with a favourable endgame. The d5-pawn will remain under pressure, which can be increased by ♖e5 or ♖c1-c5, doubling the rooks at the same time and capturing one of the open files, or a pawn advance on both wings. The text-move, however, encounters other problems.

17 ♗xd5 exd5 18 ♛b3! (D)

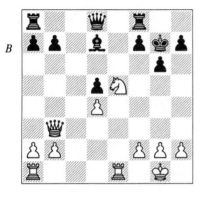

This time the isolated pawn was successfully blockaded, but behind it, White has obtained active piece-play, and can force a better endgame.

18...f6

18...♗c6 19 ♖ac1 is hardly more inviting. Of course, the text-move permanently weakens Black's king position, so major-piece endgames will involve additional difficulties.

19 ♘d3 ♗f5

It is too late for 19...♗c6 because 20 ♘c5 wins material. Black must give up a pawn.

20 ♛xb7+ ♖f7 21 ♛a6 ♖b8 22 ♖e2 ♗xd3 23 ♛xd3

A pawn down and with his king's defences compromised, Black has paid the price for his inadequate treatment of the opening phase involving an isolated pawn. White now succeeds in demonstrating how difficult it is to defend such positions.

23...♛a5 24 h3 ♖b4 25 b3 ♛b6 26 ♖d1 a5 27 ♛e3 a4 28 ♖d3 axb3 29 axb3 ♖b7 30 ♛e8 ♖xb3 31 ♖xb3 ♛xb3 32 ♖e7+ ♖xe7 33 ♛xe7+ ♔g8 34 ♛xf6 ♛b1+ 35 ♔h2 ♛b8+ 36 f4 ♛e8 37 ♛e5 ♛f7 38 g4 h6 39 f5 gxf5 40 gxf5 ♔h7 41 ♔g3 ♛b7 42 ♔f4 ♛c6 43 ♛e7+ ♔h8 44 ♔e5 ♛c1 45 f6 ♛e3+ 46 ♔d6 ♛a3+ 47 ♔e6 ♛xh3+ 48 ♔f7 1-0

Karpov – Uhlmann
Madrid 1973
French Defence

1 e4 e6 2 d4 d5 3 ♘d2 c5 4 exd5 exd5 5 ♘gf3 ♘c6 6 ♗b5 ♗d6 7 dxc5 ♗xc5 8 0-0 ♘ge7 9 ♘b3 ♗d6 10 ♗g5 (D)

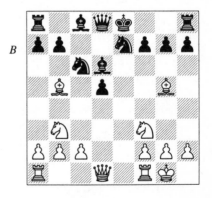

This position from the French Tarrasch is one of the most instructive

for a student of our topic. The d5-pawn
is well protected by numerous black
pieces and weakening it is a subtle
task.

The continuation Karpov used to
apply in the 1970s is in keeping with
the general strategic plan. We shall yet
speak of it, but let us mention in passing that exchanges slowly undermine
the stability of an isolated pawn. What
Karpov has in mind is the manoeuvre
♗g5-h4-g3, in order to exchange the
dark-squared bishops, which will be to
the detriment of the d5-pawn. This is
perfectly logical, although later experience warned that the intended manoeuvre is somewhat slow and the
alternative follow-up 11 ♖e1 prevailed.

10...0-0 11 ♗h4 ♗g4

11...♕b6 comes into consideration,
but the text-move is logical as well.

12 ♗e2 ♗h5

As long as so many pieces stand
behind the d5-pawn it is a healthy
pawn, and White's pressure on it is
barely perceptible. However, just one
wrong step can change the picture
significantly. Although, for instance,
12...♕b6 looks natural, it would have
brought a series of unwanted exchanges, leading to an endgame in
which the d5-pawn starts to feel shaky:
13 ♗xe7 ♘xe7 14 ♕d4 ♕xd4 15
♘fxd4. Instead, 12...♖e8 13 ♖e1 ♕b6
is satisfactory. In that case, 14 ♗xe7
would be met by 14...♖xe7 15 ♕xd5
♘b4.

13 ♖e1 ♕b6 14 ♘fd4 ♗g6

Considering constantly the nature
of the isolated pawn, we see that these
are logical reactions by both sides:

White is looking for exchanges, and
Black avoids them.

15 c3

Another logical step. The square in
front of the isolated pawn is White's
strong square; he wants to control it
fully.

**15...♖fe8 16 ♗f1 ♗e4 17 ♗g3 ♗xg3
18 hxg3 a5?!** *(D)*

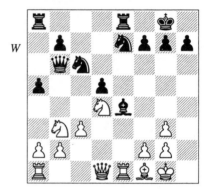

We are discussing here a very delicate position in which even impercep-
tibly wrong steps can turn the tables.
Uhlmann's last move is a blank shot. It
turns out that it offers a weak square,
b5, for nothing. We shall see why.

19 a4! ♘xd4 20 ♘xd4 ♘c6

We see now that 20...♕xb2 does
not work due to 21 ♘b5 or 21 ♗b5,
followed by f3, winning material.
18...a5 was intended to exert pressure
on d4, but it missed its target. White
will now use the b5-square to seize the
initiative.

21 ♗b5 ♖ed8

Black obstinately continues to fo-
cus on the firm white point at d4, but
perhaps it was premature to leave the

e-file. 21...♗g6 came into consideration.

22 g4 ♘xd4

While undoubtedly consistent with the previous play, this is one of those 'obvious' possibilities players should think twice before adopting.

23 ♕xd4 ♕xd4 24 cxd4 ♖ac8

24...♔f8 looks more natural in order to prevent the penetration of the seventh rank, but it is not clear what Black can do against the doubling of rooks on the e-file.

25 f3 ♗g6 26 ♖e7 b6

26...♖c2 comes into consideration.

27 ♖ae1 h6

The immediate 27...h5 is better.

28 ♖b7 ♖d6 29 ♖ee7

White's pair of rooks on the seventh rank is paralysing. Black's position is critical.

29...h5 30 gxh5 ♗xh5 31 g4 ♗g6 32 f4 *(D)*

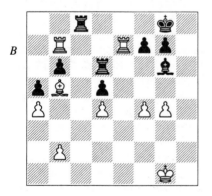

That's it. The plan started by 25 f3 has been carried out perfectly.

32...♖c1+ 33 ♔f2 ♖c2+ 34 ♔e3 ♗e4

34...♖e6+ 35 ♖xe6 fxe6 36 ♖xb6 ♖xb2 37 ♖xe6 is no better.

35 ♖xf7 ♖g6 36 g5 ♔h7 37 ♖fe7 ♖xb2 38 ♗e8 ♖b3+ 39 ♔e2 ♖b2+ 40 ♔e1 ♖d6 41 ♖xg7+ ♔h8 42 ♖ge7 1-0

One of the best games Karpov ever played. I remember watching a group of grandmasters analysing it. For a long time, they could not grasp the reason for Black's loss. In the battle against the isolated pawn, White achieved an advantageous endgame by exploiting small, barely perceptible errors by his opponent. To parry an immediate central thrust is not enough. Looming behind the intricacies of the opening there are always endgames whose nature and destiny are often decided in the most sensitive phase when opening turns into middlegame. In our game, Black was not up to his difficult task.

Rubinstein – Tartakower
Marienbad 1925
Queen's Gambit Accepted

1 d4 e6 2 ♘f3 d5 3 c4 ♘f6 4 ♘c3 dxc4 5 e3 a6 6 a4 c5 7 ♗xc4 ♘c6 8 0-0 cxd4 9 ♘xd4 ♘xd4?! 10 exd4 ♗e7

Without discussing the niceties of the opening phase, let us just note that a somewhat unusual course of events has led to the well-known position with one difference: a pair of knights has been exchanged, making possible a rather uncommon, early breakthrough in the centre...

11 d5 exd5 12 ♘xd5 ♘xd5 13 ♗xd5 *(D)*

This time the advance of the mobile pawn has brought about a position

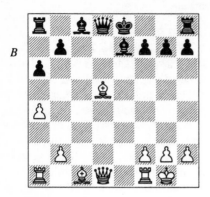

B

characterized by a strong, dominant bishop on d5, targeting both the opponent's wings: since White is always half a step in front of his adversary, such an advantage cannot be taken lightly.

13...0-0 14 ♕f3 ♗d6

By aiming at h2, Black indirectly defends the b7-pawn.

15 ♖e1

Probably expecting 15...♕b6, Rubinstein prepares 16 ♖e8. White is better: his development is superior, and his pressure against the b7- and f7-pawns grants him an initiative.

15...♕h4 16 h3 ♕b4

Tartakower was not a patient man, ready to defend his material balance tenaciously. The active sally by his queen prepares to parry 17 ♖e8 by 17...♗e6, now viable because White's first rank is not defended. However, it also exposes the queen.

17 ♖d1 ♖b8 18 b3 ♗e6

The type of clever answer one could expect from Tartakower. He ignores the threatened 19 ♗a3, which he can meet by 19...♕b6 20 a5 ♕c7, hoping that a

major-piece endgame will offer drawing chances. However, Rubinstein sets his opponent a more difficult task...

19 ♗xe6 fxe6 20 ♕e2 ♗c5

Black hopes to extricate himself from his predicament by gaining counter-pressure against f2 in return for the e6-pawn.

21 ♕xe6+ ♔h8 22 ♗a3

Not 22 ♗e3 ♖be8, etc.

22...♕a5 23 ♖d5 ♗xf2+ 24 ♔h1 ♕c3 25 ♖c1 ♕f6 26 ♕xf6 ♖xf6

So in spite of his imaginative defence, Tartakower faces a difficult endgame. The g7-pawn is exposed and the seventh rank defenceless.

27 ♖d7 ♗e3?

This makes things easier for White. However, either 27...♖b6 28 ♗b2 or 27...b6 28 ♗b2 ♖g6 29 ♖cc7 ♖g8 will sooner or later lead to collapse.

28 ♖xb7 ♖b6 29 ♖xb6 ♗xb6 30 ♖c6 h5 31 ♗d6 ♖b7 32 b4 a5 33 b5 ♔h7 34 g4 hxg4 35 hxg4 ♔g8 36 ♔g2 ♔f7 37 ♔f3 ♗d8 38 ♔e4 ♔e8 39 ♔d5 g5 40 ♔e6 ♗b6 41 ♖c8+ ♗d8 42 ♗c5 ♖b8 43 ♖c6 ♖b7 44 b6 ♖b8 45 ♖c7 ♗xc7 46 bxc7 ♖c8 47 ♗b6 ♖a8 48 ♗a7 1-0

This game, played with Rubinstein's inimitable simplicity, is highly instructive. We see how an isolated pawn, when poorly restrained by the opponent, breaks through, and enables White to transform his initiative into a dominant strategic piece on a central square. The outcome is a superior endgame for White. Strong pieces on the central squares are yet another consequence of the mobile central pawn that one should fear.

Spassky – Avtonomov
Leningrad 1949
Queen's Gambit Accepted

1 d4 d5 2 c4 dxc4 3 ♘f3 ♘f6 4 e3 c5 5 ♗xc4 e6 6 0-0 a6 7 ♕e2

The eternal question is whether to prevent Black's expansion on the queenside or to allow it. The fashion changes, but the question remains.

7...b5 8 ♗b3 ♘c6?!

I have a personal preference for the lines based on ...♘bd7.

9 ♘c3

In case of 9 ♖d1 there is the well-known 9...c4 10 ♗c2 ♘b4 and the bishop will be beheaded.

9...cxd4

Better is 9...♗e7.

10 ♖d1 ♗b7 11 exd4 ♘b4 *(D)*

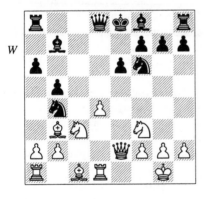

Black must have been quite satisfied with his position. He controls the seemingly strong square in front of the isolated pawn and needs just a tempo before he can castle, when he will have achieved an ideal position. However, appearances can be deceptive.

The fact that he lost time developing his queenside and delaying the natural development of the kingside proves fatal. White's pieces are ideally posted to support the following bolt from the blue.

12 d5! ♘bxd5

If 12...♘fxd5?, then 13 a3 decides.

13 ♗g5 ♗e7 14 ♗xf6 gxf6 15 ♘xd5 ♗xd5 16 ♗xd5 exd5 17 ♘d4

Like in the Tartakower game, the central thrust is followed by the appearance of a powerful piece in the centre. The white knight dominates the board. This fact in itself, coupled with Black's shattered pawn-formation, defines our position as totally lost for Black. And so it was...

17...♔f8 18 ♘f5 h5 19 ♖xd5 ♕xd5 20 ♕xe7+ ♔g8 21 ♕xf6 1-0

White's knight entered the battle via the vacant square in the wake of the break. It is a common motif to keep the initiative and crown what the isolated pawn started.

Steinitz – von Bardeleben
Hastings 1895
Giuoco Piano

1 e4 e5 2 ♘f3 ♘c6 3 ♗c4 ♗c5 4 c3 ♘f6 5 d4 exd4 6 cxd4 ♗b4+ 7 ♘c3 d5?!

Later experience confirmed that 7...♘xe4 8 0-0 ♗xc3 is correct.

8 exd5 ♘xd5 9 0-0 ♗e6

From the days of Gioacchino Greco we know that 9...♘xc3 10 bxc3 ♗xc3 loses to 11 ♕b3 ♗xa1 12 ♗xf7+ ♔f8 13 ♗a3+ ♘e7 14 ♗h5 g6 15 ♘g5 ♕e8 16 ♖e1, etc. Black, therefore, closes the open file and tries to finish his development as quickly as possible.

10 ♗g5 ♗e7

White is better developed and seeks to preserve an initiative via exchanges.

11 ♗xd5 ♗xd5 12 ♘xd5 ♕xd5 13 ♗xe7 ♘xe7 14 ♖e1

Now Black will be unable to castle – the king must try to survive in the centre.

14...f6 15 ♕e2

Probably planned and executed quickly; otherwise White might have considered 15 ♕a4+ ♔f7 (15...♕d7 loses to 16 ♕b4, while 15...c6 loses to 16 ♕a3 ♕d7 17 ♖xe7+, etc.) 16 ♘e5+! fxe5 17 ♖xe5 ♕d6 18 ♕c4+ ♔f8 19 ♖ae1 with tremendous pressure against Black's uncoordinated pieces.

15...♕d7 (D)

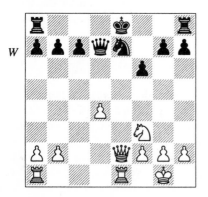

16 ♖ac1

This position attracted the attention of numerous commentators. They discussed 16 d5 ♔f7 17 ♖ad1, when 17...♘xd5 loses to 18 ♘g5+, but there is the stronger 17...♖ad8. Paul Keres indicated 16 ♕e4 c6 17 ♖e2 ♔f7 18

♖ae1 ♘d5 19 ♕h4. There is also 16 ♖ad1 ♔f7 (16...c6 17 d5) 17 ♕c4+, when 17...♘d5 loses to 18 ♘e5+ fxe5 19 dxe5. Fine, but I am happy that Steinitz played exactly as he did.

16...c6

Black was hoping for some sort of artificial castling and perhaps a comfortable endgame due to the potentially weak d4-pawn. Perhaps he considered what was later proposed as the saving move – 16...♔f7, but it would not have been so easy to evaluate what happens after 17 ♘g5+ fxg5 18 ♕f3+, e.g. ♔g8 19 ♕xb7 ♕d5 20 ♖xc7. Even the apparently simple 18...♘f5 19 g4 leads to positions in which White keeps the initiative (19...♖hf8 20 ♕b3+ ♔g6? 21 ♖e6+ ♖f6 22 gxf5+ ♔xf5 23 ♕h3+ winning; 19...♖ae8 20 gxf5 or 20 ♖e5; 19...c6 20 ♖c5; 19...♖hd8 20 gxf5 or 20 ♕b3+). In comparison with all that confusion, the text-move must have seemed consistent and to promise security; vain hopes...

17 d5!

This strong move has two main aims: to open another file for his rook and to vacate the d4-square for the knight. Like a battering-ram, the isolated pawn opens the gate, via which the cavalry attacks.

17...cxd5 18 ♘d4 ♔f7 19 ♘e6 ♖hc8

19...♖ac8 loses to 20 ♕g4 g6 21 ♘g5+ ♔e8 22 ♖xc8+, etc.

20 ♕g4 g6 (D)

The scene is set for one of the unforgettable combinations of chess history.

21 ♘g5+ ♔e8 22 ♖xe7+! ♔f8

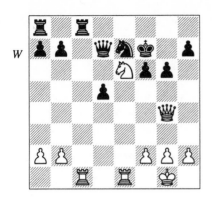

W

22...♔xe7 loses to 23 ♖e1+ ♔d6 24 ♕b4+ ♔c7 25 ♘e6+, etc., but Black continues to find clever answers based on the weakness of White's back rank. Unfortunately for him, they were just temporary solutions...

23 ♖f7+ ♔g8 24 ♖g7+ ♔h8 25 ♖xh7+ 1-0

Here von Bardeleben effectively resigned by leaving the hall and not returning, leaving Steinitz to show the finish of the combination: 25...♔g8 26 ♖g7+ ♔h8 27 ♕h4+ ♔xg7 28 ♕h7+ ♔f8 29 ♕h8+ ♔e7 30 ♕g7+ ♔e8 31 ♕g8+ ♔e7 32 ♕f7+ ♔d8 33 ♕f8+ ♕e8 34 ♘f7+ ♔d7 35 ♕d6#.

The breakthrough d5 did not yield immediate results but opened the way for a strong initiative based on the knight manoeuvre. This proved fatal for Black.

Kasparov – Ivanchuk
Linares 1999
Queen's Gambit Accepted

1 d4 d5 2 c4 dxc4 3 ♘f3 e6 4 e3 c5 5 ♗xc4 a6 6 0-0 ♘f6 7 ♗b3 ♘c6 8 ♘c3

cxd4 9 exd4 ♗e7 10 ♖e1 0-0 11 a3 ♘a5 12 ♗c2 b5 13 d5!**

We have seen this sequence of moves in the game Kramnik-Anand, annotated above. Kramnik-Anand was played later and Black was in a better situation than Ivanchuk in Linares, facing a position he had not been able to consider in the peace of his home. As we saw, Anand came up with an improvement – 13...♖e8; Ivanchuk had to find an answer at the board...

13...♘c4?!

The d5 advance is worrying Black and it is not a big secret why he plays this move: expecting 14 ♗g5, he plans in reply 14...♘b6, when 15 ♕d3 can be met by 15...♘bxd5.

14 ♕d3!

Played also with deep consideration for the d5 advance. 14...♘b6 is excluded by the strong reply 15 ♘d4 and the tension is kept.

14...♖e8 15 a4

Black is ready to meet 15 ♘g5 cold-bloodedly by 15...exd5 16 ♘xh7 g6, but I imagine he did not foresee this stab on the queenside.

15...exd5 16 axb5 a5 17 b3 ♘d6 18 ♘d4 ♗b7 19 f3 *(D)*

In a couple of moves the position has been thoroughly changed. Instead of the threats to Black's king, which distinguished Kramnik's victory over Anand, our position is characterized by a number of static features. The first thing to notice is that the situation in the centre has been turned upside down. Now it is Black with an isolated pawn or, we should now say, burdened with an isolated pawn; it is

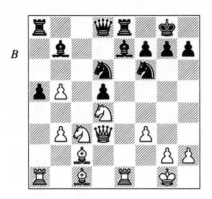

well protected at the moment, but blockaded beyond hope of getting back its mobility. Together with the pawn there is the light-squared bishop on b7 also blocked by its own d5-pawn. Apart from that, there is another weak spot in Black's camp – the a5-pawn, defended well enough for the moment but potentially shaky. In comparison, White's doubled pawns on the b-file do their duty: the b3-pawn controls the c4-square, and the b5-pawn squeezes Black. The f3-pawn denies the black knights the coveted e4-square. All that White needs now is to improve the position of his bishops, which have lost their primary targets on the kingside and are looking for a better view.

19...Rc8 20 Na4

Cautious and logical: by controlling c5 and b6 White increases his spatial advantage as well as avoiding any inconveniences on the g1-a7 diagonal.

20...Bf8 21 Bg5 g6 22 Qd2

The light-squared bishop must be taken care of; it needs the d3-square.

22...Rxe1+ 23 Rxe1 Nde8

Ivanchuk sets a nice trap which White passes by calmly.

24 Re2!

After 24 Rxe8? Qxe8 25 Bxf6 Bb4, 26 Qc1 Ba3 leads to a repetition of moves. Kasparov demonstrated 26 Qf2? Be1 27 Qf1 Qe3+ 28 Kh1 Bh4!, when Black turns the tables.

24...Bb4 25 Qe3 Rc7 26 Bd3 (D)

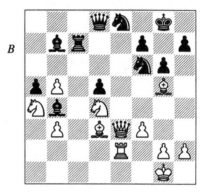

All very consistently played. Having decided that any minor-piece endgame is in his favour, White happily agrees to the exchanges.

26...Re7 27 Qc1 Rxe2 28 Bxe2 Qe7 29 Qe3 Qxe3+ 30 Bxe3

The truth about endgames begins with pawns. Once you damaged your pawn-structure you have to live with it. In our game they are a limiting factor for Black.

30...Nd7 31 Nc6 Bxc6 32 bxc6 Nb8

32...Ne5 33 Bb6 or 32...Nf8 33 Nc5 would not offer any more hope for Black.

33 Bb6 Bd6 34 Nc3 Bc7 (D)

35 Bf2?

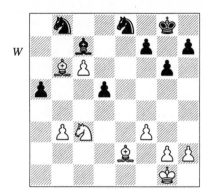

At the very end, after a long series of brilliant positional solutions, White stumbles. At first it's not easy to notice it and Ivanchuk misses a concealed point. This serves as a reminder that a game of chess is not finished until the scoresheets are signed.

If White had played 35 ♗c5 then resignation would have been Black's only reasonable option.

35...d4 36 ♘d5 1-0

However, just at the moment when Ivanchuk gave up he could continue 36...♘xc6 37 ♗b5 ♘b4 38 ♘xb4 ♘d6, regaining his piece with chances to save his skin, as Jan Timman pointed out in detailed analysis. To us it matters little. The fine points we were looking for in the search for truth about the isolated pawn are all there – in the imaginatively played opening and deep transition into the middlegame, relying on motifs and ideas which emphasize the most instructive elements of the characteristic position.

In Kasparov-Ivanchuk as well as most of the games we have analysed,

the advance of the central pawn is often seen early in the opening. Against a cautious and well-prepared opponent that task is as a rule difficult to carry out successfully. I offer for the reader's attention two games by Grandmaster Gligorić, where he demonstrates his expertise in the delicate positions of the Queen's Gambit Accepted.

Gligorić – Portisch
Yugoslavia – Hungary, Pula 1971
Queen's Gambit Accepted

1 d4 d5 2 c4 dxc4 3 ♘f3 ♘f6 4 e3 e6 5 ♗xc4 c5 6 0-0 a6 7 a4

No doubt consistent, because it emphasizes Black's basic problem – the development of his queen's bishop. Still, in view of the pawn-formation which will arise in the centre in a few moves, when the breakthrough will be definitely thwarted by the obvious manoeuvre ...♘b8-c6-b4, it is understandable that the continuation is not so popular today.

7...♘c6 8 ♕e2 cxd4 9 ♖d1 ♗e7 10 exd4 0-0 11 ♘c3

As 11 ♗g5 ♘d5 leads to unwanted simplifications, it is better to postpone the development of the queen's bishop.

11...♘d5

The alternative was 11...♘b4 again with intention of meeting 12 ♗g5 by 12...♘fd5. Of course, White would proceed with the stronger 12 ♘e5, keeping some pressure.

12 ♗d3

The bishop will be more useful on the b1-h7 diagonal.

12...♘cb4 13 ♗b1 b6

13...♘f6 is possible, but less good is 13...♗d7, which allows 14 ♕e4 g6 15 ♘e5 with pressure in the centre and on the kingside. For example: 15...♗f6 16 ♕f3 ♗g7 17 ♕g3 followed by h4 gives White the initiative, as shown by a number of games.

14 a5

A couple of days earlier in the same match Gligorić chose 14 ♘e5, but after 14...♗b7 15 ♖a3 ♖c8 16 ♘xd5 ♕xd5 17 ♖g3 f5 Black slammed shut the gates to his king. The text-move was the fruit of home analysis.

14...♗d7?! *(D)*

While preventing ♘a4, Black forgets that b7 is the natural place for his bishop. Correct is 14...bxa5 15 ♘e5 ♗b7 with a good game.

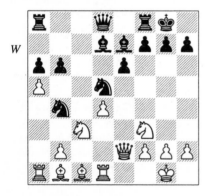

It is instructive to watch the sensitive relationships between pawns and pieces. As long as they stay in harmony, the effects are positive. As soon as disharmony between them is inadvertently caused, the position suffers. We sense at once that the bishop is out of place on d7.

15 ♘e5 bxa5 16 ♖a3

With the bishops blocking normal coordination on the first rank, the third rank becomes a natural exit. In the type of positions we are analysing, the rook manoeuvre on the third rank is often used to good effect. The a3-rook is eyeing the kingside, and White already threatens ♗xh7+, provoking the following weakening.

16...f5 17 ♘xd5 ♘xd5 18 ♘xd7 ♕xd7 19 ♖xa5 ♘c7 20 ♗a2

There is always the other diagonal. White begins strong, lasting pressure on Black's weaknesses. His bishop-pair begins to be felt.

Note also that all the time, together with the other pieces, the d4-pawn takes part in the events. Quietly, almost unnoticed, it controls key central squares and supports an important central piece, offering White a spatial advantage, but first and foremost it is the opponent's constant worry.

20...♗d6 21 ♗c4 ♔h8 22 ♕f3 ♗b4 23 ♖a1 a5

Black defends well and gets rid of one of his weak points, but at the same time White succeeds in moving his pieces forward into dominant positions.

24 ♗f4 ♘d5 25 ♗e5 ♖fc8 26 ♕e2 ♕b7 27 h3 ♖c6 28 ♖ac1 ♖ac8 29 ♗xd5!

The correct decision. Exchanges do not make things easier for Black, due to his lasting weaknesses.

29...exd5 30 ♖xc6 ♕xc6 31 ♖d3

Again the third rank is a convenient route for White's rooks.

31...♕d7

Note that the thoughtless 31...♕c2 would be punished by 32 ♗xg7+.

32 ♖g3 ♗f8 33 b3

Preventing ...a4, a useful measure in the endgame.

33...♖a8 34 ♕c2 ♖c8 35 ♕d2 ♖a8 36 ♕g5 ♔g8 37 ♖f3 (D)

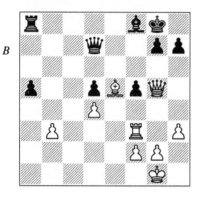

Forcing a further weakening.

37...g6 38 ♖c3 ♕d8 39 ♕c1 ♗d6 40 ♕f4 ♗xe5 41 ♕xe5 ♖a7 42 ♖c5

This was the sealed move.

42...♖e7

Black will eventually lose a pawn. 42...♖d7 43 ♖b5 ♔f7 is best met by the quiet 44 g3, since 44 ♖b8 ♕c7 puts up resistance.

43 ♖xd5 ♕c7 44 ♕xc7 ♖xc7 45 ♖xa5 ♖b7 46 ♖a3 ♖b4 47 d5 ♔g7 48 ♔f1 ♔f6 49 ♔e2 ♔e5 50 ♔d3 ♔xd5 51 ♔c3 ♖e4 52 ♖a4 ♖e2 53 ♖d4+ ♔c5 54 b4+ ♔b5 55 ♖d5+ ♔c6 56 ♖d2 ♖e1 57 f3 ♖g1 58 ♔d4

It was important for White to win this game. I remember we analysed in two groups exchanging information, because the time was limited. All the small details were taken care of and no

surprise was possible. The threatened penetration of the kingside combined with the passed pawn now decides quickly.

58...♖e1 59 ♖c2+ ♔b6 60 ♔d5 ♖e3 61 ♖c6+ ♔b5

If 61...♔b7 then 62 ♖e6.

62 ♖c7 h5 63 ♖b7+ ♔a4 64 ♔c4 ♔a3 65 ♖a7+ ♔b2 66 ♖g7 1-0

Gligorić – Szabo
European Team Ch, Hamburg 1965
Queen's Gambit Accepted

1 d4 d5 2 c4 dxc4 3 ♘f3 ♘f6 4 e3 e6 5 ♗xc4 c5 6 0-0 a6 7 a4

I already spoke of the hole on b4, facilitating the blockade of the isolated pawn later on. It cannot be emphasized enough that whatever you do on the wings has repercussions in the centre.

7...♘c6 8 ♕e2 cxd4 9 ♖d1 ♗e7 10 exd4 0-0 11 ♘c3 ♗d7?!

One prefers Portisch's move from the previous game, 11...♘d5, or even 11...♘b4, with the idea of preventing ♗d3, as well as the obvious motive of controlling the d5-square. In both lines Black should aim to develop his queen's bishop on b7, its natural position against the d4-pawn.

12 ♗f4!

One of the key questions in our variation is the development of the dark-squared bishop. In general, it belongs on g5, but here simplifying ideas like ...♘d5, or even ...♘h5 at a proper moment, dissuaded White and he started to resort to Gligorić's continuation. White's decision is based on the state of the central pawn and its future.

12...♘b4 13 ♘e5

13 d5 is possible, but after a series of exchanges Black would simply play ...♕e8, dissipating White's pressure.

13...♗e8

After 13...♗c6 14 ♘xc6 bxc6 15 a5 White keeps the better chances. Despite that, it seems to me the right way for Black to play, because sooner or later the bishop will have to leave its shelter.

14 ♗g5 (D)

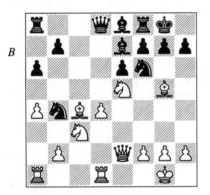

Despite the loss of tempo, this move is now good. It is to Gligorić's credit that he discovered this subtle nuance.

14...♘fd5 15 ♗xd5 ♘xd5 16 ♘xd5 ♗xg5

16...exd5 is a dubious reaction in view of 17 ♗xe7 ♕xe7 18 ♕f3, reminding us of Gligorić's game versus Eliskases: the knight would be superior to the bishop.

17 ♘c3

Relying on his centralized knight, White plans d5, opening the position

to his advantage. In chess, that which cannot be done directly, sometimes can be done with a loss of time. One should remain open to such possibilities.

17...♗c6 18 ♘xc6 bxc6 19 a5

So finally Black could not avoid the passive position with pawns on a6 and c6, but in a somewhat worse situation.

19...♗e7 20 ♕c4 ♕d6 21 ♘a4 ♖fd8 22 ♖ac1

22 ♘b6 ♖a7 23 ♖ac1 brings about the same position as in the game, while avoiding the possibility in the next note.

22...♕b4

Black could play 22...♗f6, when 23 ♘b6 can be met by 23...♖ab8 and 23 ♘c5 by 23...♕d5.

23 ♘b6 ♖a7 24 ♕xc6 ♕xa5

24...♕xb2? loses to 25 ♘c8.

25 d5 (D)

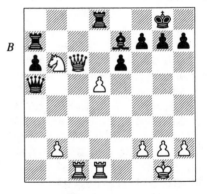

Finally comes this thrust, but with great strength, because the black forces have lost their normal coordination.

25...exd5 26 ♘xd5

The basic threat is ♖a1, which must be parried very precisely.

26...♔f8?

26...♖b8 is essential. At first glance it seems that White should also have a forced win here, but after 27 ♕c8+? ♖xc8 28 ♘xe7+ ♔f8 29 ♘xc8, there is 29...♖b7, when 30 ♖c5? loses to 30...♖d7!. The planned 27 ♖a1 yields only a draw after 27...♕c5 28 ♖xa6 ♖xa6 29 ♕xa6 ♖xb2 30 ♕c8+ ♗f8. It takes some time to realize that White should turn to exerting positional pressure. In this respect, 27 ♘c7 appears good, cutting the a7-rook out of play, denying Black's queen the important b5-square and preparing ♖d7 followed by ♖cd1, with play against f7 and Black's back rank. Then the cautious 27...♗f8 seems appropriate (27...♕b6 28 ♖d8+ ♗f8 29 ♕xb6 ♖xb6 30 ♘d5 is unpleasant, while 27...♗f6 28 b4 causes other problems).

27 b4 1-0

If 27...♕b5, then 28 ♘xe7, etc.

An impressive game, played consistently through all the complications and keeping in mind unequivocally what is good for the isolated pawn and what increases its potential.

The games we have analysed so far represent the isolated pawn at its best. Mobile and aggressive, in full harmony with other pieces, it has been a symbol of initiative and action. Unfortunately, as I hinted in the prologue, pawns live double lives, isolated pawns particularly so. To understand fully what they really are, we shall watch them in less fortunate circumstances.

Regedzinski – Rubinstein
Lodz 1917
Queen's Gambit

1 d4 d5 2 ♘f3 ♘f6 3 c4 e6 4 ♗g5 ♘bd7 5 ♘c3 ♗e7 6 e3 0-0 7 ♗d3

An experienced modern master would more likely continue 7 ♕c2, 7 ♖c1 or 7 cxd5 followed by ♗d3.

7...dxc4 8 ♗xc4 a6 9 0-0 b5 10 ♗d3 ♗b7 11 ♕e2 c5 12 ♖ad1 cxd4 13 exd4 ♘b6

Owing to White's superficial play, Black has achieved all that he can hope for in this variation. He was allowed to expand on the queenside, develop his minor pieces on their optimal squares and blockade the isolated pawn firmly. The d5-square is Black's strong square to be used at will by his pieces.

14 ♘e4?

Of course, the move to make was 14 ♘e5, trying to compensate for White's superficial development and to activate his pieces in such a manner that the potential weakness at d4 is less exposed. The text-move is a very instructive error of the sort I alluded to earlier in the book. In order to play an active role, isolated pawns need good support from pieces. Without them, their isolation is accentuated. Regedzinski does not understand the nature of his d4-pawn and chooses exactly the path he should avoid.

14...♘xe4 15 ♗xe7 ♕xe7 16 ♗xe4 ♖fd8 17 ♖d3

Another pointless move.

17...♗xe4 18 ♕xe4 ♖ac8

The exchanges have visibly weakened the d4-pawn. As if that were not enough, Black's dominance on the open file predicts a very difficult endgame for White.

19 ♖fd1 ♘d5 20 ♖3d2

White has settled for the most passive defence.

20...♘f6 21 ♕e3 ♕b7 22 h3 h6 23 ♖e2 ♕d5 24 b3 ♕d6

I have always admired Rubinstein's simplicity of thought. First he chased White's queen from the centre in order to provoke a further weakening by ...♕d5. Now he vacates the d5-square again, this time for his knight. The value of such strong squares lies exactly in the fact that one can use them for different pieces and different purposes.

25 ♖c1 ♘d5 26 ♕d2 ♕f4! *(D)*

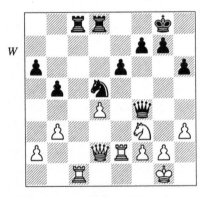

What White did not understand, Black does: the further into the endgame, the more difficult White's position will become.

27 ♖c2 ♕xd2 28 ♖exd2 ♖xc2 29 ♖xc2 ♘b4 30 ♖b2 ♖c8

The penetration of the rook on the only open file will prove decisive.

31 ♔f1 ♖c1+ 32 ♔e2 ♖a1 33 ♔d2 ♖xa2 34 ♖xa2 ♘xa2

Material is won. Only some attention is now needed.

35 ♘e5 ♘b4 36 ♘d7 f6 37 g3 ♔f7 38 ♘b6 ♔e7 39 ♔c3 a5 0-1

The lesson is crystal clear: when you own an isolated pawn in the centre, do not exchange pieces! The game we have just examined is a perfect example of what should not be done. For teaching purposes, such games are precious.

Botvinnik – Zagoriansky
Sverdlovsk 1943
English Opening

1 c4 c5 2 ♘f3 ♘f6 3 ♘c3 e6 4 e3 ♗e7 5 b3 0-0 6 ♗b2 d5 7 cxd5 ♘xd5 8 ♘xd5 exd5?!

One would expect 8...♕xd5.

9 d4 cxd4

In case of 9...♕a5+ or 9...♗f6 White continues 10 ♕d2 playing in both lines to create a potentially weak pawn on d5.

10 ♕xd4

Looking forward to the exchange of bishops, White provokes ...♗f6.

10...♗f6 11 ♕d2 ♘c6 12 ♗e2 ♗e6 13 0-0 ♗xb2 14 ♕xb2 ♕a5 15 ♖fd1

The plan in similar situations is quite simple: first, build maximum pressure on the isolated pawn, tying the opponent's forces to passive defence.

15...♖fd8 16 ♖d2 ♖d7 17 ♖ad1 ♖ad8 18 h3 h6 19 ♘e5

Again crystal clear: the fewer pieces there are on the board, the more exposed the d5-pawn will be.

19...♘xe5 20 ♕xe5 ♕c5 21 ♗f3 b6
22 ♕b2 ♖c8 23 ♕e5 ♖cd8 24 ♖d4

Following the old recommendation that a pawn weakness should be immobilized. Besides, the rook on the fourth rank can be put to good use on the wings.

24...a5 25 g4! *(D)*

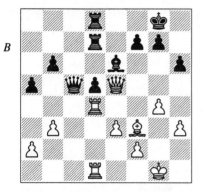

A move to remember, played at an important moment. The position is highly instructive for the method applied against a blockaded isolated pawn. At the moment when all Black's forces are tied to the defence of the lame d5-pawn, White opens another front on the kingside. Attacks of this kind are in principle very dangerous because they are undertaken when the passive position of the defender's pieces diminishes his prospects of putting up resistance.

25...♕c6

Note that Black cannot oppose the attack by 25...♕d6? because after the exchange of queens, e4 wins material – another reason why the d5-pawn must be blockaded.

26 g5 hxg5

Somebody suggested that Black should play 26...♕c2, trying to bring at least one piece back to defend the kingside. It may be so, but only temporarily. That which is in principle bad, says an old Latin proverb, by the passage of time cannot be improved.

27 ♕xg5 f6

With the g-file open, Black's castled position can only be temporarily defended.

28 ♕g6 ♗f7 29 ♕g3 f5

This will only help White, but it is difficult to recommend anything substantially better against the pressure exerted on the g-file.

30 ♕g5 ♕e6 31 ♔h1 ♕e5 32 ♖g1 ♖f8 33 ♕h6 ♖b8 34 ♖h4 ♔f8 35 ♕h8+ ♗g8 36 ♖f4 ♖bb7 37 ♖g5 ♖f7 38 ♕h5 ♕a1+ 39 ♔h2 g6 40 ♕xg6 ♗h7 41 ♕d6+ ♖fe7 42 ♕d8+ 1-0

Korchnoi – Karpov
World Ch match (game 9),
Merano 1981
Queen's Gambit

1 c4 e6 2 ♘c3 d5 3 d4 ♗e7 4 ♘f3 ♘f6 5 ♗g5 h6 6 ♗h4 0-0 7 ♖c1

Grandmaster Uhlmann used this move-order so as to meet the Tartakower Variation, 7...b6, with 8 cxd5 ♘xd5 9 ♗xe7 ♕xe7 10 ♘xd5 exd5 11 g3 ♗e6 12 ♗g2, when the fianchettoed bishop is well placed against Black's pawn-centre. Later Black countered his idea by postponing ...♗e6 and keeping at his disposal ...♗a6. Karpov, however, came up with a simpler idea...

7...dxc4 8 e3

On 8 e4 Beliavsky demonstrated 8...♘c6 9 ♗xc4 ♘xe4.

8...c5 9 ♗xc4 cxd4 10 exd4 ♘c6 11 0-0 ♘h5! *(D)*

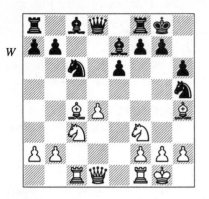

One of those simple reactions typical of Karpov's play and implying a deep understanding of the position in the centre. Although unwilling to do so, White has no choice but to exchange the dark-squared bishops, limiting significantly his chances of active play in the middlegame.

12 ♗xe7 ♘xe7 13 ♗b3?!

This is too tame to satisfy the urgent needs of the position. When we see the whole game and look back at it, we must come to the conclusion that White's initial advantage is gone and his wisest course is 13 d5, leading to exchanges and a draw. With the white pieces, one is naturally reluctant to seek a draw at such an early stage of the game, but objective evaluation of the position should prevail over emotions.

If White decides to continue fighting, then the text-move is certainly not the one on which he should pin his hopes. 13 ♖e1 has been tried, but it does not convince me. I am sure that a realist like Tigran Petrosian would not hesitate to offer a draw. We shall soon see why.

13...♘f6 14 ♘e5 ♗d7 15 ♕e2 ♖c8 16 ♘e4?

Black has blockaded the isolated pawn just as in the lines of the Queen's Gambit Accepted, but with one crucial difference: the dark-squared bishops have been exchanged, a fact which favours Black. Further exchanges are just grist to Black's mill. Instead of the natural 16 ♖cd1, White himself is looking for exchanges and the consequences will be all too plain to see.

16...♘xe4 17 ♕xe4 ♗c6 18 ♘xc6 ♖xc6 19 ♖c3

Korchnoi's last move was also criticized and 19 ♖xc6 suggested as better, but I doubt this very much, because 19...bxc6 would isolate the d4-pawn for good. We have known since the 1921 Lasker-Capablanca match (see the next game) what an impossible task the defence of such a pawn and such a position represent.

19...♕d6 20 g3

There is no meaningful job for the rook on the kingside.

20...♖d8 21 ♖d1 ♖b6

So as to make it possible for Black to play ...♕d7 and ...♖d6, exerting maximum pressure on the d4-pawn.

22 ♕e1 ♕d7 23 ♖cd3 ♖d6 24 ♕e4 ♕c6 25 ♕f4 ♘d5 26 ♕d2 ♕b6 27 ♗xd5?!

Played again against principles. As I have emphasized many times: the fewer pieces there are on the board, the lonelier isolated pawns become. 27 a3 is not appealing, but what must be done must be done. It is a wrong conviction, refuted many times, that a major-piece endgame offers the best saving chances. On the contrary, it is the simplest route to debacle.

27...Xxd5 28 Xb3 Wc6 29 Wc3 Wd7 30 f4 *(D)*

In order to prevent ...e5 White must weaken his castled position and that is the beginning of the end. Karpov plays with great precision and although we could criticize some of Korchnoi's following moves, we cannot propose anything substantially better.

30...b6 31 Xb4 b5 32 a4 bxa4 33 Wa3 a5 34 Xxa4 Wb5 35 Xd2 e5!

This advance was sooner or later unavoidable. The position opens up and the white king remains unprotected.

36 fxe5 Xxe5 37 Wa1 We8 38 dxe5 Xxd2 39 Xxa5 Wc6 40 Xa8+ ❖h7 41 Wb1+ g6 42 Wf1 Wc5+ 43 ❖h1 Wd5+ 0-1

A game of masterful moves and conspicuous errors, but all of them highly instructive!

Lasker – Capablanca
World Ch match (game 10),
Havana 1921
Queen's Gambit

1 d4 d5 2 c4 e6 3 ♘c3 ♘f6 4 ♗g5 ♗e7 5 e3 0-0 6 ♘f3 ♘bd7 7 Wc2

This is Rubinstein's move, which often intends queenside castling and kingside action.

7...c5 8 Xd1

Confronted by an energetic reply in the centre, White changes his plan. As a matter of fact, the consistent 8 0-0-0 is more dangerous for Black.

8...Wa5

Black does not fear 9 cxd5 ♘xd5 10 ♗xe7 ♘xe7 11 ♗d3 ♘f6, as this gives Black good play. The exchange of the dark-squared bishops favours him. Besides, 8...cxd4 seems premature in view of 9 ♘xd4.

9 ♗d3 h6 10 ♗h4 cxd4

Commentators later pointed out that after 10...dxc4 11 ♗xc4 ♘b6 White's bishop would have to be satisfied with the uglier view from e2.

11 exd4 dxc4 12 ♗xc4 ♘b6 13 ♗b3 ♗d7 14 0-0 Xac8

The impatient 14...♗c6 is insufficient because of 15 ♘e5 ♗d5 16 ♘xd5 ♘bxd5 17 We2 Xac8 18 f4, threatening f5 with promising activity.

15 ♘e5

With Black's reply in mind, we can say that the alternative 15 We2 was better.

15...♗b5 16 ♖fe1 ♘bd5

The game has developed into a complex struggle around the central squares and the isolated pawn. Black has succeeded in restraining the d4-pawn, by establishing a firm point on d5.

This position inspired numerous commentators in those days and one of them, the famous Hungarian player Gyula Breyer, recommended the following variation: 17 ♗xf6 ♗xf6 (not 17...♘xf6 due to 18 ♘g6) 18 ♗xd5 exd5 19 ♘g4 (Lasker's 19 ♕f5 also proves insufficient in view of 19...♗c6 20 ♘g4 ♗g5 21 f4 g6) 19...♗g5 20 f4 and now 20...♗xf4 21 ♕f5 ♗c7 22 ♘xd5 ♔h8 23 ♘xh6 gxh6 24 ♘f6 ♔g7 25 ♘h5+. Years were to pass until another dedicated analyst came up with improvements introduced by 20...♗h4.

I quote these analyses because they are essential for the understanding of the complex relationships in the centre.

17 ♗xd5 ♘xd5 18 ♗xe7 ♘xe7 19 ♕b3 ♗c6 20 ♘xc6 bxc6! *(D)*

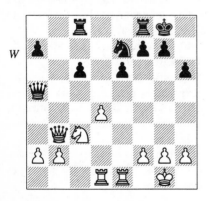

A most interesting endgame is in front of us. Both sides are burdened with isolated pawns, but the thoughtful analyst will soon come to the conclusion that it is White who will have to fight an uphill struggle. The reason: his central isolated pawn is weaker than the c6-pawn. Besides, Black has a semi-open file at his disposal on which additional pressures can be built.

21 ♖e5 ♕b6 22 ♕c2?! ♖fd8 23 ♘e2?!

Lasker's last two moves were criticized as too passive, especially 23 ♘e2, where 23 ♘a4 was suggested. It is true, by positioning his knight on a4 White would thwart a later minority attack, but on the other hand his d4-pawn would be weaker. The fact is that the position is much easier to play for Black, because his plan is clear. White, on the contrary, must sit and wait.

23...♖d5 24 ♖xd5

This is a hasty decision; the exchange in principle favours Black. In our case there is an additional consideration: Black gets rid of his isolated pawn, while the d4-pawn remains subject to pressure.

24...cxd5 25 ♕d2 ♘f5 26 b3 h5

Many commentators noted that this move should have been prepared by 26...g6, as White could now cause inconvenience, though not alleviate his difficulties entirely, by 27 ♘g3.

27 h3 h4

Now White's kingside is blocked, the d4-pawn in constant need of defence, and the open file is dominated by Black's major pieces – just to sum up the visible inconveniences.

28 ♕d3 ♖c6 29 ♔f1 g6 30 ♕b1 ♕b4 31 ♔g1 a5 *(D)*

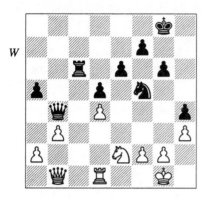

We have seen this method before. When the maximum pressure has been built on a weak point and opponent's forces tied to its defence, it is usually necessary to open another front. Playing against Zagoriansky, as we saw, Botvinnik attacked on the kingside. Capablanca starts a minority attack which will sooner or later result in another weak point in White's camp. To hold a position with two weak points will be twice as difficult – simple logic.

32 ♕b2 a4 33 ♕d2 ♕xd2 34 ♖xd2 axb3 35 axb3 ♖b6 36 ♖d3 ♖a6

Rooks are always attracted by open files and the chance to break through to their seventh rank. Here Black's rook is offered both incentives.

37 g4 hxg3 38 fxg3 ♖a2 39 ♘c3 ♖c2 40 ♘d1 ♔e7 41 ♘e3 ♖c1+ 42 ♔f2 ♘c6 43 ♘d1 ♖b1

One can never be too careful: after 43...♘b4 44 ♖d2 ♖b1 45 ♘b2 ♖xb2 46 ♖xb2 ♘d3+ 47 ♔e2 ♘xb2 48 ♔d2 the knight is trapped.

44 ♔e2? ♖xb3 45 ♔e3 ♖b4 46 ♘c3 ♘e7 47 ♘e2 ♘f5+ 48 ♔f2 g5 49 g4 ♘d6 50 ♘g1 ♘e4+ 51 ♔f1 ♖b1+ 52 ♔g2 ♖b2+ 53 ♔f1 ♖f2+ 54 ♔e1 ♖a2 55 ♔f1 ♔g7 56 ♘e3 ♔g6 57 ♖d3 f6 58 ♖e3 ♔f7 59 ♖d3 ♔e7 60 ♖e3 ♔d6 61 ♖d3 ♖f2+ 62 ♔e1 ♖g2 63 ♔f1 ♖a2 64 ♖e3 e5 65 ♖d3 exd4 66 ♖xd4 ♔c5 67 ♖d1 d4 68 ♖c1+ ♔d5

...and the hopeless resistance was finally broken.

0-1

Karpov – Vaganian
Skopje 1976
French Defence

1 e4 e6 2 d4 d5 3 ♘d2 c5 4 exd5 exd5 5 ♘gf3 a6 6 dxc5 ♗xc5 7 ♘b3 ♗b6

When Black withdraws the bishop on this diagonal, its refuge is usually a7 (i.e. 7...♗a7). Then 8 ♗g5 is met by 8...♘f6 9 ♘fd4 0-0 10 ♗e2 ♕d6, getting rid of the pin, when the d5-pawn feels well.

8 ♗d3 ♘e7

8...♕e7+ seems to me logical.

9 0-0 ♘bc6 10 ♖e1

The standard procedure against Black's dark-squared bishop. White prepares ♗e3, a thematic exchange of pieces and a small step towards the desired endgame.

10...♗g4 11 c3

First, block the pawn!

11...h6 12 h3 ♗h5 13 ♗e3 0-0

Black is unable to avoid the exchange by playing 13...♗c7 because then 14 g4 is too strong.

14 ♗xb6 ♕xb6 15 ♕e2 ♖fd8 16 ♖ad1 a5 *(D)*

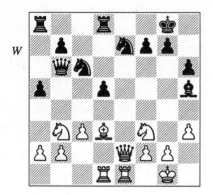

At first glance the text-move causes some inconvenience, but the impression is false.

17 &b1

It is not difficult to see the idea behind the withdrawal of the bishop. 17...a4 can now be met by 18 ♘bd4 ♘xd4 19 ♖xd4, when 19...♘c6 fails to 20 ♖xd5, Black's back rank being vulnerable. Of course, the aim is to control the strong square d4.

17...&xf3 18 ♕xf3 a4 19 ♘d4 ♕xb2

Black could not resist the temptation of the b2-pawn or perhaps the feeling that something is dubious about his position made him to look for some compensation. As a consequence his king falls under attack.

20 ♘xc6 ♘xc6 21 ♕f5 g6 22 ♕f6

White threatens &xg6, and 22...♖e8 is not enough to parry the threat because 23 &xg6 fxg6 24 ♕xg6+ ♔f8 25 ♕f6+ ♔g8 26 ♖e6 decides. With Black's queen astray, it is impossible for him to defend his naked king.

Note that when an isolated pawn is successfully blocked, as a rule there is

a chance to switch to action on the wings. The weaker side, concentrating on the defence of the pawn, is often left defenceless on the wing.

22...♖d7 23 &f5! *(D)*

23 ♖e3 is too slow due to 23...♕a3, when the queen retreats in time, but the text-move is a killer leaving Black no hope.

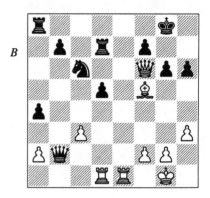

23...♖e7

23...gxf5 fails to 24 ♖d3 f4 25 ♕xf4, etc.

24 ♖xe7 ♘xe7 25 &d3 ♘f5 26 &xf5 gxf5 27 ♖e1 ♕xa2 28 ♕xh6!

Vaganian had set a refined trap, which Karpov evidently saw through. After 28 ♖e3 f4 29 ♕xf4 ♕b1+ 30 ♔h2 a3 31 ♖g3+ there is 31...♕g6 and the passed pawn will save Black.

28...a3 29 ♕g5+ ♔f8 30 ♕f6 ♔g8 31 ♕xf5 ♕d2 32 ♖e7 ♖f8 33 ♕g4+ ♔h7 34 ♖e5 ♕h6 35 ♖h5 ♖a8 36 ♕f5+ ♔g7 37 ♖xh6 ♔xh6 38 ♕f6+ ♔h7 39 ♕xf7+ ♔h8 40 ♕xb7 1-0

A number of the games we have analysed emphasized the significance of the opponent's strong square in front of the isolated pawn. Very often the measure of one's influence on it makes the difference between success and failure. In that sense the games played in the French Tarrasch are particularly revealing and deserve our attention.

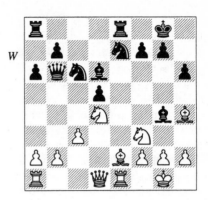

Karpov – Korchnoi
Candidates match (game 4),
Moscow 1974
French Defence

1 e4 e6 2 d4 d5 3 ♘d2 c5 4 exd5 exd5 5 ♘gf3 ♘c6 6 ♗b5 ♗d6 7 dxc5 ♗xc5 8 0-0 ♘e7 9 ♘b3 ♗d6 10 c3

One of the logical possibilities applied by Karpov in his matches against Korchnoi. White bases his strategy in the opening phase on achieving full control of his strong square d4.

10...♗g4

A natural reaction. By pinning the knight, ready to exchange it at any moment, Black starts his battle for counter-pressure on the same d4-square.

11 ♘bd4 0-0 12 ♗e2

In later games of the same match Karpov gave preference to 12 ♕a4 but 12...♗h5 13 ♗e3 ♕c7 14 h3 ♘a5, planning ...♘c4, kept the balance.

12...♖e8 13 ♖e1 a6 14 ♗g5 h6 15 ♗h4 ♕b6 *(D)*

Having developed harmoniously, Korchnoi takes a correct decision to throw all his weight on the point d4.

16 ♕b3 ♗c5 17 ♕xb6 ♗xb6 18 ♗d3

It is already clear that there is no way for White to keep the stronghold at d4.

18...♔f8 19 a3 ♘xd4 20 ♘xd4 ♗xd4 21 cxd4 ♘f5 22 f3 ♘xh4 23 fxg4 ♘g6

The scene is clearer now. Black has succeeded in nullifying White's pressure in the centre without making other concessions (compare the game Karpov-Uhlmann, Madrid 1973).

24 g3

Playing White, players often indulge in a false sense of security that often leads to the abyss. Instead of securing a draw by 24 ♗xg6, Karpov strangely enters an endgame that is advantageous to his opponent.

24...♘e7 25 ♗f1 ♘c6 26 ♗g2 ♖xe1+ 27 ♖xe1 ♖d8 28 ♔f2 ♖d6 29 ♖d1 ♔e7 30 b4 ♖d8 31 ♔e3 ♔d6 32 ♖f1 f6 33 ♖c1 ♖c8 34 ♖c5 ♘e7 35 ♗f1?!

This is a serious error. 35 ♖xc8 followed by a4 was called for.

35...♖e8 36 ♔d2 f5 37 ♗e2

37 gxf5 ♘xf5 activates the knight, which then threatens to enter the game via e3.

37...fxg4 38 ♗xg4 ♖f8 39 ♖c2 g6 40 ♔e3 h5 41 ♗h3 ♘c6 42 ♖d2 b5?!

If Black prepares ...♖e8+ by 42...g5, then White's defence is not so easy.

43 ♗g2 a5 44 h4 axb4 45 axb4 ♖e8+ ½-½

White intended 46 ♔f4 ♘xb4 47 ♔g5 ♖e3 48 g4, etc.

Sometimes the strong square in front of the isolated pawn belongs completely to one's opponent. One can just watch him parading his minor and major pieces as it pleases him. When possible, however, the pressure exerted on it repays itself in the form of positional equality, or even more, if circumstances allow it...

L. Schmid – Portisch
Olympiad, Nice 1974
French Defence

1 e4 e6 2 d4 d5 3 ♘d2 c5 4 ♘gf3 ♘c6 5 exd5 exd5 6 ♗b5 ♗d6 7 dxc5 ♗xc5 8 0-0 ♘e7 9 ♘b3 ♗d6 10 ♗g5 0-0 11 ♗h4

We have seen already this sequence of moves. The idea is the exchange of dark-squared bishops by ♗g3.

11...♗g4 12 ♗e2 ♖e8 *(D)*

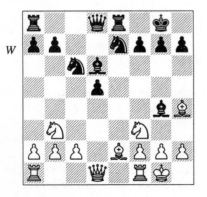

An improvement in comparison with the game Karpov-Uhlmann, Madrid 1973, which we discussed earlier in this book.

13 ♖e1

13 ♗g3 would finally accomplish White's planned manoeuvre, but then 13...♗xg3 14 hxg3 ♕b6, with ...♖ad8 and ...♘f5 to follow, gives Black satisfactory play.

13...♕b6 14 ♘fd4

14 c3 is met by 14...♘f5 with full control of the d4-square, while 14 ♗xe7 backfires in view of 14...♖xe7 15 ♕xd5 ♘b4.

14...♗xe2 15 ♖xe2 ♗e5

This too has been made possible by 12...♖e8. The pressure exerted on d4 will force White to give up the blockade. Portisch has succeeded in solving the thematic problem of the central squares.

16 ♘xc6 ♘xc6 17 c3 a5

Here, in somewhat different circumstances, this move seizes the initiative, because 18 a4 loses to 18...♗xh2+.

18 ♖b1 a4 19 ♘d2 ♕b5 20 ♗g3 ♗f6

Black has managed to turn the tables: now it is he who is in command of the centre.

21 ♖xe8+ ♖xe8 22 ♕f1 ♕c5 23 ♖e1 ♖d8

One does not voluntarily exchange active pieces.

24 a3 h6 25 ♕d3 ♕b6 26 ♕c2 ♕b5 27 ♗c7?!

27 ♘f3 is more natural.

27...♖c8 28 ♗f4?

28 ♗g3 was indispensable. The text-move loses a pawn.

28...♘d4 29 ♕d1 ♘e6 30 ♕g4 h5 31 ♕f5 ♖e8 32 ♘f3 ♕xb2 33 ♗e5 ♗xe5 34 ♘xe5 ♘d8 35 h3 g6 36 ♕d7 ♖xe5 37 ♕xd8+ ♔g7 38 ♖xe5 ♕c1+ 39 ♔h2 ♕f4+ 40 g3 ♕xe5 41 ♕a5 h4 42 ♕c5 hxg3+ 0-1

In view of 43 fxg3 b6, etc.

Portisch demonstrated masterfully yet another motif in the attempt to control the isolated pawn and keep the positional balance. Quite often, however, the side playing against an isolated pawn can resort to tactical solutions, thwarting the standard plans of his adversary and compromising the array of his forces. It is worthwhile giving some thought to the events characterizing the following games...

Botvinnik – Euwe
Hastings 1934/5
Caro-Kann Defence

1 c4 c6 2 e4 d5 3 exd5 cxd5 4 d4 ♘f6 5 ♘c3 ♘c6 6 ♗g5 e6 7 ♘f3 dxc4

In a few moves the play transposes from one opening to another. One must be constantly alert to such possibilities. We shall see in what measure Euwe's decision was correct.

8 ♗xc4 ♗e7 9 0-0 0-0 10 ♖c1

Decades of grandmaster practice has taught us that on c1 the rook is of little use to White. Today one would continue 10 a3, preparing ♕d3, ♖ad1 and ♖fe1. Besides, in the Queen's Gambit Accepted the bishop on g5 is in the wrong place. It should be at e3, making possible ♘e5. In transposing from one variation to another, Black was more cunning.

10...a6

A good reply. The planned ...b5 followed by the fianchetto of the queen's bishop corresponds to the general strategy of blockade in the centre.

11 ♗d3 h6

White's previous move did not prevent 11...b5 because after 12 ♘xb5 axb5 13 ♖xc6 ♗b7 Black takes on a2. Therefore, that was Black's simplest choice.

12 ♗e3

We have reached a critical phase of the game. White could choose 12 ♗h4, intending to create threats by ♗b1 and ♕d3, as we have seen in a number of games.

12...♘b4 13 ♗b1 b5 14 ♘e5 ♗b7 15 ♕d2 ♖e8

The opening phase is over, and Black has achieved his strategic aims. He dominates d5, and the d4-pawn has become a potential weakness.

16 f4?!

Since in comparison with Botvinnik's win over Vidmar the chances of attack are significantly reduced, the more moderate 16 f3 was a healthier choice.

16...♘bd5 17 ♘xd5 ♕xd5 18 f5 ♗d6! *(D)*

Very strong indeed! The point e5 is shaky.

19 fxe6 ♖xe6 20 ♗f5

White cannot contemplate 20 ♘f3 ♖ae8 or 20 ♗f4 ♗xe5.

20...♖e7 21 ♗h3 ♗xe5 22 dxe5 ♕xe5 23 ♗f4 ♕d5 24 ♕xd5

If in his previous calculations White considered the sacrifice 24 ♗xh6 gxh6 25 ♕xh6, he now had to give up the

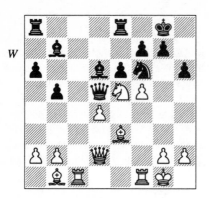

W

idea because of the counterattack with 25...Ξe2.

24...Ξxd5 25 Ξd2 Ξae8 26 b3 Ξe2

Black has won the theoretical duel and starts to convert his material advantage into victory.

27 Ξf2 ♘f6 28 ♗a5 Ξxf2 29 ♔xf2 ♘e4+ 30 ♔f1 ♘g5 31 ♗d7

31 ♗g4 offers more resistance.

31...Ξe7 32 ♗f5 Ξe5 33 ♗b1 Ξe4

Euwe makes use of his advantage in exemplary fashion. Note the manoeuvre ...♘f6-e4-g5!

34 ♗xe4 ♘xe4 35 Ξc6

More precise was 35 Ξc8+ followed by ♗e1 in order to thwart the penetration of the rook.

35...Ξf5+ 36 ♔e1 Ξf2 37 a4 Ξxg2 38 Ξxa6

After 38 ♗c7 some concentration is still needed: correct is 38...Ξb2, but not 38...bxa4 39 bxa4 Ξa2 40 a5 (not 40 Ξxa6? Ξa1+).

38...bxa4 39 bxa4 Ξxh2 40 Ξa8+ ♔h7 41 ♗b6 Ξa2 42 a5 h5 43 a6 h4 44 a7 h3 45 ♗g1 ♘f6 46 ♔d1 ♘g4 47 Ξe8 h2 48 ♗xh2 Ξxa7 49 ♗b8 Ξa8 50 Ξd8 ♘e5 51 ♗c7 Ξxd8+ 52 ♗xd8

♔g6 53 ♔e2 ♔f5 54 ♔e3 ♔g4 55 ♗c7 ♘f3 56 ♔f2 f5 0-1

The health of the centralized knight at e5 depends on the d4-pawn and vice versa. They succeed or fall together.

Another game from the 1930s is also a small lesson on tactical play in the same variation...

Hasenfuss – Flohr
Kemeri 1937
Caro-Kann Defence

1 e4 c6 2 d4 d5 3 exd5 cxd5 4 c4 ♘f6 5 ♘c3 ♘c6 6 ♗g5 e6 7 ♘f3 dxc4 8 ♗xc4 ♗e7 9 0-0 0-0 10 Ξc1 a6 11 a3

The famous Radio Erevan would say: White played well; the only problem is that he put his pieces in the wrong place and at the wrong time.

11...b5 12 ♗a2 ♗b7 13 ♕d3 ♘d5 (D)

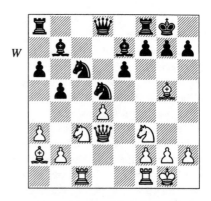

W

14 ♘e4?

White would like to exploit the inviting weakness at c5. He did not like 14 ♗xe7 ♘cxe7 15 ♘e4 because of 15...♘f4. On the other hand 14 ♘xd5

♗xg5 or 14 ♗b1 f5, when the attractive e4-square is out of reach, did not appeal to him. These considerations must have pushed Hasenfuss into an erroneous step. Looking at the position objectively, 14 ♗xd5 appears logical; an advantage is there or it is not there, but it cannot be forced upon the position. The punishment follows at once...

14...♘cb4! 15 ♕b1

Taking on b4 would just cost a pawn.

15...♘xa2 16 ♕xa2 ♗xg5 17 ♘exg5 h6 18 ♘e4 ♘f4 19 ♖ce1 ♗d5 20 b3 f5 21 ♘ed2 ♕f6 22 ♔h1

Played in order to meet ...♕g6.

22...♖ac8 23 ♕b1

23 ♖c1 was not at White's disposal due to 23...♕g6 24 g3 ♕g4.

23...♘xg2 24 ♔xg2 ♕g5+ 25 ♔h1 ♕xd2 26 ♖e3 ♕xd4 0-1

Szabo – Petrosian
Bamberg 1968
Nimzo-Indian Defence

1 d4 ♘f6 2 c4 e6 3 ♘c3 ♗b4 4 e3 0-0 5 ♗d3 d5 6 ♘f3 c5 7 0-0 ♘c6 8 a3 cxd4 9 exd4 dxc4 10 ♗xc4 ♗e7

Having been confronted with 8 a3, Petrosian has entered a risky continuation for Black. We have already examined similar positions in a few games and the comparison will be useful to the reader.

11 ♖e1 ♗d7 12 ♗a2

A logical retreat. On a2 the bishop cannot be attacked by ...♘a5 and it can switch immediately to the other important diagonal, namely b1-h7.

12...♖c8 13 ♕d3 ♖e8 14 ♘e5

At this point it seems better to develop the queenside.

14...g6 15 ♗g5 (D)

One would prefer 15 ♗h6.

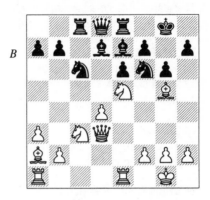

15...♘h5!

Black chooses the proper moment for this move. White was finishing his preparations for the breakthrough in the centre, but Black succeeds in diminishing the pressure. His move reminds us of Karpov's reaction in one of his match games versus Korchnoi (p.36). This simplifying move is characteristic of many positions in the Queen's Gambit and it is useful to remember it.

16 ♗xe7 ♕xe7 17 ♘c4

In case of 17 d5 there is 17...♘xe5 18 ♖xe5 ♕d6 with level play but 17 ♖ad1 makes a better impression than the somewhat unnatural text-move.

17...b5!

Since 18 ♘xb5 is well answered by 18...♘b4, the sudden advance of the b-pawn thwarts the imminent danger of the breakthrough.

18 ♘e3 b4 19 ♘e4 ♘f6

Petrosian does not miss a single chance: the exchange of knights would alleviate difficulties in the centre.

20 ♘c4 ♖cd8 21 ♘xf6+?

21 ♘ed6 would be more unpleasant for Black. In general, exchanges help the side lacking space and air.

21...♕xf6 22 ♘d6 ♖e7

This will keep the rook in play.

23 ♖ad1 ♗e8 24 ♘xe8

24 ♘e4 is not better, in view of 24...♕g7.

24...♖exe8

The fog has lifted: the isolated pawn remains under pressure and it cannot move.

25 ♕a6 ♘xd4 26 ♕xa7

26 axb4 ♘c2 27 ♖xd8 ♖xd8 28 ♖f1 ♘xb4 29 ♕xa7 ♕xb2 30 ♗c4 ♖c8 does not bring White relief.

26...b3 27 ♗b1 ♘c2 28 ♖xd8 ♖xd8 29 ♖f1 ♕xb2

By skilfully defending a passive position and making use of White's little inconsistencies, Petrosian has slowly turned the position to his advantage. The far-advanced passed pawn guarantees victory.

30 ♕b6 ♖d5 31 a4 ♕c3 32 h3 ♔g7 33 g3 ♖a5 34 h4 ♖xa4 35 h5 gxh5 36 ♕d8 h6 0-1

The skill demonstrated by Petrosian in defence is worth analysing in detail.

Some General Observations

Studying this short selection of games we have learnt what an uncertain life an isolated pawn leads. The centre characterized by such a pawn-formation, therefore, requires sober evaluation and most careful treatment. The position is so sensitive that even small errors, which may be imperceptible to an inexperienced eye, cause grave difficulties. At the same time the reader must have become aware of the fact that each of these central situations, no matter how similar they may seem, is different. A pawn advance on the wing or one piece placed at a different position can change everything. Strict, constantly valid rules how to play these positions remain, therefore, out of reach, no matter how many examples we examine.

However, the reader must also have noticed that some general guidance can be applied, covering a very large number of possible cases. These general maxims are the only directions we can depend upon. If we absorb them by studying typical cases, if they are a fruit of our analytical work, all the better. So in order to formulate some general advice we can trust, we start from our simple, practical observations.

Studying our topic we are soon aware that there exist two types of central isolated pawns: one movable, aggressive; the other immovable, controlled and blockaded. These cases result in utterly different situations.

If the breakthrough is possible, as a rule, it releases a remarkable amount of energy, which is manifested in several typical cases:

a) Attack on the opponent's castled position, carried out after direct, combined threats on the diagonals b1-h7 and a2-g8, and often supported by threats on the open e-file;

b) Penetration of the king's knight in the footsteps of advancing isolated pawn;

c) Transformation of the initiative into a strong, active centralized piece;

d) Transformation of the initiative into a better endgame.

In all these cases, and the record does not leave room for any doubt, the side which successfully prepares and carries out a central thrust achieves a very high percentage of wins. The conclusion is self-evident: a central isolated pawn must be blockaded.

We have seen that it takes patience, precision in the choice of the move-order and sometimes cunning, too, if we wish to be successful. The counter-measures against an isolated pawn are concentrated on the full domination over the square in front of the pawn. If such a balance of power is reached in the centre, the side with the isolated pawn will create activity based on his mobile pieces: in the first place a dominant centralized knight, supported by the isolated pawn, or a rook manoeuvre on the third rank, coupled with bishops exerting pressure on the diagonals towards the opponent's castled position. Note, however, that such activity does not come of itself. As a rule, it is a fruit of better development, a spatial advantage and actively posted pieces.

The side fighting against an isolated pawn, on the contrary, must try to simplify the position through exchanges, constantly watching that no central thrust is possible. Unquestionable authority over the square in front of the pawn is an imperative.

Taking all this into consideration, one can never emphasize enough two crucial maxims:

1) As the side with the isolated pawn, save your pieces; do not exchange them lightly, because an isolated pawn needs company badly. At the same time stay alert to all the possible tactical blows inspired by the breakthrough, even at the cost of making a sacrifice.

2) When playing against the isolated pawn, try to blockade the isolated pawn, concentrating your effort on the strong square in front of it, reduce material (most exchanges are welcome) and try to reach an endgame, because it is not a natural habitat for an isolated pawn and because in endgames, as a rule, it becomes a lame duck, an immovable target.

And finally, White or Black, when playing a position characterized by an isolated pawn in the centre, should after each move ask the essential question: can the pawn advance or not? And the next question: what can I do to prepare the breakthrough? Or vice versa: what can I do to stop it for good or make it innocuous?

During a game much will depend on how seriously you ask these questions and how responsible your answers are.

2 Isolated Pawn Couples and Hanging Pawns

Having discussed isolated pawns in the centre, we reach a new subject. We shall now discuss a pair of central pawns unsupported by other pawns on the neighbouring files. They appear usually as the consequence of two pawn exchanges in the centre or, very often, as descendants of an isolated pawn, after an exchange on the neighbouring file. It takes just a move from an isolated pawn to reach an isolated pair of pawns (called an 'isolated pawn couple') and one step further to what we call hanging pawns, a pair of pawns on the fourth rank (or if Black on the fifth rank). Being such close relatives, they inherit and share some strikingly similar qualities. Let us first pay attention to an isolated pawn couple.

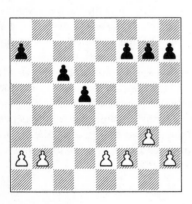

Here we have one of the typical cases of an isolated pawn couple. An isolated pawn lived on d5 and an exchange on c6 united them for common action and destiny. What we notice first in the diagram is the hole on c5 and an experienced eye associates it at once with a potential weakness.

On the contrary, if the c6-pawn steps forward to c5, we have the position of the next diagram.

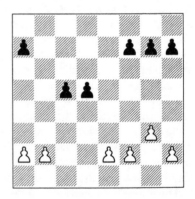

The difference is small, just a detail in Black's pawn-formation, and yet we associate it at once with aggressive advance in the centre. The following grandmaster games will confirm our first impressions and offer some basic answers.

Rubinstein – Salwe
Lodz 1908
Queen's Gambit

1 d4 d5 2 c4 e6 3 ♘c3 c5 4 cxd5 exd5 5 ♘f3 ♘c6 6 g3 ♘f6 7 ♗g2

Due primarily to the enthusiasm of its inventor, Dr Tarrasch, some crucial problems of this sensitive variation were solved at the beginning of the 20th century, but many nuances remained to be understood at the time when our game was played. The pressure on the d5-pawn caused by the fianchetto of the light-squared bishop is evidently a major factor in the position. Today we know it and deal with it cautiously. The modern main line continues 7...♗e7 8 0-0 0-0 9 ♗g5 and only then does Black cede in the centre by 9...cxd4. Salwe cedes at the wrong moment...

7...cxd4?! 8 ♘xd4 ♕b6

By exerting pressure on d4 at a moment when White cannot fortify it, Black provokes ♘xc6, when his d-pawn will no longer be isolated. It seems a logical decision, but we shall soon see how costly it really was.

9 ♘xc6 bxc6 10 0-0 ♗e7 11 ♘a4! *(D)*

Black has managed to unite his pawns, but at the cost of time and development – he is yet to castle, and the c5-square is weak. It is toward that square that White directs his forces. On a4, the knight controls c5 and defends the b2-pawn, making possible further pressure on c5 by ♗e3 and along the c-file.

11...♕b5 12 ♗e3 0-0 13 ♖c1 ♗g4

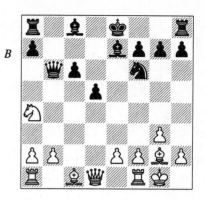

B

At first glance this is a normal developing move. Still, after further consideration we notice that it allows quick, concentrated pressure on the c-file.

14 f3

An ugly move, but only until we discover its true purpose. Already here Rubinstein had in mind the manoeuvre ♖f2-c2, which will definitely fix the isolated pawn couple c6-d5 in all their passivity.

14...♗e6 15 ♗c5

When we are stronger on some square, it is useful to exchange the pieces that defend it. Such exchanges make the weakness evident.

15...♖fe8 16 ♖f2 ♘d7 17 ♗xe7 ♖xe7 18 ♕d4

With the dark-squared bishops exchanged, Black tries to use his knight to cover his weakness, but the dominant, centralized queen reinforces White's dominance over the critical c5-square.

18...♖ee8

In case of 18...♖c8 White, naturally, would not greedily grab the pawn by

19 ♕xa7 because 19...c5 changes the scene to his detriment. Instead, the quiet 19 ♘c5 would thwart any attempt at freeing Black's game.

19 ♗f1 ♖ec8 20 e3 ♕b7 21 ♘c5 ♘xc5 22 ♖xc5

So the minor pieces have disappeared from the board and the blockade on the dark squares grows stronger move by move.

22...♖c7 23 ♖fc2 ♕b6 24 b4 *(D)*

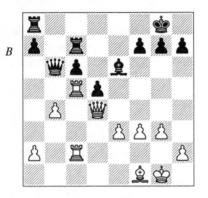

The threat of b5 will provoke another weakness after 24...a6. This offers another important lesson: the pawns around weak squares become weak and shaky as time passes and weaknesses multiply. It is exactly to that relentless process that we owe numerous victories on the basis of weak squares.

24...a6 25 ♖a5 ♖b8

After the exchange on d4 a pawn would fall.

26 a3 ♖a7 27 ♖xc6

Finally White's spatial advantage is transformed into a tangible material advantage.

27...♕xc6 28 ♕xa7 ♖a8 29 ♕c5 ♕b7 30 ♔f2 h5 31 ♗e2 g6 32 ♕d6 ♕c8 33 ♖c5 ♕b7 34 h4 a5 35 ♖c7 ♕b8 36 b5 a4 37 b6 ♖a5 38 b7 1-0

In its simplicity a magnificent game to analyse and learn from. An isolated pawn couple, if caught unawares and firmly blockaded, demonstrates the same weakness we discovered in isolated pawns when they could not advance and died slowly in desperate passivity in the resulting endgames.

Balashov – Dreev
Russia Cup, Samara 1998
Caro-Kann Defence

1 c4 c6 2 e4 d5 3 exd5 ♘f6 4 ♘c3 cxd5 5 cxd5 ♘xd5 6 ♘f3 ♘xc3 7 bxc3 g6 8 d4

Here we have the pawn-formation from the previous game as if seen in a mirror. Our isolated pawn couple is on c3 and d4, while Black's pressure comes from the dark-squared bishop and on the semi-open c-file.

8...♗g7 9 ♗d3 ♘c6 10 0-0 0-0 11 ♗e4

In a couple of moves this bishop will return to d3, giving the impression of aimless play. 11 ♖e1 was a legitimate alternative, but little can change some basic facts: the pressure on the pawn couple remains strong and it is difficult to imagine how their status could be improved. At the same time Black's plan is self-evident, and Grandmaster Dreev carries it out smoothly in the next few moves...

11...♗d7 12 ♖e1 ♖c8 13 ♗g5 ♖e8 *(D)*

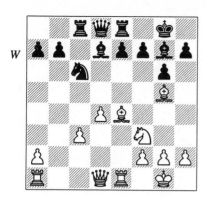

14 ☐c1?!

A critical moment. White sounds the retreat with bleak prospects ahead in an endgame burdened with three pawn-islands of which the central island will remain under constant pressure. One would prefer the more active 14 d5 ♘a5 15 d6 although after 15...♗f6 16 ♗xf6 exf6 White's passed pawn is well blockaded. Then 17 ♗d5 would give some meaning to White's previous play.

14...♘a5 15 ♗d3 ♘c4 16 ♕b3

White continues to watch the slow degradation of his position. It is true, 16 ♕e2 is not appealing in view of 16...♗e6, but 16 ♗xc4 ☐xc4 17 ♘e5 seems indispensable. The text-move allows Dreev to continue stifling his opponent.

16...b5 17 ♗xc4 ☐xc4 18 ♘d2

Now 18 ♘e5 ♗xe5 19 dxe5 exposes White's king to attack after the reply 19...☐g4.

18...☐a4 19 ♘e4 ♗c6 20 ☐cd1?
(D)

The disease has spread on the light squares and a meaningful plan is not easy to recommend. We can just note that the text-move is an obvious error losing material. 20 ♘c5 ☐c4 21 f3 continues resistance in adverse circumstances.

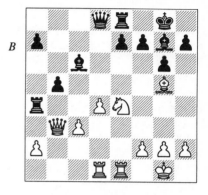

20...♗d5! 21 ♕b1

21 ♕xb5 loses to 21...☐a5.

21...☐xa2

A loss of material is the punishment for White's passive set-up in the centre and visible lack of initiative.

22 ♘c5 a6 23 ♘d3 ☐a4 24 ♘b4 ♗b7 25 f3 ♕c7 26 ♕b3 e6 27 ☐a1 ☐c8 28 ♗d2 ☐xa1 29 ☐xa1 ♕d6 30 ♗e3 e5 31 ☐d1 exd4 32 ♗xd4 ♗xd4+ 33 ☐xd4 ♕c5 34 ♘a2 ☐e8 35 ♕d1 a5 36 ♕d2 ♔g7 37 ♘c1 ♗d5 38 ♘d3 ♕b6 39 h4 h5 40 ♔h2 ♗c4 41 ♘f4 a4 42 ♕f2 ♕f6 0-1

It is not a rare situation for the side with the isolated pawn couple to fall into a disadvantageous position because of the latent pawn weakness. However, much depends on whether the backward pawn can advance and turn the couple into hanging pawns, acquiring mobility and strength. Have a look at the following game...

Reshevsky – Donner
Santa Monica 1966
Nimzo-Indian Defence

1 d4 ♘f6 2 c4 e6 3 ♘c3 ♗b4 4 e3 c5 5 ♗d3 d5 6 ♘f3 0-0 7 0-0 dxc4 8 ♗xc4 ♘bd7

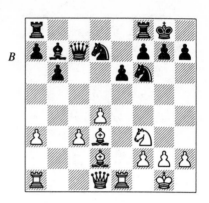

In those days 8...♘c6 9 a3 ♗a5 was also explored with passion, but the feeling prevailed that the position of the knight on d7 was sounder.

9 ♗d3

In case of 9 a3 cxd4 10 exd4 ♗xc3 followed by ...♕c7 Black would have pressure on the c-file, which the text-move avoids. In later years, however, 9 ♕e2 followed by ♖d1 became more popular.

9...b6

If 9...a6, then 10 a3 ♗a5 11 ♕e2 and White can meet 11...b5 by 12 b4.

10 a3 cxd4

After 10...♗xc3 11 bxc3 ♗b7 12 ♖e1 ♗e4 White avoids the exchange by 13 ♗f1, planning ♘d2.

11 exd4 ♗xc3 12 bxc3 ♗b7 13 ♖e1 ♕c7 14 ♗d2 (*D*)

Before he plays c4 Reshevsky wants to prepare it cautiously. The opening phase by both players is characterized by attention to the quality of the isolated pawn couple.

14...♖fe8 15 ♕e2 ♖ac8 16 ♖ac1 ♗d5

Since it will be difficult to organize any meaningful pressure on the hanging pawns, provoking their appearance is a loss of time.

17 c4 ♗b7

When playing 16...♗d5 perhaps Donner intended 17...♗xf3 18 ♕xf3 e5 19 d5 ♘c5, but then understood that 20 ♗f5 followed by ♖c3 and ♗g5 is unpleasant for Black. Whatever the case, Reshevsky has achieved what Salwe and Balashov could only dream of. Well supported by numerous pieces, White's bishop-pair conspicuous among them, the lame isolated pawn couple has metamorphosed into aggressive hanging pawns. From now on Black will have a constant worry in his mind: just like their father, the isolated pawn, this couple on the fourth rank is ready to strike at any moment. Apart from the real threats they pose, they are psychological burden, too.

18 a4 ♕c6

One would expect the natural move 18...h6. The idea of taking the a4-pawn is bizarre.

19 ♗f4 ♕xa4 20 ♖a1 ♕c6 21 ♖xa7 ♖a8 22 ♖xa8 ♖xa8 23 h3

A useful little move. Black should reply by taking the same measure, i.e. 23...h6. Instead he decides to play 'actively' and falls under a strong attack.

23...♖a3? *(D)*

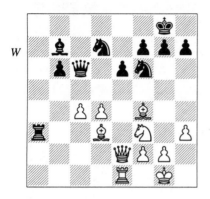

24 d5!

White's motive for the breakthrough is Black's weakened back rank. Now decisive things happen, while the a3-rook can only watch. One should never disregard the constant menace, whenever confronted by two bad boys on the fourth rank.

24...exd5 25 cxd5 ♕xd5

25...♘xd5? loses at once to 26 ♗b5 or 26 ♕e8+ ♘f8 27 ♗xh7+. Remember: when the position opens there are, as a rule, some diagonals via which the more active side can attack.

26 ♗c4 ♕c5 27 ♗xf7+! ♔xf7 28 ♕e6+ ♔g6 29 ♗d6

White has a substantially simpler win by 29 ♘h4+ ♔h5 30 ♖e5+! ♕xe5 31 ♗xe5 ♔xh4 32 ♗xf6+ ♘xf6 33 ♕e7.

29...♕a5?!

Black can put up a better fight by 29...♕c3, though White still wins by very precise play. After 30 ♘h4+ ♔h5

31 ♘f5 (threatening 32 ♕f7+ g6 33 g4+ ♘xg4 34 ♕xh7+, mating) Black has to play 31...♖a4, when he is a whole piece up, but his king is astray in enemy territory. Then:

a) 32 ♘xg7+ ♔g6 33 ♕f5+ (33 ♖e3 ♕xe3 does not change much) is a direct attempt to finish Black off rapidly, which works after 33...♔xg7 34 ♕g5+ ♔h8 35 ♖e7 ♘g8 36 ♗e5+, but Black can reply 33...♔h6, when 34 ♖e5 is insufficient due to 34...♕c1+ 35 ♔h2 ♕f4+. It is certainly consoling that 34 ♘e6 is possible, when Black has nothing better than 34...♕xe1+ 35 ♔h2 ♕xe6 (not, of course, 35...♖a5?? allowing 36 ♗f4#), with a dubious position in spite of his enviable material reserves.

However, having caught the black king in such a delicate situation, one is not ready to let him escape...

b) 32 ♖e3! appears to win easily, but 32...♕c1+ 33 ♔h2 g6 puts up new barriers. 34 f3 is parried by 34...♕c2, 34 ♗e7 by 34...♕c6, and 34 f4 ♕c2 (not 34...♗xg2?? 35 ♘g3+ ♔h4 36 ♗e7 ♕c6 37 ♕g4#) is far from clear. Fortunately, 34 ♘g3+ ♔h4 (34...♔g5 loses to 35 f4+ ♔h4 36 ♘f5+, and 34...♔h6 to 35 ♗f8+ ♘xf8 36 ♕xf6) 35 ♖e5 keeps the king stranded. Then 35...♘xe5 (35...♕c6 36 ♘e4 forces mate; 35...♖a1 loses to 36 ♘f1) gives White a choice of wins: 36 ♗xe5 ♘d5 37 ♗d6!, threatening ♗e7+ and ♘e4, or 36 ♕xf6+ ♔g5 37 ♕g7, when the threats can no longer be parried.

30 ♘e5+ ♘xe5 31 ♖xe5 ♖a1+ 32 ♔h2 ♕a8 33 ♕f5+ ♔f7 34 ♖e7+ ♔g8 35 ♗e5

After an impressive sequence of forcing moves, Black is pushed into a corner without an exit. If 35...♕f8 White wins by 36 ♕e6+ ♔h8 37 ♗xf6, etc.

35...♖e1 36 ♖xg7+ 1-0

The game is a striking lesson on the difference between the isolated pawn couple and their close relatives, hanging pawns. The following games will strengthen the first impressions.

Gligorić – Keres
Yugoslavia – USSR, Zagreb 1948
Nimzo-Indian Defence

1 d4 ♘f6 2 c4 e6 3 ♘c3 ♗b4 4 e3 c5 5 ♗d3 b6 6 ♘f3 ♗b7 7 0-0 0-0 8 ♗d2

There is little sense in 8 a3 in view of the simple 8...♗xc3 9 bxc3 ♗e4.

The text-move takes into consideration the attempt at simplification by 8...♗xc3 9 ♗xc3 ♘e4, when Gligorić had in mind 10 ♗xe4 ♗xe4 11 dxc5 bxc5 12 ♕d6. However, Black has at his disposal better answers, so in later years 8 ♘a4 gained preference.

8...cxd4

8...d6 is a serious alternative.

9 exd4 d5 10 cxd5 ♗xc3?!

10...♘xd5 is possible, also keeping open the long h1-a8 diagonal, because 11 ♘xd5 ♗xd2 12 ♘xb6 axb6 is obviously not good for White.

11 bxc3 ♕xd5

11...exd5 12 ♗g5 has its drawbacks for Black, but the text-move brings about the standard case of an isolated pawn couple which is converted into hanging pawns at once.

12 c4 ♕d6 13 ♗c3 ♘bd7

13...♘g4 obviously fails against 14 ♗xh7+, so Black must settle for routine developing moves.

14 ♖e1 ♖ac8 15 h3 ♖fd8 16 ♖e3 ♘h5? *(D)*

In the first game of the same match Keres played 16...h6, no doubt a useful and appropriate move in such positions. This time Black was not cautious enough.

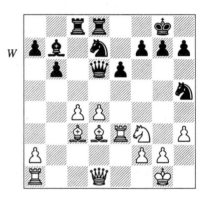

17 d5!

White is able to strike before the knight reaches the f4-square. The tactical stroke is based on 17...exd5 18 ♘d4, when the knight attacks in the footsteps of the advancing pawn (the motif so often repeated in positions with an isolated pawn). At the same time the tremendous power of White's bishops is unleashed towards the black king, creating all sorts of threats.

17...♘c5 18 ♘g5 g6 19 ♗e2 ♘g7 20 ♕d4

Now it is the queen's turn to make use of the strong d4-square. The defence of the king, based on the pair of knights on d7 and f6, has been thrown into disorder. White's domination of the a1-h8 diagonal foreshadows a quick collapse...

20...♕f8 21 ♕h4 h5 22 ♗g4!

One would think it was Keres attacking.

22...f5 23 ♘xe6 ♘gxe6 24 dxe6 ♖e8 25 ♗xh5 ♕h6 26 ♕f6 f4 27 ♕f7# (1-0)

This was again a successful case of an isolated pawn couple advancing into battle array before the blocking pressure could be organized and exerted on them. In most cases, however, the hanging pawns appear as the result of a double pawn exchange in the centre.

Nimzowitsch – Tarrasch
St Petersburg 1914
Queen's Gambit

1 d4 d5 2 ♘f3 c5 3 c4 e6 4 e3 ♘f6 5 ♗d3

This is rather an unusual move-order, which Black could exploit by 5...dxc4, with a tempo-up version of a Queen's Gambit Accepted.

5...♘c6 6 0-0 ♗d6 7 b3 0-0 8 ♗b2 b6 9 ♘bd2 ♗b7 10 ♖c1

The position is reminiscent of a Queen's Indian line with the differences that the black knight is posted more actively on c6 instead of d7, and that the dark-squared bishop is in the proper place, making ...♕e7 possible.

10...♕e7 11 cxd5 exd5 12 ♘h4

White invests time provoking a weakening of Black's kingside: a costly investment in our case because the prospects of any action on the

a1-h8 diagonal are still in the realm of dreams.

12...g6 13 ♘hf3 ♖ad8 14 dxc5? bxc5 *(D)*

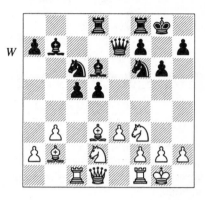

So at the moment when opening passes into middlegame, a pair of hanging pawns have appeared on the fifth rank. We can say that in principle the creation of such pawns makes sense only when one is able to build pressure on them in such a way that their dynamic potential cannot bear fruit. In our game Nimzowitsch has not brought about these conditions and his strategy in the opening must be considered faulty. 14 dxc5 was a most serious error.

15 ♗b5 ♘e4 16 ♗xc6 ♗xc6 17 ♕c2 ♘xd2 18 ♘xd2

Perhaps White nourished some illusions about making use of the long a1-h8 diagonal, but the dramatic course of the game renders his conception a disaster.

18...d4! *(D)*

While closing the diagonal of the b2-bishop, Black opens diagonals for

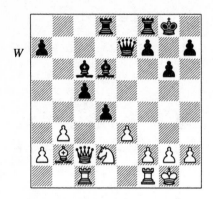

his own mighty bishops; we witness the typical moment when the mechanism of the hanging pawns is put into action.

19 exd4?

Natural caution suggests 19 e4, but White decided wrongly to accept the challenge.

19...♗xh2+!

19...♗xg2 20 ♔xg2 ♕g5+ is also effective.

20 ♔xh2 ♕h4+ 21 ♔g1 ♗xg2!

The connoisseurs must have said "déjà vu", thinking of Lasker's combination produced a quarter of a century earlier, but of course there are always some new details.

22 f3

22 ♔xg2 does not work due to 22...♕g4+ 23 ♔h2 ♖d5 24 ♕xc5 ♖h5+ 25 ♕xh5 ♕xh5+ 26 ♔g2 ♕g5+, when the knight falls.

22...♖fe8

Black indirectly defends the bishop and threatens ...♖e2, which cannot be parried by 23 ♕d3 due to 23...♕g3 24 ♘e4 ♖xe4.

23 ♘e4 ♕h1+ 24 ♔f2 ♗xf1 25 d5

The last desperate attempt. 25 ♖xf1 obviously loses the queen, while 25 ♘f6+ ♔f8 26 ♘xe8 ♖xe8 achieves nothing.

25...f5 26 ♕c3 ♕g2+ 27 ♔e3 ♖xe4+

The final blow.

28 fxe4 f4+ 29 ♔xf4 ♖f8+ 30 ♔e5 ♕h2+ 31 ♔e6 ♖e8+ 32 ♔d7 ♗b5# (0-1)

Mate of a refugee.

Kasparov – Portisch
Nikšić 1983
Queen's Indian Defence

1 d4 ♘f6 2 c4 e6 3 ♘f3 b6 4 ♘c3 ♗b7 5 a3 d5 6 cxd5 ♘xd5 7 e3 ♘xc3 8 bxc3 ♗e7 9 ♗b5+ c6 10 ♗d3 c5 11 0-0 ♘c6 12 ♗b2

The b2-square is a natural position for the dark-squared bishop. Its eventual target is Black's kingside, but in the meantime it is there to support the advance in the centre: White's hanging pawns, when they arise, will need full protection and support.

12...♖c8 13 ♕e2 0-0 14 ♖ad1 ♕c7

14...cxd4 15 exd4 keeps on the board d- and c-pawns.

15 c4!

This is clearly stronger than 15 e4, which can be countered by the natural 15...♘a5.

15...cxd4

Note that 15...♗f6 fails to 16 d5; the strength of the b2-bishop is already felt across the board.

16 exd4 ♘a5 *(D)*

Portisch was counting on his counterplay against the c4-pawn. However,

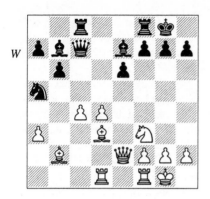

the exposed black kingside remains at the mercy of the white bishops. A sacrificial thrust in the centre is in the air and an experienced player will smell such occasions at once.

17 d5!

As usual in the circumstances, the breakthrough is based on tactical lines: 17...♘xc4 would be punished by 18 ♕e4 g6 19 ♗xc4 ♕xc4 20 ♕e5 f6 21 ♕xe6+ ♖f7 22 ♖c1 ♕a6 23 d6 with a large advantage for White; the far-advanced passed pawn must decide. We have in front of us an excellent example of the damage done by hanging pawns – Black's whole kingside is under devastating attack.

17...exd5 18 cxd5 ♗xd5 19 ♗xh7+! ♔xh7 20 ♖xd5 ♔g8 21 ♗xg7! ♔xg7 22 ♘e5

Motifs repeat; sacrifices remind us of older games whose wisdom we are trying to absorb. How to defend a naked king? 22...f5 23 ♖d7 makes things worse. 22...♕c2 fails to the shrewd 23 ♕g4+ ♔h7 24 ♖d3 ♖c3 25 ♕f5+ (or simply 25 ♕h3+) 25...♔g7 26 ♖g3+. The more stubborn 22...♖h8 is refuted

by 23 ♕g4+ ♔f8 24 ♕f5 f6 25 ♖e1. Therefore...

22...♖fd8 23 ♕g4+ ♔f8 24 ♕f5 f6

24...♗d6 is met by 25 ♕f6. If Black plays 24...♗xa3, then 25 ♖d7 ♖xd7 26 ♘xd7+ ♔e7 27 ♖e1+ ♔d8 28 ♘e5.

25 ♘d7+ ♖xd7 26 ♖xd7 ♕c5 27 ♕h7 ♖c7

White was threatening ♖xe7. Black not only parries the threat but also sets a hidden trap: 28 ♖d3? would allow the frightening 28...♕xf2+. One can never be cautious enough!

28 ♕h8+ ♔f7 29 ♖d3 ♘c4 30 ♖fd1 ♘e5?

After 30...♗d6 (best) 31 ♖h3 Black has serious problems.

31 ♕h7+ ♔e6 32 ♕g8+ ♔f5 33 g4+ ♔f4 34 ♖d4+ ♔f3 35 ♕b3+ 1-0

Exciting chess, yet it is the rational building of the position, White's harmonious development and full cooperation of pieces and pawns, that makes it possible and even look so simple.

Korchnoi – Karpov
World Ch match (game 1),
Merano 1981
Queen's Gambit

1 c4 e6 2 ♘c3 d5 3 d4 ♗e7 4 ♘f3 ♘f6 5 ♗g5 h6 6 ♗h4 0-0 7 e3 b6 8 ♖c1 ♗b7 9 ♗e2 ♘bd7 10 cxd5 exd5 11 0-0 c5 12 dxc5?

In Hort-Karpov, Amsterdam 1981, White played 12 ♕c2, which is certainly better. Korchnoi commits the same error we encountered in the game Nimzowitsch-Tarrasch. To put it concisely, one should never create hanging pawns if the conditions do not exist to expose them to strong pressure and thus to control them.

12...bxc5 *(D)*

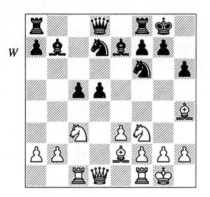

A useful comparison occurs to me. In the game Yusupov-Ljubojević, Tilburg 1987, this position occurred with one, seemingly unimportant, difference: White's bishop was on f4 and ...h6 had not been played. Owing to the position of the bishop on f4, White was able to continue 12 ♘e5, preparing ♗f3 and offering an advantageous exchange of knights. The pressure was there. In our game Black's central pawns are strongly supported by pieces and all of a sudden they represent an imminent danger.

13 ♕c2 ♖c8 14 ♖fd1 ♕b6

When the pressure on the pawns is feeble, their owner, as a rule, can move his pieces to active positions. He commands more space.

15 ♕b1

The beginning of a rather artificial manoeuvre, convincing us that there is something basically wrong with the white position.

15...♖fd8 16 ♖c2 ♕e6 17 ♗g3

17 ♖cd2 would be met by 17...♘e4.

17...♘h5 18 ♖cd2 ♘xg3 19 hxg3 ♘f6

Now that White's dark-squared bishop has been eliminated, Black can comfortably sit and wait for the proper moment to take action in the centre.

20 ♕c2 g6 21 ♕a4 a6 22 ♗d3

White has spent quite a lot of time manoeuvring his queen to a4, where, as we shall find out, it stands badly. This move is the beginning of another manoeuvre, by which White brings the bishop to a2 in order to increase the pressure on the d5-pawn.

22...♔g7 23 ♗b1 ♕b6 24 a3 *(D)*

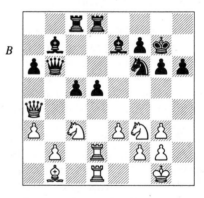

Korchnoi, of course, is well aware that the hanging pawns are extremely dangerous if set in motion, but he evidently believes they cannot advance. Karpov proves the opposite:

24...d4!

One is somewhat sceptical about this move at first glance. It seems that White can grab the pawn, but 25 exd4 does not work due to a tremendous response – 25...♗c6. Since 26 dxc5 fails to 26...♗xa4, to be followed by ...♗xd1, the queen must move. 26 ♕c2 loses to 26...♗xf3 27 gxf3 (or 27 dxc5 ♗xd1) 27...cxd4 28 ♘a4 ♕b5, while 26 ♕c4 loses to 26...cxd4 27 ♘a4 ♕b5. In my opinion White overlooked the intermediary ...♗c6 and when he saw it, it was too late. White had no choice but to enter an ugly situation.

25 ♘e2 dxe3 26 fxe3 c4 27 ♘ed4 ♕c7 28 ♘h4 ♕e5 29 ♔h1 ♔g8

Black's spatial advantage combined with White's undefended pawn-islands make it a routine job.

30 ♘df3 ♕xg3 31 ♖xd8+ ♗xd8 32 ♕b4 ♗e4 33 ♗xe4 ♘xe4 34 ♖d4 ♘f2+ 35 ♔g1 ♘d3 36 ♕b7 ♖b8 37 ♕d7 ♗c7 38 ♔h1 ♖xb2 39 ♖xd3 cxd3 40 ♕xd3 ♕d6 41 ♕e4 ♕d1+ 42 ♘g1 ♕d6 43 ♘hf3 ♖b5 0-1

Keres – Taimanov
USSR Ch, Moscow 1951
Queen's Gambit

1 c4 ♘f6 2 ♘f3 e6 3 ♘c3 d5 4 e3 ♗e7 5 b3 0-0 6 ♗b2 b6 7 d4 ♗b7 8 ♗d3 dxc4

Almost a quarter of a century later the same opponents met in Tallinn, 1975. They were sitting near my board and when they started to play I remembered this old encounter and watched the opening with interest. On that occasion Taimanov was more cautious: he played an early ...c5, then ...cxd4 and kept his strong point d5, refusing to open the long a1-h8 diagonal. Taimanov had learnt his lesson. Here he creates hanging pawns,

forgetting the quantity of evil energy they can produce.

9 bxc4 c5 10 0-0 cxd4 11 exd4 ♘c6 12 ♕e2?! *(D)*

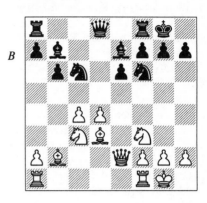

As far as the d4-pawn is concerned, this is tactically correct because after 12...♘xd4? 13 ♘xd4 ♕xd4 a hidden trap is set in motion: 14 ♘d5! ♕c5 15 ♗xf6 gxf6 (or 15...♗xf6 16 ♕e4) 16 ♕g4+ ♔h8 17 ♕h4. However, after the text-move Black had at his disposal 12...♘b4, when Keres showed that after 13 ♗b1 ♗xf3, 14 ♕xf3 ♕xd4 15 a3 ♘a6 16 ♕b7 fails after the unexpected 16...♗d6 17 ♕xa6 ♗xh2+ 18 ♔xh2 ♕h4+ 19 ♔g1 ♘g4. Therefore, he examined 14 gxf3 ♕xd4 15 ♘e4 with attacking prospects. It is curious that following Keres's recommendation, Grigorian-Karpov, USSR Ch, Moscow 1976 continued 15...♕d8 16 ♖d1 ♕c7 17 ♘xf6+ ♗xf6, when, instead of 18 ♗xh7+, looking for a draw, Grigorian played 18 ♗xf6 gxf6 19 ♗xh7+ and ended up in an unfavourable endgame after 19...♔g7 20 ♖d4 ♖h8 21 ♖g4+ ♔f8.

Naturally, allowing the exchange of the light-squared bishop on d3 diminishes White's attacking potential while his central pawns lose the lion's share of their support. We can, therefore, conclude that 12 ♕e2 was an error of which, as we shall see, Taimanov did not take advantage.

12...♖e8?! 13 ♖fd1 ♖c8 14 ♖ac1 ♕d6

Black seeks more living space by moving his queen to f4. After 14...♘b4 15 ♗b1 ♗xf3 White can continue 16 gxf3. It is a better version than above, but White's kingside is damaged for good. So it was still a better choice.

15 ♗b1 ♕f4 16 d5!

The time has come in spite of the possible inconveniences on the e-file. We enter a chaotic battle, of the type which Keres liked from his young days and played with stunning cold-bloodedness.

16...exd5 (D)

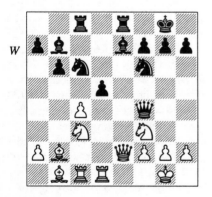

17 cxd5

Keres thought for a long time considering the consequences of 17 ♘xd5

♘xd5 (he rightly dismissed 17...♕h6 18 ♖e1) 18 cxd5 ♗f6 19 dxc6 ♖xe2 20 cxb7. It is worth putting down what he saw and why at the end of long calculation he gave it up and settled for a more secure route to advantage. Here is what Keres himself wrote:

"a) 20...♖xc1 21 ♖xc1 ♗d8 (or 21...♖e8 22 ♖c8 ♕a4 23 g3 ♕d7 24 ♗f5 winning) 22 ♖c8 ♕d6 23 g3 ♖xb2 24 ♗e4 winning.

"b) 20...♖ce8 21 ♗xf6 (not 21 ♖c8? ♗xb2 22 ♖dd8 *[we may add that White still wins by 22 ♗d3 and 23 ♗b5]* 22...♕c1+ 23 ♖xc1 ♖xd8 24 ♖c8 ♖ee8) 21...gxf6 (21...♕xf6 22 ♖c8 ♕e6 23 ♖cd8 or 21...♕b8 22 ♘d4!) 22 ♖c8 ♔g7 23 b8♕ (23 ♖dc1 ♕d4!) 23...♕xb8 24 ♖xb8 ♖xb8 25 g3 with a won endgame.

"c) 20...♖b8 21 ♗e5! ♖xe5 22 ♘xe5 g6 (or 22...♕xe5 23 ♖c8+ ♕e8 24 ♖dc1 ♗e5 25 ♖xe8+ ♖xe8 26 ♖e1 winning) 23 ♘d7 (not 23 ♖c8+ ♔g7 24 ♖xb8 ♗xe5 with dangerous counterplay) 23...♖xb7 24 g3 ♕f3 25 ♗e4!.

"d) 20...♖f8 21 ♗a3 (21 ♗xf6 ♕xf6 22 ♖c8 ♖ee8 and then 23 b8♕ ♖xc8 24 ♕xa7 ♕b2 or 23 ♖dc1 ♕e6 with good chances to save the game) 21...♗e7 22 ♗xe7 (not 22 ♖c8 ♗xa3 23 ♖dd8 ♕c1+!) 22...♖xe7 23 ♖c8 g6 24 b8♕ ♕xb8 25 ♖xb8 ♖xb8 and White's advantage in the endgame may prove inadequate."

After 17 ♘xd5 ♘xd5 18 cxd5 ♗f6 Keres put in brackets the alternative 19 ♕c2 ♗xb2 20 dxc6 ♗xc1!. However, Nunn later found 21 ♕xh7+ ♔f8 22 cxb7 ♖cd8 23 ♕h8+ ♔e7 24 ♖e1+ ♔d7 25 ♗f5+ ♕xf5 26 ♖xe8 ♖xe8 27

♕xe8+ ♔xe8 28 b8♕+ and the pawns on a7 and b6 fall.

This is an impressive list of mind-spinning lines. I cite Keres because I would like the reader to be fully aware of the stunning amount of energy released by a breakthrough in the centre.

17...♘b8

17...♘b4!? can be met by 18 ♖d4 (18 a3? ♗c5!) 18...♕b8 19 ♕d2 ♖cd8 20 ♘h4, with attacking chances.

18 ♖d4 ♕d6 19 ♖cd1 ♗f8

The central thrust has transformed White's more active pieces and spatial advantage into another form of advantage: a passed pawn on the d-file, mobile, squeezing and well supported. At the same time White's bishop-pair exerts obvious pressure on Black's kingside. Considering that, 19...♘bd7 was essential for the king's protection.

20 ♘e4 ♘xe4 21 ♖xe4 ♖xe4 22 ♕xe4 ♕h6

After 22...g6 23 ♘g5 White would also keep attacking chances.

23 ♘g5 ♗d6 24 h4 ♘d7 25 ♕f5 ♘f6 26 ♗xf6

26 ♘xf7 is simpler.

26...gxf6 27 ♘xf7 ♕c1 28 ♕xh7+ ♔f8 29 ♘xd6 ♕xd1+ 30 ♔h2 ♕xd5 31 ♘xb7 ♕e5+ 32 g3 ♖c7 33 ♕h8+ ♔f7 34 h5 ♖xb7 35 ♕h7+ ♔e6 36 ♕xb7 ♕xh5+ 37 ♔g2 1-0

Keres's win over Taimanov repeats the standard themes of previous games, and throws light on the preconditions for the breakthrough, on the attacking motifs on the diagonals, the strength of bishops unleashed by the thrust, and the transformation of an advantage into other forms.

However, the hanging pawns do not always have enough support to succeed in their primary mission. They can be used in a quieter manner, emphasizing their positional values. The following games offer information on the subject...

Korchnoi – Ivkov
Interzonal tournament, Sousse 1967
Bogo-Indian Defence

1 d4 ♘f6 2 c4 e6 3 ♘f3 ♗b4+ 4 ♘bd2 d5 5 a3 ♗e7 6 e3 0-0 7 ♗d3 b6

The fianchetto is Black's natural way to develop, while also preparing ...c5. 7...♘bd7 has the same idea in mind, and if 8 b4 then 8...a5.

8 b3 ♗b7 9 ♗b2 c5 10 0-0 cxd4 11 exd4 ♘bd7 12 ♖e1

When the pawn-structure in the centre takes this shape, ♕e2 is a good choice for White, leaving the squares e1 and d1 for the rooks in support of the central pawns.

12...♖e8 13 ♘e5 dxc4

White has a spatial advantage, which encourages Black to seek exchanges. As a rule, a responsible decision, but Ivkov evidently hopes he will be able to control the dynamic force of the central pawns.

14 bxc4 ♘xe5 15 ♖xe5 ♗f8 *(D)*

Black evaluates correctly that his kingside may fall under attack. He therefore prepares to fianchetto his dark-squared bishop, which would bring not only more security to the king, but also counter-pressure against the d4-pawn.

16 a4

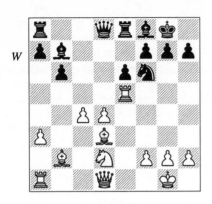

It is difficult to imagine White carrying out a central thrust under reasonable conditions. The pawns, therefore, will be used to control the central space, while action takes place on the wings. The minority attack on the queenside should create a pawn weakness in Black's camp.

16...g6 17 a5 ♗g7 18 ♖e1

There is little point in 18 ♖b5.

18...♘h5?!

An alluring move, seeking to attack d4 as well as g2. However, although commentators passed by this move in silence, we have reached a critical moment of the game. The further course of events shows beyond doubt that the pressure on White's hanging pawns must be prepared more carefully. In my opinion 18...♕c7 was the proper choice. Black's knight is destined for d7, not h5.

19 ♗e4 ♗xe4 20 ♘xe4 ♖c8 21 ♕b3!

Very good: in case of 21...♗xd4 22 ♗xd4 ♕xd4 23 ♖ad1 ♕xc4 24 ♕xc4 ♖xc4 25 ♘d6 ♖ec8 (or 25...♖cc8) 26 a6 White wins.

21...f5?! 22 ♘g3 ♘xg3 23 hxg3 bxa5?!

Two poor decisions in three moves will make Black's life harder. 21...f5 weakens the position, while 23...bxa5 exposes the a-pawns for good.

24 ♖ed1 ♕c7 25 c5 ♖b8 26 ♕a2 ♕c6 27 ♗c3 ♖e7 28 ♕xa5 *(D)*

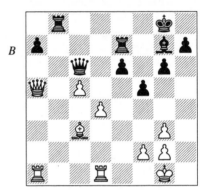

Material equality has been restored, while White has maintained a healthier pawn-structure. Notice how his central pawns, well protected all the time, played the role of watchful guard, while action was successfully taken on the wing. The result is White's passed pawn on the c-file and Black's isolated a7-pawn.

28...♖d7 29 ♕a6 ♖c8 30 ♕c4 ♕d5 31 ♕xd5 ♖xd5 32 f4

32 ♖xa7 would not be met by 32...♖cxc5 because of 33 ♖xg7+, but the simple 32...e5 would suffice. What follows is Korchnoi's usual skilful play in the endgame, and is worth perusing closely.

32...♖d7 33 ♔f1 ♖c6 34 ♔e2 ♗f6 35 ♖a4 g5 36 ♖da1 gxf4 37 gxf4

♖cc7 38 ♖b1 ♖c8 39 g3 h5 40 ♖ab4 ♔f7 41 ♖b7 ♔e8 42 ♔d3 ♗d8 43 ♔c4 a5 44 ♖b8 ♖xb8 45 ♖xb8 ♔e7

45...♖a7 would invite an amusing end: 46 c6 a4 47 ♗a5.

46 ♖a8 ♖b7 47 c6 ♖b1 48 ♖a7+ ♔d6 49 ♖d7+ ♔xc6 50 ♖xd8 ♖g1 51 d5+ exd5+ 52 ♖xd5 ♖xg3 53 ♖xa5 h4 54 ♖xf5 ♖f3 55 ♗e5 ♖a3 56 ♖h5 h3 57 ♖h6+ ♔d7 58 ♔d5 ♖f3 59 ♖h7+ ♔d8 60 ♔e6 1-0

O. Bernstein – Capablanca
Exhibition game, Moscow 1914
Queen's Gambit

1 d4 d5 2 c4 e6 3 ♘f3 ♘f6 4 ♘c3 ♗e7 5 ♗g5 0-0 6 e3 ♘bd7 7 ♖c1 b6

The introductory move of the so-called 'Orthodox Fianchetto'. Black intends to solve his basic development problem – that of his queen's bishop. Comparing the position with similar situations in the opening phase, we shall notice that the early development of the queen's knight left a hole on c6 – a motif to make use of.

8 cxd5 exd5 9 ♕a4

It is interesting that earlier, in Capablanca-Teichmann, Berlin 1913, Capablanca himself produced the strong 9 ♗b5 ♗b7 10 0-0, and after 10...a6 11 ♗a4, it became clear that the intended 11...c5 would be met by 12 ♗xd7 ♕xd7 13 dxc5 bxc5 14 ♘a4. Equally, in case of 10...c5, 11 ♗xd7 ♕xd7 12 dxc5 bxc5 13 ♗xf6 ♗xf6 14 ♘e4 refutes Black's play. What Capablanca knew the others did not know. The strong players were luckier then, because there were no 'Informators'

and discs to teach their opponents what to play.

9...♗b7

In Capablanca-Lasker, World Ch match (game 5), Buenos Aires 1921, Lasker chose 9...c5 10 ♕c6 ♖b8 11 ♘xd5 ♗b7 12 ♘xe7+ ♕xe7 with compensation in his active position and chances to equalize.

10 ♗a6

A logical move weakening the complex of light squares.

10...♗xa6 11 ♕xa6 c5

Black could choose the more placid 11...c6 12 0-0 ♕c8, but he had no peaceful intentions in this game.

12 ♗xf6

Not necessary at this moment. 12 0-0 should be preferred.

12...♘xf6 13 dxc5 bxc5 14 0-0 ♕b6 15 ♕e2 c4! *(D)*

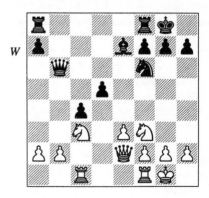

Powerful logic stands behind this simple move. Hitherto we have analysed classic cases of breakthrough. In our position Black's standard task of preparing ...d4 is impossible with his dark-squared bishop posted passively at e7. Black therefore evaluates his position realistically. Since he can exert pressure on the semi-open b-file, emphasizing the backwardness of the b2-pawn, Black moves his c-pawn and creates the preconditions for squeezing further his opponent in defence. At the same time the move, ceding the d4-square to White, implies an exceptional psychological effect. In normal circumstances it is only after successful pressure that hanging pawns can be blockaded. Bernstein has got it for free and he is happy to land his knight on d4 and formulate his plan on the basis of it. Thus, as we shall see, he continues in the wrong direction.

16 Ĩfd1?!

Although the hanging pawns are blocked, they are dangerous, because they offer Black an obvious spatial advantage, and a lot of manoeuvring space. If White had evaluated his position correctly he would have chosen 16 e4 to break up the couple and seek equality in a sequence of exchanges.

16...Ĩfd8 17 ♘d4

Bernstein again has a chance to play 17 e4, but he evidently thought he was standing better.

17...♗b4

Owing to the move ...c4 Black's passive bishop gets an active role.

18 b3

18 ♕c2 came into consideration, but 18...Ĩab8 maintains the pressure. Bernstein finally must have felt that things were getting out of control and he tried to simplify through exchanges.

18...Ĩac8 19 bxc4 dxc4 20 Ĩc2 ♗xc3

The passed pawn is a major hope for Black. Its road must be cleared.

21 Ĩxc3 ♘d5 22 Ĩc2 c3 23 Ĩdc1 Ĩc5 24 ♘b3 Ĩc6 25 ♘d4 Ĩc7 26 ♘b5

White becomes greedy. Many commentators proposed 26 ♕e1 Ĩdc8 27 ♘e2 as correct. Black has time to reply unperturbed 27...Ĩc4, but even 27...♕a5 28 e4 ♘b4 29 Ĩxc3 ♘xa2 still keeps some advantage.

26...Ĩc5 27 ♘xc3?

There was still time to go back humbly to d4.

27...♘xc3 28 Ĩxc3 Ĩxc3 29 Ĩxc3 *(D)*

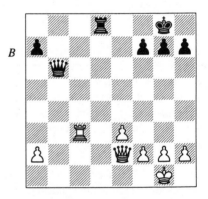

29...♕b2! 0-1

White resigned, struck by a thunderbolt.

Bertok – Fischer
Interzonal tournament,
Stockholm 1962
Queen's Gambit

1 d4 d5 2 c4 e6 3 ♘c3 ♗e7 4 ♘f3 ♘f6 5 ♗g5 0-0 6 e3 h6 7 ♗h4 b6 8 cxd5

♘xd5 9 ♗xe7 ♕xe7 10 ♘xd5 exd5
11 ♗e2 ♗e6 12 0-0 c5 13 dxc5?

My club-mate Mario Bertok was
clearly playing for a draw against a superior opponent. However, as often
happens in such circumstances, he
does it in the wrong way. He could apply the routine manoeuvre against
Black's hanging pawns, based on the
pin after ♕a4-a3 or he could choose
12 ♘e5 or 13 ♘e5 as well. The text-
move is a definite error. The exchange
on c5 is premature. It leaves a larger
choice to his opponent and Fischer
does not miss his chance to avoid the
standard positions and switch to a
more promising continuation.

13...bxc5 14 ♕a4 ♕b7! *(D)*

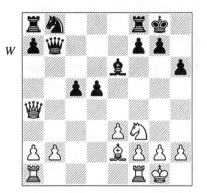

Before the knight takes its place on
d7, Fischer was allowed to move his
queen to a more active place. Missing
the correct move-order, Bertok, instead of forcing the black queen to
stay passively on e7, allowed a move
which is a part of Black's strategic
plan. The backward b2-pawn and the
semi-open b-file dictate future events.

15 ♕a3 ♘d7 16 ♘e1

White is already in difficulties. 16
♖ac1 ♖fb8 17 ♖c2 ♗f5 18 ♖d2 ♘f6
favours Black, but the text-move is in-
effective as well.

16...a5 17 ♘d3 c4

Like Capablanca, Fischer had that
rare ability to find simple, straightforward moves, which, as a rule, are part
of equally simple and straightforward
plans. Since he was able to move the
queen to b7, the subsequent course of
action has all been self-explanatory.

18 ♘f4 ♖fb8 19 ♖ab1

At first glance, the consistent course
seems to be 19 ♗f3 ♘f6 20 ♖fd1.
Having invested several tempi to bring
the knight to f4, White had a chance
to exert counter-pressure on the d5-
pawn. Unfortunately, the b2-pawn is
more valuable and the bargain after
20...♕xb2 21 ♕xb2 ♖xb2 and the following exchanges on d5 cannot please
White: the passed pawn on the c-file
runs towards promotion with dire consequences.

Fischer was of the opinion that 19
♘xe6 fxe6 20 ♗g4 was White's best
option.

19...♗f5 20 ♖bd1 ♘f6 21 ♖d2

After 21 ♗f3 Fischer considered
21...♕xb2 22 ♕xb2 ♖xb2 23 ♘xd5
♘xd5 24 ♗xd5 (or 24 ♖xd5 ♗e6 25
♖c5 ♖c8) 24...♖c8 25 e4 ♗e6 26
♗xe6 fxe6 27 a4 c3, etc., as well as the
alternative 21...♗e4 22 ♗xe4 ♘xe4.

21...g5

Simple but decisive. White's passivity will be exposed fully once the
pressure on the d5-pawn is removed.

22 ♘xd5

Giving up a piece for little compensation is quite desperate, but 22 ♘h5 ♘e4 23 ♖c2 ♕b4, threatening ...♘g3, would be of little help to White.

22...♘xd5 23 ♗xc4 ♗e6 24 ♖fd1 ♘xe3 25 ♕xe3 ♗xc4 26 h4 ♖e8 27 ♕g3 ♕e7 28 b3 ♗e6 29 f4 g4 30 h5 ♕c5+ 31 ♖f2 ♗f5 0-1

We are taught again that the timing of the birth of hanging pawns is of great importance. If at the moment of their origin it is not possible to exert some meaningful pressure on them, we can be quite certain that we missed the right time.

Some preconditions must be fulfilled in order to control their dynamic options. We shall throw some light on the subject in the following games. In order to give as credible a message as possible, let us stay with the same variation used by Bertok, but now in the hands of two great champions.

Spassky – Pachman
Capablanca memorial, Havana 1962
Queen's Gambit

1 d4 ♘f6 2 c4 e6 3 ♘f3 d5 4 ♘c3 ♗e7 5 ♗g5 0-0 6 e3 h6 7 ♗h4 b6 8 cxd5 ♘xd5 9 ♗xe7 ♕xe7 10 ♘xd5 exd5 11 ♗e2 ♗e6 12 ♘e5 c5 13 0-0 *(D)*

Comparing with the game Bertok-Fischer, we conclude beyond any doubt that by playing ♘e5 White causes more difficulties to his opponent.

13...♖d8?!

This will make his further development difficult. 13...♘d7 seems natural. Instead, 13...c4 is met by 14 b3, when 14...b5 fails to 15 a4 and 14...♘d7 to

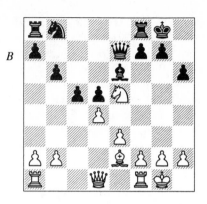

15 ♘xd7 ♕xd7 16 bxc4 dxc4 17 e4, in both cases with advantage to White.

14 ♖c1 f6?!

This is grist to White's mill, but note that 14...c4 fails again, this time to 15 ♗f3 b5 16 b3.

15 ♘g6 ♕d6 16 dxc5

Having accumulated Black's small mistakes, White finally exchanges at c5, but at a moment when, thanks to his better development, he can exert maximum pressure on the pawns.

15...bxc5 17 ♘f4 ♗f7 18 ♕c2 ♘d7 19 ♖fd1 d4

If Black parries the obvious threat – ♘xd5 – by 19...♔h8, then there is no answer to 20 ♗f3. Pachman achieves the breakthrough, but under adverse circumstances.

20 ♗c4 ♗xc4 21 ♕xc4+ ♔h7

Or 21...♔h8 22 ♘g6+ ♔h7 23 ♕d3.

22 b4! *(D)*

Exposed to pressure, Black's central pawns were first forced to advance and now they will fall apart.

22...♖ac8

22...cxb4 loses material after 23 ♖xd4.

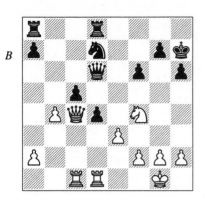

B

23 ♘e6

Possible because the black king is exposed to checks on h7.

23...♘e5 24 ♕c2+ d3 25 ♘xd8 ♕xd8 26 ♕b2 c4 27 h3 ♕b6 28 a4 g5 29 ♔f1 ♔g7 30 ♕d4 c3

If 30...♕xb4, then 31 f4 followed by ♖xd3.

31 ♖xd3 ♘xd3 32 ♕d7+ 1-0

After 32...♔g6 33 ♕xd3+ f5 34 g4 White wins easily.

Fischer – Spassky
World Ch match (game 6),
Reykjavik 1972
Queen's Gambit

1 c4 e6 2 ♘f3 d5 3 d4 ♘f6 4 ♘c3 ♗e7 5 ♗g5 0-0 6 e3 h6 7 ♗h4 b6 8 cxd5 ♘xd5 9 ♗xe7 ♕xe7 10 ♘xd5 exd5 11 ♖c1 ♗e6

It is hardly necessary to mention that 11...♕b4+ 12 ♕d2 leads to a favourable endgame for White.

12 ♕a4 c5 13 ♕a3

Resorting to the old queen manoeuvre, White waits for a better moment to create hanging pawns. In the meantime he will look for ways to exert pressure on them.

13...♖c8 14 ♗b5 *(D)*

A provocative move found by Furman. Instead the quiet 14 ♗e2 would be best met by 14...a5. In Szilly-Marović, Wijk aan Zee 1972, after 15 0-0 ♕a7 16 dxc5 bxc5 17 ♖c3 ♘d7 18 ♖fc1 ♖cb8 (preventing ♘d4 and justifying the positioning of the queen on a7 by the planned ...♕b7 or ...♕b6) 19 ♘e1 a4 20 ♘d3 c4 21 ♘f4 ♘f6 22 ♗f3 ♕b6 Black stood better. Capablanca's play against Bernstein was known to me and preparing for the game I found ...♕a7 and the subsequent plan in 5 minutes.

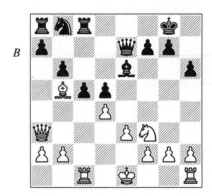

B

14...a6?!

This will prove inadequate. Later, in Timman-Geller, Hilversum 1973, Geller played the strong 14...♕b7, sacrificing a pawn for the initiative. After 15 dxc5 bxc5 16 ♖xc5 ♖xc5 17 ♕xc5 ♘a6 18 ♗xa6 ♕xa6 19 ♕a3 ♕c4 20 ♔d2 ♕g4 21 ♖g1 d4 Timman was in deep trouble.

15 dxc5 bxc5 16 0-0 ♖a7

This is as unnatural as it looks. 16...♕b7 was preferable.

17 ♗e2 ♘d7 18 ♘d4

Comparing the text with Bertok's play, the importance of the proper time for exchanges is self-evident. Fischer is able to use the central squares to his advantage, exerting pressure on the newly born couple.

18...♕f8

18...♘f6 was unanimously accepted as more logical.

19 ♘xe6 fxe6 20 e4! *(D)*

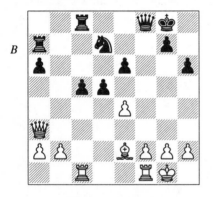

White has succeeded in building up pressure on the hanging pawns. Now 20...♘f6 would come too late, as 21 e5 ♘d7 22 f4 gives White a clear advantage.

20...d4?

Wiser after the event, many commentators were of the opinion that 20...c4 was better, when Fischer had in mind 21 ♕h3 with the initiative. After the text-move, White achieves what he strives for in general when trying to tame the hanging pawns. Being in firm control of the squares in front of them,

White has sapped their aggressive potential. Apart from that, there is the inviting c4-square for the light-squared bishop.

21 f4 ♕e7 22 e5

Again the best: fix the weakness on e6!

22...♖b8 23 ♗c4 ♔h8 24 ♕h3 ♘f8

If Spassky calculated that he would be able to control the strong e4-square with his knight, he missed the point. He was given no peace until his knight was pushed back to defend his weak e6-pawn. The bishop on c4 is the czar of the position.

25 b3 a5 26 f5

The beginning of the end: Black's king is not in a safe refuge any more. Having won the battle against the hanging pawns, Fischer has achieved an overwhelming strategic advantage.

26...exf5 27 ♖xf5 ♘h7 28 ♖cf1 ♕d8 29 ♕g3 ♖e7 30 h4 ♖bb7 31 e6 ♖bc7 32 ♕e5 ♕e8 33 a4 ♕d8 34 ♖1f2 ♕e8 35 ♖2f3 ♕d8 36 ♗d3 ♕e8 37 ♕e4 ♘f6 38 ♖xf6 gxf6 39 ♖xf6 ♔g8 40 ♗c4 ♔h8 41 ♕f4 1-0

Although the hanging pawns made a part of the scene for a short period of the game and soon became a larger unit, it is their destiny which sticks in the memory after a brilliant lesson given by Fischer. The very moment Spassky's central pawns were blocked and their energy drained away by the loss of mobility, White won his battle. The basic themes of this encounter are of importance for the full understanding of the hanging pawns and we shall continue our discussion in the next game...

Romanishin – Psakhis
USSR Ch, Moscow 1983
Queen's Indian Defence

1 ♘f3 ♘f6 2 c4 b6 3 d4 e6 4 g3 ♗a6 5 ♘bd2 d5 6 ♗g2 ♗e7 7 0-0 0-0 8 ♘e5 c5

8...♗b7 is the alternative, but not fearing the pressure on the long light-square diagonal, Black carries out the routine ...c5 at an early phase of the game. The passive position of White's queen's knight on d2 must have had something to do with Psakhis's decision.

9 dxc5

Years ago my attention was drawn to the game Sosonko-Portisch, Tilburg 1981. Sosonko continued 9 ♘b3, which complicates Black's development. After 9...♗b7 10 dxc5 bxc5 11 cxd5 Portisch had to accept an isolated pawn in the centre and play 11...♗xd5. If he had chosen 11...exd5 then 12 ♗g5 would have caused serious problems. The hanging pawns are under heavy fire, and there is no good solution.

9...bxc5

In a number of later games I noticed Black choosing 9...♗xc5 10 cxd5 exd5, when 11 ♘df3, followed by b3 and ♗b2, comes into consideration.

10 b3 ♗b7

This is necessary in order to complete development; besides, there is no job for the bishop at a6.

11 cxd5 exd5 12 ♗b2 a5 *(D)*

So we have again one of the innumerable positions featuring hanging pawns in the centre. This time they are under pressure which might increase

easily. For instance, had Black continued 12...♘bd7, White could have played 13 ♘dc4, making use of the pin to activate all his forces. Notice that the pin is frequently used against such central formations.

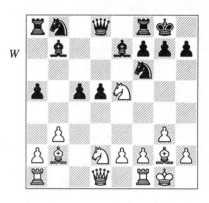

13 e4!? d4

We have already concluded that hanging pawns are mobile and dangerous by their nature, but if they are blockaded, they become weak. If Black accepts the pawn by 13...♘xe4 then 14 ♘xe4 dxe4 15 ♕c2 f5 16 ♖ad1 ♕e8 17 ♕c3 gives White the initiative.

14 ♘ec4

That is what we talked about. The dynamic potential of the central pawns has gone.

14...♘fd7 15 ♖e1 ♘b6 16 ♘xb6 ♕xb6 17 ♘c4 ♕d8 18 ♗c1!

It is very important to improve the position of the dark-squared bishop. Its proper place is now d2, from where it thwarts the expected manoeuvre ...♘d7-b6, securing a dominant position for his knight and keeping an eye on the a5-pawn.

18...♘d7 19 ♗d2 ♖a6

It is not easy to find a good plan for Black. He vacates a8 for his queen, probably with a later ...f5 in mind.

20 a4

Again: fix the potential weakness!

20...♕a8 21 ♕c2 *(D)*

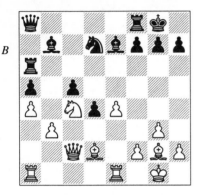

21...♗d8

21...f5 does not work due to 22 ♘xa5 ♖xa5 23 ♗xa5 ♕xa5 24 exf5 ♗xg2 25 ♖xe7, which explains Black's bishop move.

22 ♗f4

Taming Black. 22...f5 would now be met by 23 ♘d6.

22...♗e7 23 ♗f1

The final solution against ...f5.

23...♕c8 24 f3 ♕d8 25 ♗d2

Avoiding ...♗g5.

25...♖a8 26 ♗d3 g6 27 ♖e2 ♘b8 28 ♖f1 ♘c6 29 f4

The fruit of White's good strategy is a pawn-majority on the kingside.

29...♘b4 30 ♗xb4 cxb4 31 ♕d1 ♖c8 32 ♖d2 ♗c5 33 ♖e1 ♖e8 34 ♖de2 ♔g7 35 h3 ♖c6 36 ♔h2 ♖ce6 37 ♕c2 ♗a7 38 e5

Only now is everything ready for the decisive steps.

38...♗f3 39 ♖f2 ♗d5 40 f5 gxf5 41 ♖xf5 ♖h6 42 ♕d2 ♗c5 43 ♖f6 ♖h5 44 ♕f4 ♗e6 45 g4 1-0

Once the battle against the hanging pawns was won, the rest was a routine technical job carried out well by Romanishin with some nice little points instructive for our topic.

Korchnoi – Geller
Candidates match (game 5), Moscow 1971
Queen's Gambit

1 d4 d5 2 c4 e6 3 ♘c3 ♗e7 4 ♘f3 ♘f6 5 ♗g5 0-0 6 e3 h6 7 ♗h4 b6 8 ♗e2 ♗b7 9 ♗xf6 ♗xf6 10 cxd5 exd5 11 0-0 ♕e7

White has ceded the bishop-pair to his opponent early on, relying on his pawn-formation to keep the diagonals closed. Black, on the contrary, wants to open those same diagonals for his bishops. 11...c5 is too presumptuous and can be met energetically by 12 dxc5 bxc5 13 ♕b3; the pressure on the central pawns is already there.

12 ♕b3

In expectation of ...c5 White's queen takes an active position, at the same time vacating the d1-square for his rook. It is clear that in a couple of moves the game will be characterized by Black's hanging pawns on the fifth rank. It is of great importance to meet them properly developed.

12...♖d8

Another necessary move in support of ...c5.

13 Rad1 c5

Grandmaster Suetin proposed 13...c6 14 &d3 ♘d7 15 Rfe1 ♘f8 with a passive but firm position, but Geller was a fearless player, ready to accept any challenge.

14 dxc5 &xc3 15 ♕xc3 bxc5 16 Rc1

Both players have achieved what they wanted. Black has carried out ...c5, while White is ready to exert maximum pressure on the central pawns. The further course of the game will demonstrate whether the pawns represent a liability for Black or a menace to White.

16...♘d7 17 Rc2

A useful move in similar positions. White will be able to double rooks on either the c- or the d-file at will.

17...Rab8?!

Rooks seek open and semi-open files by their nature. We have seen in similar positions that counter-pressure could be built on the backward b2-pawn. Here, however, there is no such possibility. Besides, the rook can be useful on the a-file, supporting a later ...a5.

At the same time, since the d5-pawn is well protected and can be further supported by ...♘f6, all the attention should be given to the c5-pawn. Therefore one could expect Black to play 17...Rdc8.

18 b3 ♕e6 19 Rd1 ♕b6?! *(D)*

Now 19...Rbc8 was logical: there is no target on the b-file. Black probably had in mind ...a5, missing his opponent's continuation, which is of extraordinary strength...

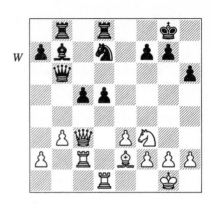

20 ♘e1!

Having aimed his heavy artillery towards the hanging pawns, White takes the opportunity to engage all his forces against the couple stuck in the centre. White threatens &g4, trying to remove the vital defender on d7. At the same time the knight is moved to d3, where it will act in full harmony with the other white pieces.

20...Rbc8

The support comes too late, as several tempi have been lost, and it comes at the wrong moment, when the bishop is expected at g4.

21 &g4 ♕g6 22 &h3 Rc7

22...d4 fails to 23 exd4 cxd4 24 ♕g3, when White's pressure is stronger than Black's support.

23 ♘d3 ♘f6 24 ♕a5 ♘e8 25 Rxc5 Rxc5 26 ♘xc5 1-0

Simple and impressive! Korchnoi played consistently all the game, fully concentrating on the central pawns. First he restricted their movement, then engaging literally all his forces built maximum pressure on the unfortunate couple, after which he could just gather the fruits of his work. Note also the instructive errors committed by Geller, who failed to provide the proper protection and support the hanging pawns always require.

Some General Observations

Our analysis of hanging pawns leads to unequivocal conclusions, which do not differ much from those we reached about isolated pawns. They share the same origin and they share some basic characteristics. Both are weapons of attack if actively assisted, and both are helpless targets when the protection is inadequate and assistance fails; both feel well accompanied by numerous pieces and both show signs of exhaustion when material is reduced.

The games we have analysed teach us very clearly that the dynamic energy hidden in hanging pawns is very great. Whenever they can advance in the centre with full support, the position opens up and the pieces assisting the breakthrough, especially bishops, become extremely active and quite often the opponent's king is within their long reach. In most cases on such occasions some concealed tactical possibilities spring up and then any reaction in general comes too late to prevent the harm their advance causes. One must be fully aware of their damaging potential and evaluate very carefully when to create such pawns in the centre and when to preserve a healthy dose of caution and to avoid them.

I shall always remember a scene in the press-room of the Banja Luka tournament in 1979. Two players were stubbornly defending a dubious position against two potent white pawns on the fourth rank but whatever they tried, it failed. Tigran Petrosian was quietly watching the proceedings and one of the analysts finally turned to him for help: "What would you do in this position?". Petrosian replied, "I would never accept such a position!"

And, indeed, if some preconditions are not fulfilled, if the pressure one is able to put on the hanging pawns is light, then, as Petrosian put it simply, do not enter such a position. On the other hand, if one can develop actively and, by putting pressure on the pawns, force their advance or turn them by exchange into an isolated pawn, controlled and blockaded, all the negative sides of the pawn-formation become apparent.

Naturally, the success of such a plan depends primarily on the activity of our pieces and the amount of pressure we manage to put on the hanging pawns as soon as they appear in the centre. In most cases some late defensive measures won't do. The central pawn-unit's ability to pierce defences surpasses by far that of an isolated pawn at its best.

In comparison with isolated pawns, hanging pawns offer some other advantages, too. They transform more easily into mobile passed pawns; also, when a central thrust is not possible, their influence and control of the central squares is greater, which makes it possible to take action on the wings. The side possessing hanging pawns often uses the neighbouring semi-open files to put pressure on the backward pawns which occur regularly on them. On such occasions one of the hanging pawns may advance in order to squeeze the backward pawn to the maximum, even at the cost of the strong square offered to the opponent.

In general we can say that hanging pawns are associated with a spatial advantage and that strong counter-measures against such a mobile, aggressive unit are not very often at the opponent's disposal.

Naturally, when we succeed in forcing their advance and, using strong squares in front of them, halt their action, they get stuck and the menace they represent is gone. The frontal pressure combined with the pin on the diagonal proves to be the best means to achieve an advantageous position.

The characteristic, instructive games presented to the reader point to a terse warning: fear the dynamic potential of the hanging pawns and be aware of their static weakness.

The story of the isolated pawn couple is not quite the same. An isolated pair of pawns does not represent an immediate danger to your opponent. On the contrary, the weak square associated with their appearance is more often than not a sign of potentially lasting weakness. When accepting such a couple as one's central pawn-structure, one takes on a serious responsibility. There is a crucial question one should ask at the moment they arise on the board: can the isolated pawn couple be successfully converted into hanging pawns or must the pawn-unit withstand the pressure in its present lame form? If the latter is the case, then I could repeat with Tigran Petrosian: do not accept such a position! In a conspicuously large number of cases its passive immobility leads to a dubious middlegame and quite commonly to a compromised endgame.

3 Passed Pawns

On a number of occasions in the previous two chapters we encountered intriguing cases of metamorphosis, in which isolated and hanging pawns, acquiring mobility and strength, were transformed into a new species. We call them passed pawns.

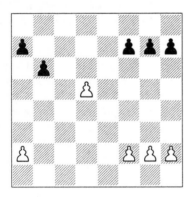

Our diagram represents a typical example of a passed pawn on a central file. It illustrates the basic definition: passed pawns have no opposing pawns in front of them on their own or neighbouring files. That is the key to understanding the power of passed pawns: their freedom of movement is the cause and explanation of the serious menace they pose. With no barriers to their advance, they run down the file towards the promotion square. In order to stop a passed pawn it takes at least a piece, which, tied to its passive duty, is missing in the battle waged on other parts of the board.

Apart from that, we can easily imagine our d5-pawn in the diagram penetrating into Black's camp, to d6 or d7, and we can imagine the cramping effect on Black's forces.

We can reach these straightforward conclusions by pure speculation, looking at the diagram and foreseeing the probable events, but if we want to know the virtues and shortcomings of a passed pawn, it will take more than that. We shall turn again to a selection of good grandmaster games for help. Our aim is to watch the passed pawn in the complex battles of the middlegame, when its best qualities come to the fore, but before we do so we shall see it in action in a couple of games remembered for outstanding endgames. It is in the elementary conditions of an endgame that the fundamental values of a piece are revealed. Our passed pawn is no exception.

Euwe – Alekhine
World Ch match (game 8),
Amsterdam 1935
Semi-Slav Defence

1 d4 d5 2 c4 c6 3 ♘f3 ♘f6 4 e3 e6 5 ♘c3 a6

Once upon a time this variation was in vogue as a sort of accelerated Meran in which Black prepares ...dxc4 followed by ...b5 and ...c5.

White's next move was a theoretical novelty at the time.

6 c5 b6?

A couple of games later Alekhine improved with the natural 6...♘bd7. He understood that 6...b6 was premature and caused serious troubles.

7 cxb6 ♘bd7 8 ♘a4 ♘xb6 9 ♗d2 ♘xa4

In later years Najdorf tried to improve on this by 9...♘bd7, but then 10 ♖c1 ♗b7 11 a3 ♗d6 12 ♗b4 leaves holes in Black's camp.

10 ♕xa4 ♕b6 11 ♖c1 ♗d7 12 ♘e5 ♕xb2 13 ♘xd7 ♘xd7 14 ♗d3!

While he was an excellent tactician, Euwe also knew how to play simply, and this game is a brilliant example of his rare skill. 14 ♕xc6 would be met by the strong 14...♗b4, while 14 ♖xc6 fails to 14...♗a3, when Black is prepared to castle or continue by ...♕b1+. Therefore, for now he develops and will retake the pawn later.

14...♖b8 15 ♔e2 ♖b6 16 ♖b1

16 ♖xc6 ♖xc6 17 ♖b1, as proposed by Alekhine, is also good.

16...♕a3 17 ♕xa3 ♗xa3 18 ♖xb6 ♘xb6 19 ♖b1 ♘d7 20 ♗xa6 ♔e7 21 ♖b3 *(D)*

21 ♗b7 ♖b8 22 ♖b3 ♔d6 would not pay. White has created an outside passed pawn and with the text-move he opens its way.

21...♗d6 22 ♗b7 c5 23 a4 ♗b8

The unpleasant thing about passed pawns is that you have to blockade

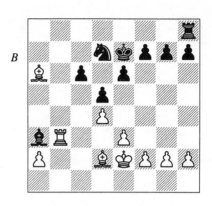

them, which implies a passive defensive posture. a7 is not an attractive place for a bishop, but no alternative is available.

24 ♖b5

24 ♗c6 ♖c8 gives White nothing.

24...♗a7 25 dxc5 ♘xc5 26 ♗b4 ♔d6 27 a5 ♔c7 28 ♗xc5

The advantage of a bishop-pair consists in the possibility of exchanging one of them at will. Here 28 a6 ♘d7 29 ♗c3 ♖g8 30 ♗d4 is met by the cold-blooded 30...♗b6.

28...♗xc5 29 ♗xd5 ♔d6

29...exd5 30 ♖xc5+ ♔d6 31 ♖c2, intending ♖a2, leads to a lost rook endgame for Black. The opposite-coloured bishops offer more hope.

30 ♗b7 ♗a7 31 a6 ♖d8 32 ♖b2 ♖d7 33 ♖d2+ ♔e7 34 ♖c2 ♖d6 35 ♖c7+ ♖d7 36 ♖c2 ♖d6 37 f4 f5

It is not easy to say how Black should best wait, but there is no doubt that black pawns on light squares, the same as White's bishop, represent an additional burden. Note that 37...♖d8 loses to 38 ♗c8 and that 37...f6 38 h4 would not make things easier.

38 Rc8 Rd8 39 Rc7+ Rd7 40 Rc3 Rd6 41 Rc7+ Rd7 42 Rc3 Rd6 43 h4 *(D)*

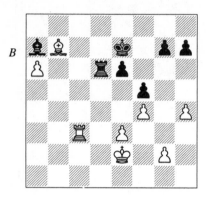

43...g6

After a couple of waiting moves, White's play becomes consistent, aiming for zugzwang. 43...Rd8 fails again to 44 ♗c8, 43...♔d7 to 44 Rc8, 43...♗b8 to 44 Rc8 Rd8 45 Rxb8, and 43...♗b6 to 44 Rc8 Rd8 45 Rc6 ♗a7 46 ♗c8.

44 Rc2 h5 45 Rc3

A good alternative is 45 Rc8 Rd8 46 Rxd8 ♔xd8 47 e4, followed by exf5 and ♗d5. The constant threats to black pawns would make it possible for White's king to penetrate to b7.

45...Rb6 46 Rc7+ ♔d6 47 Rg7 Rb2+ 48 ♔d3 Ra2 49 Rxg6 Ra3+ 50 ♔c4 ♗xe3 51 ♗d5 ♗xf4 52 Rxe6+ ♔c7 53 Rc6+ ♔b8 54 Rg6

54 Rb6+ ♔a7 55 ♔b5 fails to 55...Ra5+.

54...♗c7 55 ♗b7 ♔a7 56 Rg5 ♗d8 57 Rxh5 ♗xh4 58 Rxf5 ♔b6 59 Rb5+ ♔c7 60 Rb3 Ra5 61 ♔d4 ♗f2+ 62 ♔e4 ♔d6 63 Rd3+ ♔e6 64 ♗c8+

♔e7 65 Rd5 Ra4+ 66 ♔f5 ♗g3 67 Rd7+ ♔f8 68 a7 ♗f2 69 ♗a6 1-0

Shackled by White's distant passed pawn, Black's resistance was hopeless.

Kurajica – Karpov
Skopje 1976
Ruy Lopez

1 e4 e5 2 ♘f3 ♘c6 3 ♗b5 a6 4 ♗a4 ♘f6 5 ♗xc6 dxc6 6 ♘c3 ♗d6 7 d4 ♗b4

7...♗g4 is also quite good, but Karpov wants more.

8 ♘xe5 ♘xe4 9 0-0 ♗xc3 10 bxc3 0-0 11 ♗a3 ♘d6 12 c4 f6

White has treated the opening phase clumsily. Already Black's position is somewhat easier to play.

13 ♘g4

13 ♘d3 or 13 ♘f3 Re8 is obviously to Black's advantage.

13...Re8 14 ♘e3 ♘f5

In order to win a game of chess Black first must equalize. An experienced player in the quest for victory will not be discouraged by the presence of the opposite-coloured bishops, if at least some minimal advantage can be squeezed from the position.

15 ♘xf5 ♗xf5 16 ♕d2 ♗e6 17 ♕c3 ♕d7 18 Rfe1 ♕f7 19 ♕b2

White cannot afford to continue 19 c5 ♗xa2. A distant passed pawn on the a-file would become his lasting nightmare.

19...b6 20 c5 b5

20...♗d5 21 c4 would lead to simplifications of the type Black is trying to avoid.

21 &b4 a5 22 &d2 &d5 23 f3 &xe1+ 24 &xe1 b4 25 a4 bxa3 26 &xa3 a4 27 &b4 *(D)*

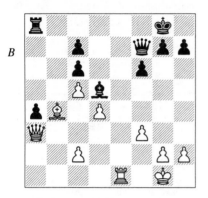

The queen is too valuable to be used as a blockader, so its place will be taken by the bishop. Owing to the opposite-coloured bishops the game is still in the balance, but the a4-pawn is the first sign of danger. From now on the dark-squared bishop will have to watch carefully.

27...&g6 28 &c3 h5 29 &a3 &e8 30 &xe8+ &xe8 31 &f2 &g6 32 &d3 &xd3 33 cxd3 h4 34 g3 &f7 35 &e3 f5 36 &f4 &g6 37 &e3

If 37 gxh4, then 37...&h5 38 &g3 g6 and White's situation becomes slippery.

37...&h5 38 &b4 g5 39 &f2 &a2 40 &a3 &b1 41 &e2 &a2 42 &c1 &e6 43 &f2 &c8 44 d5?

From the beginning of the game White has been playing for a draw. Despite passive play he has kept the balance, but now he loses patience. After 44 &e2 &a6 he saw 45 &b2 hxg3 46 hxg3 f4 47 gxf4 gxf4 48 &c1

&g5 and he did not like it because he has to give up the d3-pawn or allow ...&h4-g3. He missed what Karpov demonstrated after the game: 45 &e3 f4+ 46 gxf4 g4 47 f5. Having overlooked that possibility, White concluded he could simply give up his d3-pawn, a worthless pawn just needing protection. It was a wrong judgement.

44...cxd5 45 d4 *(D)*

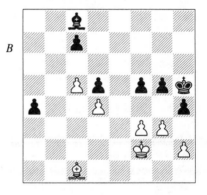

The difficulties White is facing derive from the fact that his bishop is riveted to the c1-a3 diagonal. In spite of that it seems that Black cannot improve his position because his king cannot penetrate White's position. Karpov, however, finds a hidden narrow path to victory...

45...f4!

Black threatens ...fxg3+ followed by ...h3, when the two passed pawns tie down both white pieces and the black king will just have a pleasant walk to b1. Since 46 g4+ fails to 46...&xg4 47 fxg4+ &xg4, etc., White is given no choice.

46 gxf4 g4 47 ⌐g2 ⌐f5 48 ⌐f2 gxf3 49 ⌐xf3 ⌐e4+ 50 ⌐f2 ⌐g4 51 ⌐b2

To give up the h2-pawn is even worse.

51...⌐xf4 52 ⌐c1+ ⌐g4 53 ⌐b2 c6 54 ⌐c1 ⌐h3 55 ⌐g1 ⌐g6 56 ⌐h1 ⌐h5 57 ⌐g1 ⌐d1 0-1

Karpov's king will move to e4 and there is nothing White can do about it.

The power of the passed pawn is impressive. Sometimes it looks as if it guarantees the win by its mere existence.

Alekhine – Capablanca
World Ch match (game 34),
Buenos Aires 1927
Queen's Gambit

1 d4 d5 2 c4 e6 3 ⌐c3 ⌐f6 4 ⌐g5 ⌐bd7 5 e3 c6 6 a3

White avoids the Cambridge Springs Variation, but it is now easier for Black to achieve the freeing ...c5 advance.

6...⌐e7 7 ⌐f3 0-0 8 ⌐d3 dxc4 9 ⌐xc4 ⌐d5 10 ⌐xe7 ⌐xe7 11 ⌐e4 ⌐5f6 12 ⌐g3 c5

In his book on Alekhine, Grandmaster Kotov considered this move a serious mistake, because it postpones the development of the queen's bishop, and proposed 12...b6. The fianchetto has its logic, but Capablanca's move is also logical and good.

13 0-0 ⌐b6 14 ⌐a2 cxd4 15 ⌐xd4 g6 16 ⌐c1 ⌐d7 17 ⌐e2 ⌐ac8 18 e4 e5 19 ⌐f3 ⌐g7?!

In fear eyes are large, says a proverb. Black is subconsciously afraid of the pressure on the a2-g8 diagonal and

he removes his king for no obvious reason. A simpler solution was to play 19...⌐xc1 20 ⌐xc1 ⌐c8 or 19...⌐g4 eliminating the f3-knight.

20 h3 h6 21 ⌐d2!! *(D)*

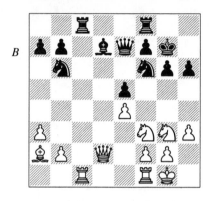

Black got rid of the feeling of insecurity caused by the a2-bishop, but he presented his opponent with a tempo, which he puts to use with an extraordinary move. Alekhine himself was proud of this quiet, subtle move which discovers almost imperceptible weaknesses. ⌐a5 is threatened, causing tensions in the seemingly peaceful waters. Sudden changes are always in some measure shocking and it is not strange that even the great Capablanca does not find the proper reply.

21...⌐e6?!

An alternative is 21...⌐c6, with a counterattack on the e4-pawn, but White has conjured up a brilliant tactical threat – 22 ⌐h4, when 22...⌐xe4? is met by 23 ⌐hf5+ gxf5 24 ⌐xf5+ ⌐g6 25 ⌐xh6+ and mate next move, while 22...⌐xe4 23 ⌐e3 ⌐xc1 24 ⌐xc1 ⌐d8 25 ⌐xe4 ⌐xe4 26 ⌐xe4

🗷d4 27 ♘xg6 is worse for Black than the game continuation.

It was Lasker who showed the correct defence – 21...♘a4.

22 ♗xe6 ♕xe6 23 ♕a5 ♘c4 24 ♕xa7 ♘xb2 25 🗷xc8 🗷xc8 26 ♕xb7 ♘c4 27 ♕b4 *(D)*

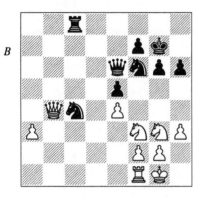

So at the end of complications we have the position we are interested in, characterized by an outside passed pawn on the a-file. From now on all Black's efforts will be concentrated on the attempt to stop that pawn.

27...🗷a8 28 🗷a1 ♕c6 29 a4 ♘xe4 30 ♘xe5!

Black is persistent in his defence and diabolically inventive. In case of 30 ♘xe4 ♕xe4 31 🗷c1 🗷c8 32 ♘xe5?? Capablanca had in mind 32...♘e3 33 ♕xe4 🗷xc1+ 34 ♔h2 ♘f1+ and the queen falls.

30...♕d6

Again the best.

31 ♕xc4 ♕xe5 32 🗷e1 ♘d6 33 ♕c1 ♕f6 34 ♘e4 ♘xe4 35 🗷xe4

Excellent defence has helped Black to avoid the worst and by a series of

'only' moves reach a major-piece endgame, hoping to blockade the passed pawn. Unfortunately for him, it is a daunting task.

35...🗷b8 36 🗷e2

Act one: put the rook behind the pawn to force Black into passivity.

36...🗷a8 37 🗷a2 🗷a5 38 ♕c7 *(D)*

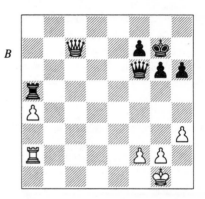

Act two: gain control of the long dark-square diagonal, because only by combining threats against the king and to advance the pawn can White succeed.

38...♕a6 39 ♕c3+ ♔h7 40 🗷d2

The threat of 🗷d8 indirectly defends the pawn.

40...♕b6 41 🗷d7 ♕b1+

We should notice that 41...🗷a7 is out of the question: the queen endgame is easily lost.

42 ♔h2 ♕b8+ 43 g3 🗷f5

Act three: advance the pawn constantly threatening mates.

44 ♕d4

The queen has found a dominant position controlling all the board.

44...♕e8 45 🗷d5 🗷f3

The exchange of rooks is again out of the question, because with the white queen on the long light-square diagonal the king is well protected and the promotion of the pawn unstoppable.

46 h4

Threatening h5 exacts new concessions. Note also another hidden trap: 46 ♔g2 is met by 46...♖a3 47 ♖d8 (47 a5 ♕c6) 47...♖xa4 48 ♕f6 ♖a6.

46...♕h8 47 ♕b6!

In principle the exchange of queens suits White, but not at the moment when the black rook can attack the passed pawn from behind. Naturally, if Black now continued 47...♕f6, White would exchange queens and bring about the ideal position by ♖d2-a2.

47...♕a1 48 ♔g2 ♖f6 49 ♕d4

Act four: White reaches a won rook endgame.

49...♕xd4 50 ♖xd4 ♔g7 51 a5 ♖a6 52 ♖d5 ♖f6 53 ♖d4 ♖a6 54 ♖a4 ♔f6 55 ♔f3 ♔e5 56 ♔e3 h5 57 ♔d3 ♔d5 58 ♔c3 ♔c5 59 ♖a2 ♔b5 60 ♔b3 ♔c5 61 ♔c3 ♔b5 62 ♔d4 ♖d6+

Black manages to free his rook, but the penetration of the white king will be decisive.

63 ♔e5 ♖e6+ 64 ♔f4 ♖a6 65 ♔g5 ♖e5+ 66 ♔h6 ♖f5 67 f4 ♖c5 68 ♖a3 ♖c7 69 ♔g7 ♖d7 70 f5 gxf5 71 ♔f6 f4 72 gxf4 ♖d5 73 ♔g7 ♖f5 74 ♖a4 ♔b5 75 ♖e4 ♔a6 76 ♔h6 ♖xa5 77 ♖e5 ♖a1 78 ♔xh5 ♖g1 79 ♖g5 ♖h1 80 ♖f5 ♔b6 81 ♖xf7 ♔c6 82 ♖e7 1-0

This battle of giants is another lesson on the vitality of a passed pawn. Even when attacked by superior forces it survives; threats on both wings keep it going unperturbed.

Naturally, there are no sacred rules that are always valid. Even in the endgame their value changes according to circumstances. We can say that in general a central passed pawn is less dangerous than a distant one, which is easily explained. Its blockader is not lost on the edge of the board, and so can fulfil other functions as well. Sometimes the passed central pawn is itself in danger and an example will help us to remember this fact.

Gipslis – Korchnoi
USSR Ch, Riga 1970
French Defence

1 e4 e6 2 d4 d5 3 ♘d2 c5 4 exd5 exd5 5 ♘gf3 ♘c6 6 ♗b5 ♗d6 7 0-0 cxd4 8 ♘b3 ♘e7 9 ♘bxd4 0-0 10 b3 ♗g4 11 ♗b2 ♕b6 12 ♗e2 ♖ad8 13 h3 ♗h5 14 ♕d2 ♖fe8 15 ♖ad1 ♗g6 16 ♖fe1 ♗c5 17 ♗f1 ♗e4 18 a3 ♘xd4 19 ♘xd4 ♕g6

Black has neutralized White's attempts to create pressure on the isolated pawn by skilful counterplay with his pieces and counter-pressure on d4. By switching the queen to g6, he vacates b6 for the bishop and finds a new target on c2.

20 ♖e3 ♗xd4 21 ♗xd4 ♘f5 22 ♖c3 b6 23 a4 h6

23...♘xd4 is erroneous in view of 24 ♕xd4 ♗xc2 25 ♖g3 ♕h6 26 ♖c1 ♗xb3 27 ♖c6.

24 ♖c1 ♕g5 25 ♖d1 ♖c8 26 f3 ♘xd4 27 ♕xg5 hxg5 28 ♖xc8 ♖xc8 29 fxe4 ♘xc2 30 exd5? *(D)*

Played under the spell of the passed pawn and its excellent endgame record.

It would all be fine if the following exchange could be avoided and the bishop survived. Correct is 30 ♖xd5 ♘e3 31 ♖d3 with level play.

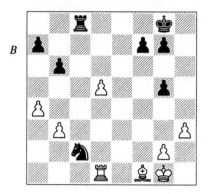

After the text-move, the pawn is exposed because its support is weak. It is obvious that the black king will blockade it, and this keeps the black rook mobile. When you combine these facts you easily conclude that the passed pawn is in mortal danger.

30...♘e3 31 ♖d3 ♘xf1 32 ♔xf1 ♔f8 33 d6

Otherwise 33...♔e7 followed by ...♔d6 would lead to the quick loss of the pawn.

33...♖d8 34 a5 f6 35 ♔e2 ♔f7

The pawn is doomed.

36 ♖c3 ♔e6 37 axb6 axb6 38 ♖c7 ♖d7 39 ♖c6 ♖xd6 40 ♖c7 g6 41 ♔e3

41 ♖g7 would be met by 41...♖d4 42 ♖xg6 ♔f7 43 ♖h6 ♔g7 44 ♖h5 ♖b4.

41...♔f5 42 ♖c4 ♔e5 43 ♖c8 ♖d5 44 b4

Black threatened 44...♖c5. White's problem, apart from being a pawn

down, is the perilous situation of his b-pawn.

44...♖b5 45 ♖e8+ ♔d6 46 ♖d8+ ♔e6 47 ♖d4 ♖e5+ 48 ♔f3 b5!

Precise play. White will not be able to keep his rook on the fourth rank, which means that the b4-pawn is also lost.

49 ♖d8

49 g3 f5 threatens 50...♖d5, while 49 g4 ♖e1 has no reply (50 ♔f2 ♔e5, etc.).

49...♖f5+ 50 ♔e3 ♖f4 51 ♖e8+ ♔d7 52 ♖g8 ♔e7

White will win the g6-pawn, but at the cost of the rook becoming an outcast on the h-file.

53 ♖xg6 ♔f7 54 ♖h6 ♔g7 55 ♖h5 ♖xb4 56 g3 ♖b3+ 57 ♔f2 b4 58 h4 ♖b2+ 59 ♔f3 ♖h2 0-1

White resigned in this hopeless situation.

The passed pawn, the pride of the position in so many endgames, failed here. Its king was far away and it fell prey to the active black king and rook. This serves as an excellent warning against prejudice of any kind. We must keep in mind that there are no sacred rules and that each case of the passed pawn must be seen as a unique case.

Pillsbury – Gunsberg
Hastings 1895
Slav Defence

1 d4 d5 2 c4 c6 3 e3 g6 4 ♘c3 ♗g7 5 ♘f3 ♘f6 6 ♗d3 0-0 7 ♘e5

White avoids 7 0-0 due to 7...♗g4, but for no good reason. Although the play is closed, sooner or later White's two bishops will find their diagonals. After 7 0-0, 7...♗e6 is more appealing; the same reply could also be applied against the text-move.

7...dxc4 8 ♗xc4 ♘d5 9 f4 ♗e6 10 ♕b3 b5 11 ♗xd5 ♗xd5 12 ♘xd5 ♕xd5 13 ♕xd5 cxd5 14 ♘d3 ♘d7 15 ♗d2 ♖fc8 16 ♔e2 e6 17 ♖hc1 ♗f8 18 ♖xc8 ♖xc8 19 ♖c1 ♖xc1 20 ♗xc1 ♗d6

White has achieved a minimal advantage based on the potentially strong c5-square. Of course, it is too little, but Black helps to undermine his own position in the following moves...

21 ♗d2 ♔f8 22 ♗b4 ♔e7 23 ♗c5 a6?! 24 b4 f6 25 g4 ♗xc5 26 bxc5 ♘b8? (D)

Black could have played better at several points in this sequence of moves: 22...♗xb4, 23...a5 or 24...♘xc5 and even now 26...a5 would avoid the following catastrophe.

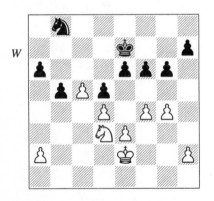

It is true that it's very easy to miss White's concealed tactical idea. Black was hoping to play ...♘c6 with an

impenetrable position, but White is to move and he strikes first...

27 f5!

All of a sudden the d5-pawn becomes shaky. The threat comes from f4 and b4 and there is no way to parry both threats: 27...exf5 28 gxf5 g5 29 ♘b4 and 27...♘c6 28 ♘f4 both lead to the same unhappy situation.

27...g5 28 ♘b4 a5 29 c6!

It is at the critical point that our passed pawn moves on decisively.

29...♔d6 30 fxe6 ♘xc6 31 ♘xc6 ♔xc6 32 e4! (D)

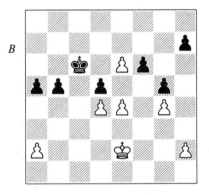

The final point! The e6-pawn gets company, while White's king can cope with the black passed pawns.

32...dxe4 33 d5+ ♔d6 34 ♔e3 b4 35 ♔xe4 a4 36 ♔d4 h5

Stronger resistance is offered by 36...♔e7 37 ♔c4 b3 38 axb3 a3 39 ♔c3 f5 40 gxf5 h5 41 b4 a2 42 ♔b2 a1♕+ 43 ♔xa1 g4 44 b5 h4 45 b6 g3 46 hxg3 hxg3 47 d6+ ♔xd6 48 b7 ♔c7 49 b8♕+ ♔xb8 50 e7, etc.

37 gxh5 a3 38 ♔c4 f5 39 h6 f4 40 h7 1-0

The tactical prowess of the passed pawn set in motion by Pillsbury is not a rare example. Combinative ideas are quite often connected with passed pawns, when their strength is fully accentuated. We shall take a look at another example.

Kasparov – Romanishin
*USSR national teams
competition 1981*
Grünfeld Defence

1 d4 ♘f6 2 c4 g6 3 ♘c3 d5 4 cxd5 ♘xd5 5 e4 ♘xc3 6 bxc3 ♗g7 7 ♘f3 c5 8 ♗e3 ♕a5 9 ♕d2 ♘c6 10 ♖c1 cxd4 11 cxd4 ♕xd2+ 12 ♔xd2 0-0 13 d5 ♖d8 14 ♔e1 ♘a5

This is a well-explored variation of the Grünfeld Defence. Let us just mention that 14...♘b4 15 ♗d2 is unattractive, as is 14...♘e5 15 ♘xe5 ♗xe5 16 f4 ♗g7 17 ♔f2.

15 ♗g5 ♗f6

Exactly what White wanted to provoke: by enticing the bishop to f6, he prevents Black from attacking his pawn-centre by ...f5 or ...e6. Later, hard-working analysts recommended 15...♗d7 16 ♗d3 f5 17 e5 ♗e8 18 d6 ♖dc8.

16 ♗d2 b6 17 ♖c7 ♗g4 18 ♗a6 e6 19 ♘g5!

It is true that White has not fully resolved his development, but Black's a8-rook and a5-knight are out of play as well. The text-move is made possible by White's well-posted pieces and a little tactical trick we should not miss: 19...exd5 20 ♘xf7 ♖d7 loses to 21 ♘h6+ ♔g7 22 ♖c8.

19...♗e5 20 ♖xf7 exd5 21 f4 ♗g7 22 f5 dxe4? *(D)*

Romanishin misses 22...gxf5 23 h3 ♗h5 24 ♖xg7+ ♔xg7 25 ♘e6+ ♔f6 26 exf5 ♖e8 27 g4 ♖xe6+ 28 fxe6 ♗g6. However, he sees a distant light at the end of the tunnel, placing his last hopes in his passed pawn.

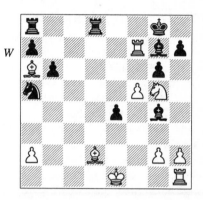

23 ♗xa5 bxa5 24 ♗c4 ♗c3+ 25 ♔f2 e3+

There is still hope: if 26 ♔xe3 then 26...♗d2+.

26 ♔g3 ♗e5+ 27 ♔xg4

27 ♔h4 would be met by the same reply.

27...♖d4+ 28 ♔h3 ♖xc4 29 f6

This will cost Black a whole piece, because 29...♖c7 does not work due to 30 ♖xc7 ♗xc7 31 f7+ ♔h8 32 ♘e6 ♗d6 33 ♖e1.

29...♗xf6 30 ♖xf6 ♖e8 31 ♖e1 e2 32 ♔g3 ♖a4 33 ♔f2 ♖xa2 34 ♘e6 a4 35 ♖b1?

35 ♘d4 should suffice for victory but White wants to weave a mating net.

35...a3 36 ♖b7 e1♕++

36...♖a1 37 ♔xe2 a2 is also sufficient to draw.

37 ♔xe1 ♖xg2 38 ♖g7+ ♔h8 39 ♖gf7

Mate is threatened and it seems unavoidable, but two passed pawns are a
vicious weapon one should never underrate.

39...h5

We shall see that 39...h6 was safer,
not ceding the h6-square to the white
rook.

40 ♔f1 ♖xh2?

The final mistake just at the moment when he was safe. 40...a2 41
♖xa7 ♖xh2 holds the draw.

41 ♖xg6 ♖xe6 42 ♖xe6 ♔g8 43 ♖xa7 1-0

Although Romanishin missed his
chance, we should not miss the message of this exciting battle: beware of
passed pawns! Either through the paralysing effect of the far-advanced and
distant passed pawns or through combinative vitality, endgames represent a
credible mirror of their natural qualities. However, it is the centre of the
board which is the proper stage for a
mobile, powerful passed pawn. We
shall test now its values in more complex circumstances.

Korchnoi – Mikenas
USSR Ch, Riga 1970
Queen's Gambit

1 d4 d5 2 c4 e6 3 ♘f3 c5 4 cxd5 exd5 5 g3 ♘c6 6 ♗g2 c4 7 0-0 ♗b4

In the normal move-order, with ♘c3
played instead of 0-0, this is the variation played and analysed by Ståhlberg

and some other Swedish masters and
named the Swedish Variation after
them. However, there is a slight difference in Korchnoi's move-order, which
amounts to significant difference on
the board. Having delayed the development of the queen's knight, White
is able to undermine the unit d5-c4...

8 b3 cxb3 9 ♕xb3 ♘ge7 10 ♗a3

Commentators pointed out that 10
♗d2 ♗xd2 11 ♘bxd2 was also favourable to White.

10...♗xa3 11 ♕xa3 0-0 12 ♘c3 ♗f5 13 ♘h4

The idea is not only to deny the
bishop its active post at f5, but also to
prepare e4.

13...♗e6 14 ♖ab1 b6 15 ♖fd1 ♘a5 16 e4 *(D)*

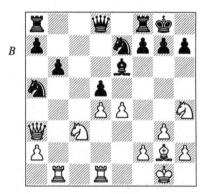

This advance was prepared by 13
♘h4 and is carried out in harmony
with the needs of White's position.
White is playing for a passed pawn on
a central file. Black cannot thwart
White's expectations but the question
is whether he will be able to hold firm
the point d5, blockading the d4-pawn.

16...dxe4 17 ♗xe4 ♘d5 18 ♖bc1 ♖c8?

Who would believe that this natural-looking move is in fact a crucial error?

19 ♗xd5! ♗xd5 20 ♘f5 ♘c4

The first hidden point lies in the fact that 20...♔h8 is refuted by 21 ♘xd5 ♕xd5 22 ♘e7 ♖xc1 23 ♘g6+, winning the exchange.

21 ♕b4

The second point: by provoking ...a5, White prevents ...♘a5.

21...a5 22 ♘e7+ ♔h8 23 ♕b3

Now 23...♕xe7 loses a piece and there is no 23...♘a5 any more. Black is forced to follow on the conceived path of Korchnoi's combination.

23...♘d2 24 ♕xd5 ♕xe7 25 ♖xd2 ♖xc3 26 ♖xc3 ♕e1+ 27 ♔g2 ♕xd2 28 ♕xf7

The third and final point. Black loses material and, what is more, he cannot afford to play 28...♖d8 because of 29 ♕d5, again playing on the weakness of the back rank. The position in the centre is cleared up, and the passed pawn has only minor obstacles to overcome.

28...♖g8 29 ♖e3

Defending the d4-pawn by the threat ♖e8 and improving the position of the rook.

29...h6 30 ♖e4 ♕c2

30...b5 puts more resistance. The d4-pawn should be stopped as long as possible.

31 ♖e6 b5

This time 31...♕d2 was better because now the quick passed pawn denies Black any chances.

32 d5 ♕xa2 33 d6 ♕d5+ 34 ♔h3 ♕c4 35 d7 ♕f1+ 36 ♔h4 g5+ 37 ♔g4 h5+ 38 ♕xh5+ 1-0

Korchnoi's combination was based on the existence of a passed pawn, which triumphs in the end. It is not by chance that tactical fireworks proved justified. The very existence of a central passed pawn is regularly based on tactical motifs. The following games will confirm that elementary lesson.

Szabo – Timman
Amsterdam 1975
King's Indian Defence

1 c4 g6 2 ♘c3 ♗g7 3 d4 d6 4 e4 ♘f6 5 f4 c5 6 d5 e6 7 ♘f3 0-0 8 ♗e2 exd5 9 cxd5 ♖e8

The Four Pawns Attack against the King's Indian is characterized by White's attempts to execute a central breakthrough. However, many tempi have been invested in the idea, leaving Black a wide choice. Sharp players may also opt for 9...b5, while those who are attracted by quiet play can choose 9...♗g4, thwarting the planned e5 advance indefinitely.

10 e5 (D)

Correct judgement. This pawn sacrifice will bring White the open f-file, quicken his development and, more importantly, create a dangerous passed pawn on the d-file.

10...dxe5 11 fxe5 ♘g4 12 ♗g5

12 e6 fxe6 13 d6 ♗d7 14 0-0 ♗c6 15 ♘g5 ♘e5 proved better for Black in Udovčić-Marović, Yugoslav Ch 1964. 12 0-0 ♘xe5 13 ♗f4 ♗f5, followed by ...♘bd7, also favours Black.

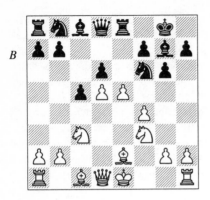

In both cases the passed pawn is successfully blockaded, so White loses the initiative.

12...f6

12...♕b6 leads to sharper play: 13 0-0 ♘xe5 (or 13...c4+ 14 ♔h1, when 14...♘f2+? 15 ♖xf2 ♕xf2 16 ♘e4 ♕b6 17 ♘d6 ♖f8 18 ♗e7 ♘d7 19 ♘xc4 gives White overwhelming power in the centre) 14 d6, when the far-advanced passed pawn represents obvious compensation for an insignificant material sacrifice.

13 exf6 ♗xf6 14 ♕d2 ♗f5

Black's queenside is undeveloped and there is no time to lose. 14...♘d7 15 0-0 ♘de5 16 ♗xf6 ♕xf6 17 ♘g5 and 14...♗xg5 15 ♕xg5 ♘e3 16 ♕xd8 ♖xd8 17 ♔f2 are dubious for Black.

15 0-0 ♗xg5 16 ♕xg5 ♘d7 17 h3 ♘e3 18 ♕h6!?

White sacrifices an exchange, entering complications in which the passed pawn has a prominent role.

18...♘xf1 19 ♘g5 ♕e7

After 19...♖e7 20 d6 the threat comes in the form of ♗c4+, when 20...♘e3 21 dxe7 ♕xe7 22 ♖e1 favours White.

20 d6 (D)

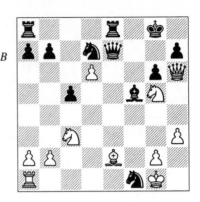

The pawn becomes troublesome.

20...♕e3+ 21 ♔xf1 ♘f8 22 ♖d1 ♖e5

Black has ideas of ...♖f5+.

23 d7 ♖d8?

Black had a fine choice of moves instead of the losing text-move. One is first attracted by 23...♕f4+ (denying White the check from c4) 24 ♗f3 (or 24 ♔e1 ♖d8 25 ♘d5 ♕c4) 24...♖d8 25 ♘e2 ♕e3, when Black is much better. 23...♗xd7 is also legitimate, e.g. 24 ♖xd7 ♖f5+ 25 ♗f3 ♘xd7 26 ♕xh7+ ♔f8 and whatever I tried Black was OK. I was quite astonished to notice that 23...♗xh3 comes into consideration too. 24 ♕xh3 ♕xg5 controls the d8-square, while 24 d8♕ loses to 24...♖f5+.

However, with a passed pawn on the seventh rank one should always be extra alert. In his quest of victory, Black underrated the d7-pawn.

24 ♗c4+ ♗e6 25 ♘xe6! ♖f5+

25...♕xh6 loses to 26 ♘xd8+ ♔g7 27 ♘e6+ ♘xe6 28 ♗xe6.

26 ♘f4+ ♔h8 27 ♘d5 ♕e4 28 ♗e2
♘e6 29 ♗f3 ♕c4+ 30 ♔g1 ♘xf4 31
♘e3 ♕e6 32 ♘xf5 ♕xf5 33 ♖e1 ♘e6
34 ♗g4 1-0

The passed pawn could be held up
in this game, but its advance introduced rich tactical play in which one
could easily lose the thread. Note also
that at the moment when the passed
pawn appeared on the d-file, Black
still had to develop his queenside.
White had a spatial advantage and
could initiate play on the kingside.

Kasparov – J. Přibyl
European Team Ch, Skara 1980
Grünfeld Defence

**1 d4 ♘f6 2 c4 g6 3 ♘c3 d5 4 cxd5
♘xd5 5 e4 ♘xc3 6 bxc3 ♗g7 7 ♘f3
b6**

Of course, 7...c5 is well known and
consistent with the king's fianchetto.
If the text-move comes into consideration it is certainly not now.

**8 ♗b5+ c6 9 ♗c4 0-0 10 0-0 ♗a6
11 ♗xa6 ♘xa6 12 ♕a4**

A serious alternative is 12 ♗g5,
with ♕d2 and ♖ad1 in mind. Black's
errant knight justifies such a concentration of forces in the centre.

**12...♕c8 13 ♗g5 ♕b7 14 ♖fe1 e6
15 ♖ab1 c5 16 d5** *(D)*

At the cost of a pawn White creates
his passed pawn. The coordinated support of his pieces justifies the decision.
We see now why the queen's rook
moved to b1: it stops the advance of
the b-pawn.

**16...♗xc3 17 ♖ed1 exd5 18 exd5
♗g7 19 d6**

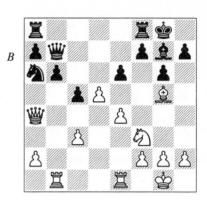

White threatens ♗e7 winning material. The fruits of the breakthrough
which resulted in the passed pawn are
very obvious. Black's pieces have lost
their coordination and are unable to
oppose the advance of the pawn.

19...f6 20 d7!

Believing in the value of his passed
pawn, White is ready to sacrifice a
whole piece. Refusing to take it does
not help, because 20...♖ad8 21 ♕c4+
♔h8 22 ♘e5 fxe5 23 ♗xd8 ♖xd8 24
♕e6 ♕b8 25 ♖b3 leads to disaster.

Whatever he does, Black's problem
remains the same. He has no way to
organize a meaningful defence, as his
forces are split in two by the ominous
presence of the passed pawn on d7.

**20...fxg5 21 ♕c4+ ♔h8 22 ♘xg5
♗f6 23 ♘e6 ♘c7**

23...♘b4 does not extricate Black
from his predicament, as 24 ♕f4 ♘c6
25 ♘xf8 ♖xf8 26 d8♕ makes use of
the pin to win material.

24 ♘xf8 ♖xf8 25 ♖d6 ♗e7 *(D)*

After 25...♗d8 there is 26 h4 ♕a6
27 ♕c3+ ♔g8 28 ♕c2, when ♖xg6+
is already in the air.

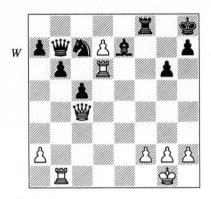

W

Unfortunately for Black, the text-move allows the pawn to deal the final blow:

26 d8♕!

Unexpected and beautiful. Since 26...♖xd8 loses to 27 ♖xd8+ ♗xd8 28 ♕f7, there is no choice...

26...♗xd8 27 ♕c3+ ♔g8 28 ♖d7 ♗f6 29 ♕c4+ ♔h8 30 ♕f4

White wins back the material, but Black, tired and confused, overlooks mate.

30...♕a6? 31 ♕h6 1-0

The passed pawn caused havoc. The explanation lies in the excellent positioning of the supporting pieces, and in the power of the passed pawn to cut the opponent's army in two, thereby making it possible for White to manoeuvre easily against the exposed enemy king.

Minić – Planinc
Zagreb 1975
Ruy Lopez

1 e4 e5 2 ♘f3 ♘c6 3 ♗b5 a6 4 ♗a4 ♘f6 5 0-0 b5 6 ♗b3 ♗b7 7 d4

White could continue solidly by 7 ♖e1, but he had in mind some earlier experiences. It was well-known that Planinc played this line.

7...♘xd4 8 ♘xd4 exd4 9 e5 ♘e4 10 c3 d3

Both players considered that after 10...dxc3 11 ♕f3, 11...♕e7 12 ♘xc3 is lost for Black, and I think they were right. Theory recommends 11...d5 12 exd6 (at the time Minić was of opinion that 12 ♘xc3 yields good compensation for the pawn) 12...♕f6, but Black does not wish to develop his opponent, all the more so since he can meet 11 ♕xd3 by 11...♘c5 and eliminate the b3-bishop – he had previously played this with success.

11 ♕f3

This was what Minić had prepared at home, preventing 11...d5 due to 12 exd6 ♘xd6 13 ♗xf7+, etc.

11...♕e7 12 ♘d2 0-0-0!?

With Planinc it was always *aut Caesar aut nihil*. After the game he did not wish even to see 12...♘c5 13 ♗d5 ♗xd5 (13...c6 14 ♘e4) 14 ♕xd5 c6 15 ♕d4, which offers better chances to White and promises Black just passive defence.

13 ♘xe4 ♕xe5 14 ♖e1 f5 15 ♕g3 ♕e8 *(D)*

It was never easy to predict Planinc's moves. The idea of sacrificing the queen is not at all obvious. Judging from the time he spent on the opening phase, Planinc thought it up at the board. His daring, resolute decision, let us not forget, is based on the almost forgotten passed pawn, which has survived deep inside White's camp.

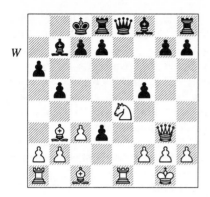

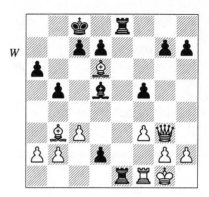

16 ♘d6+ ♗xd6 17 ♖xe8 ♖hxe8 18 ♗f4?

It was only a day later that Minić thought of the unappealing but correct 18 f4 ♗c5+ 19 ♔f1 ♖e2 20 ♗d1 giving back material and reaching an advantageous endgame.

18...d2!

The nearer to the promotion square, the nastier the tricks become. Protected by the pin of the f4-bishop, the pawn threatens mate. At this moment White still had illusions of winning the game. If he had understood that things were getting out of hand, he would have probably looked for rescue. 19 ♔f1 ♖e4 20 ♗xd6 ♖de8 21 f3 ♖e1+ 22 ♖xe1 dxe1♕+ 23 ♕xe1 ♖xe1+ 24 ♔xe1 cxd6 was the wise thing to do. Minić chose instead what seemed an easy win.

19 ♖f1 ♖e1 20 ♗xd6 ♖de8 21 f3

21 ♕d3 ♖xf1+ 22 ♕xf1 cxd6 23 f3 ♖e1 24 ♔f2 ♖xf1+ 25 ♔xf1 ♗d5 favours Black and forces White's choice.

21...♗d5! *(D)*

How to survive after this hammer-blow? Minić does not manage it, which is not surprising. Each move is a little shock for White and each revolves around the passed pawn. The idea, of course, is to weaken the defence of the promotion square, d1. To make things worse it is not only ...♗xb3 that is threatened but ...♗c4 as well.

22 ♕f4

Finally White understands that his life is at stake and that the d2-pawn is the crux of the situation. The d2-pawn must be eliminated, but in trying to do so with his queen, White relinquishes his control of another vital square – e1.

22 ♗f4, therefore, was the safest move, when Black can force a repetition of moves by 22...♖xf1+ 23 ♔xf1 ♗c4+ 24 ♔f2 ♖e2+, etc. He can try for more by 22...♗c4, when it is White's turn to produce a fine defensive manoeuvre: 23 ♗xc4 d1♕ 24 ♗d3 and the hanging bishop keeps the position together.

22...♗c4 23 h4

All he can do now is to run away, but there is still hope.

23...♖xf1+ 24 ♔h2 ♖e2

Black is not prepared to give up his precious pawn any more.

25 ♗xc7 ♖ff2 *(D)*

After the game, Minić was of the opinion that 25...♖g1 is not enough for victory, and he was right: 26 ♔xg1 ♗xb3 27 ♗a5 d1♕+ 28 ♔h2 d6 29 ♕g5 leaves the black king exposed.

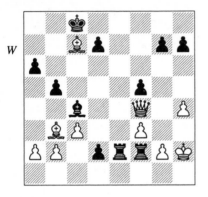

26 ♕d6?

Both players were entering time-trouble when White collapsed. As a matter of fact, the possibilities have not been exhausted and 26 ♗d1! continues resistance. After 26...♖xg2+, 27 ♔h3? loses at once to 27...♗e6!, which paralyses the white queen by the constant threat ...f4+. However, 27 ♔h1 is not that simple. 27...♖gf2 28 ♔g1 leads nowhere, hence 27...♗d5, threatening ...♖gf2, but 28 ♗b6 ♖h2+ 29 ♕xh2 ♗xf3+ 30 ♔g1 ♖xh2 31 ♔xh2 (but not 31 ♗xf3 ♖xh4 32 ♗e3 ♖h3 or 32...♖e4, etc.) 31...♗xd1 32 ♗e3 leads to a position where it is not clear how Black can win, even though 32...♗b3 33 ♗xd2 ♗xa2 gives him three extra pawns.

26...♖xg2+ 27 ♔h3 ♖h2+ 28 ♔g3 ♖eg2+ 29 ♔f4 ♖xh4+ 30 ♔xf5 ♖h6 0-1

This was a superb game. Hanging over White's destiny like the Sword of Damocles, the black passed pawn was a source of inspiration. Now it is much easier to understand what Aron Nimzowitsch meant when he said that the passed pawn was a criminal that had to be put in jail, because mild measures would not do.

Spassky – Petrosian
World Ch match (game 5),
Moscow 1969
Queen's Gambit

1 c4 ♘f6 2 ♘c3 e6 3 ♘f3 d5 4 d4 c5 5 cxd5 ♘xd5 6 e4 ♘xc3 7 bxc3 cxd4 8 cxd4 ♗b4+ 9 ♗d2 ♗xd2+

It is good to compare the course of this game with a famous old game, Rubinstein-Schlechter, San Sebastian 1912, which continued 9...♕a5 10 ♖b1 ♗xd2+ 11 ♕xd2 ♕xd2+ 12 ♔xd2 0-0, when Rubinstein's excellent 13 ♗b5, thwarting normal development and preparing to capture the open c-file, led to an obvious advantage, enhanced by the active position of White's king in the centre.

10 ♕xd2 0-0 11 ♗c4

This is the most active position for the light-squared bishop. From here it supports the advance in the centre. It is the first warning of future events.

11...♘c6

11...♘d7 is in many ways more flexible. It leaves open the a8-h1 diagonal for the black bishop, while the knight can increase the pressure on the central pawns by ...♘f6, or defend the king by ...♘f8, serve as a blockader against the advance of the d4-pawn, but it is passive. 12 0-0 b6 13 a4 ♗b7 14 ♖fe1 ♖c8 15 ♗d3 (as in Petrosian-Tal, USSR Team Ch, Moscow 1972), intending a5 with lasting pressure, emphasizes that quality.

12 0-0 b6 13 ♖ad1

When the central thrust is planned, the white rooks are most naturally placed on d1 and e1.

13...♗b7

In another famous game played later that same year, after 13...♘a5 14 ♗d3 ♗b7 15 ♖fe1 ♖c8, 16 d5! struck Black all the same. The further 16...exd5 17 e5 ♘c4 18 ♕f4 ♘b2 19 ♗xh7+! ♔xh7 20 ♘g5+ ♔g6 21 h4! put Black's king in a most difficult situation in Polugaevsky-Tal, USSR Ch, Moscow 1969.

14 ♖fe1 ♖c8 15 d5 (D)

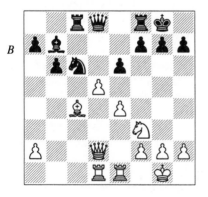

Everything is ready for White to create a passed pawn on the d-file.

15...exd5

If Black reacts by 15...♘a5, then 16 dxe6 ♕xd2 17 exf7+ ♔h8 18 ♘xd2 ♘xc4 19 ♘xc4 ♖xc4 20 e5 ♗c8 brings nothing, but simply 16 ♗d3 transposes to Polugaevsky-Tal in the note to Black's 13th move.

16 ♗xd5 ♘a5?!

A pin always causes a sense of unease, and players are inclined to get rid of it as soon as possible. However, the question occurs at once: what will the black knight do on the edge of the board? The quiet 16...♕e7 was superior.

17 ♕f4 ♕c7?!

Exchanging bishops means accepting a strong, well-supported passed pawn on the d-file, but 17...♕e7 was again better.

18 ♕f5!

Although somewhat surprising, this move is natural and strong. By threatening ♘g5, White provokes the reaction which follows.

18...♗xd5 19 exd5 ♕c2

Between two fires, direct threats to his king and the passed pawn ready to advance, Black decides that the former is his priority. He cannot solve both problems. 19...♘c4, trying to achieve the ideal blockading position on d6, fails to 20 ♘g5 g6 21 ♕h3 h5 22 ♘e4 ♘d6 23 ♘f6+ ♔g7 24 ♕g3 followed by ♕e5 and complete paralysis. The alternative defence of the kingside by 19...♕d6 20 ♘g5 ♕g6 fails after 21 ♕xg6 hxg6 22 d6, and now it is the far-advanced pawn which will paralyse Black. Spassky demonstrated 22...♘b7 23 d7 ♖cd8 24 ♖e7 ♘c5 25 ♖d6 ♘b7 (or 25...f6 26 ♘e6

♘xe6 27 ♖dxe6, and so on) 26 ♖c6 ♘c5 27 ♖c7 f6 28 ♖xc5, etc. Following the logic of this continuation, the text-move could be punished in the same way: 20 ♕xc2 ♖xc2 21 ♖e7 and the pawn cannot be stopped successfully.

20 ♕f4?! ♕xa2?!

The 20th move is characterized by a sudden lapse in concentration by both players, as they underrate the strength of the passed pawn. With Black it is psychologically more understandable. "Since I cannot stop the pawn, I shall at least grab some material" – the common reasoning in such situations. The a2-pawn is worthless and Black should have concentrated on the d-pawn. His only chance was 20...♖ce8 21 d6 ♖xe1+ 22 ♖xe1 ♕d3.

21 d6 ♖cd8 22 d7

The paralysing effect of the passed pawn announces the end. As a rule, when it advances far into the enemy camp, no coordinated defence is possible.

22...♕c4 23 ♕f5 h6 24 ♖c1 ♕a6 25 ♖c7 b5?

25...♘b3 is better in as much as it avoids the devastating reply 26 ♖e8 (see the next note), but after 26 g3 Black remains in trouble.

26 ♘d4?

White complicates things by missing the simple 26 ♖e8.

26...♕b6

Spassky's trainer, Igor Bondarevsky, showed that 26...♕d6 27 ♘xb5 ♕d2 28 ♖f1 ♘b3 29 ♖xa7 ♘d4, diminishing the pressure by exchanging knights, was more tenacious.

27 ♖c8 ♘b7

If 27...b4, then 28 ♖e8 ♕xd4 29 ♖xf8+ ♖xf8 30 ♖xf8+ ♔xf8 31 ♕c5+ – a nice little point again made possible by the far-advanced pawn.

28 ♘c6 ♘d6 29 ♘xd8 ♘xf5 30 ♘c6 1-0

Spassky's win reminds me of the following game played some years earlier and characterized by the same typical difficulties the defending side must overcome when confronted by the passed pawn.

Keres – Geller
*Candidates playoff match
(game 8), Moscow 1962*
Queen's Gambit

1 d4 ♘f6 2 c4 e6 3 ♘f3 d5 4 ♘c3 c5 5 cxd5 ♘xd5 6 e3 ♘c6 7 ♗c4 ♘xc3 8 bxc3 ♗e7 9 0-0 0-0 10 e4

By taking on c3 Black strengthened White's pawn-centre, which, using tennis terms, was probably an unforced error. Helping his opponent to build a full pawn-centre was the beginning of his problems.

10...b6 11 ♗b2 ♗b7 12 ♕e2 ♘a5

The central thrust is already in the air: d5 exd5, ♗xd5 suits White perfectly.

13 ♗d3 ♖c8 14 ♖ad1 cxd4

Not an easy decision to take. The exchange enhances the strength of the b2-bishop and, in combination with the obvious breakthrough in the centre, accentuates the aggressive stance of White's bishops, which target the exposed black kingside.

15 cxd4 ♗b4?! *(D)*

This move features a nice idea, but it is a tempo short of working. Geller's intention is 16...♗c3, which is a natural way to defend the castled position. 15...♗f6 was the only way to try to parry the massive attack the black king is facing.

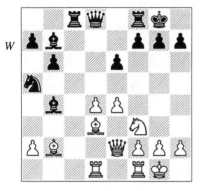

16 d5 exd5 17 exd5 ♕e7

17...♗xd5 helps White to switch his queen into direct attack by the obvious 18 ♕e5 f6 19 ♕h5, while 17...♖e8 18 ♘e5 multiplies the threats. It is probable that Geller had in mind 17...♗c3, but had to abandon the idea because of 18 ♗f5, after which the black rook has no place on the c-file.

18 ♘e5! f6

Keres pointed out 18...♗d6 19 ♕h5 g6 20 ♘g4. It is no surprise that there are no longer any useful moves for Black. White's central thrust has divided his forces and all the minor pieces are cut off on the queenside, when White opened the front on the other wing.

19 ♕h5 g6 *(D)*

20 ♘xg6 hxg6 21 ♗xg6

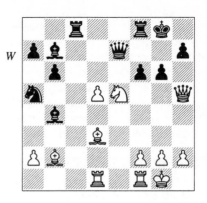

The king's defences are destroyed and the final blow comes on the third rank. 22 ♖d3 is threatened and there is little Black can do against it. 21...♗a6 prevents it, but is refuted by 22 ♗f5 or 22 d6 ♗xd6 23 ♖fe1. The other defensive try consists of moving the rook to g7, but 21...♖c7 also fails to 22 d6 ♗xd6 23 ♖fe1 ♕d8 24 ♖d4, when ♖h4 cannot be parried.

21...♕g7

21...♖c4 loses to 22 ♖d3.

22 ♖d3 ♗d6 23 f4 ♕h8 24 ♕g4 ♗c5+ 25 ♔h1 ♖c7 26 ♗h7++ ♔f7 27 ♕e6+ ♔g7 28 ♖g3+ 1-0

The striking similarity of this game and the last is not fortuitous. They share common situations, characterized essentially by the unstoppable advance in the centre and its consequences: either the king remains exposed to attack or the passed pawn advances towards the promotion square with paralysing effect on the defensive forces.

In a large number of cases the central thrust is carried out in the early phase of the game and the fruits are reaped in the middlegame. However, it is not so rare to come across games in which a passed pawn is created in the centre in the opening, but it is blockaded by pieces and only late in the game, when material is reduced, does it acquire new importance and becomes a decisive factor. Such a passed pawn is mostly the wedge of a pawn-chain or a pawn-unit. We speak of protected passed pawns and they are the theme of our next game.

Botvinnik – Tal
World Ch match (game 13), Moscow 1961
King's Indian Defence

1 d4 ♘f6 2 c4 g6 3 ♘c3 ♗g7 4 e4 d6 5 f3 0-0 6 ♗e3 e5 7 dxe5 dxe5 8 ♕xd8 ♖xd8 9 ♘d5

Having created a hole in his pawn-structure of his own free will, White must justify it, and this is the only way to do so.

9...♘xd5 10 cxd5 c6 11 ♗c4 b5

Black seizes the opportunity to expand on the queenside, at the same time increasing the pressure on the d5-pawn by the fianchetto of the light-squared bishop – a logical reaction in the circumstances. Later David Bronstein pointed out an alternative based on tactical counterchances: 11...cxd5 12 ♗xd5 ♘c6 13 0-0-0 ♘d4. Then 14 ♗xd4 exd4 15 ♘e2 is met by 15...♗f5, when 16 ♘xd4? loses to 16...♗h6+ 17 ♔b1 ♖xd5. Equally hidden and nice is 16 ♔d2 ♖ac8 17 ♖c1? ♗h6+ 18 f4 ♖xc1 19 ♖xc1 d3 20 ♔xd3 ♖xd5+ 21 ♔e3 ♖e5!, keeping an extra piece.

12 ♗b3 ♗b7 13 0-0-0 *(D)*

In later years White tried to improve on this by 13 ♖c1 provoking the exchange and succeeded after 13...cxd5 14 ♖c7 ♖d7? 15 ♖xb7, etc., as well as after 13...♖d7 14 ♘e2 cxd5 15 ♗xd5, but 13...a5, keeping the tension and seizing space, proved good for Black.

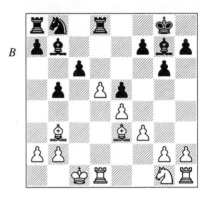

13...c5?!

Making use of the possible pin on the c-file, Black creates a queenside majority, forgetting the precious price he pays for it in the form of the strong, protected passed pawn on d5. In comparison with other passed pawns we have examined, this one is immobile, but as it is well defended, it can wait for better days.

Again, 13...a5 was the move to choose, keeping the pressure and other options.

14 ♗c2 ♘d7 15 ♘e2 ♗f8 16 ♘c3 a6?!

It is rather strange that Tal did not try a sharper line at some point. On the previous move there was 15...c4, while here he could try 16...b4 17 ♘a4 c4. Instead he settled for an apparently secure road.

17 b3! ♖ac8 18 ♗d3! ♘b6 19 ♗e2

What looked so good and solid a couple of moves earlier, is now an immobile mass of pawns with a couple of pieces behind it with no role in imminent events. Three masterful moves were enough for White to block any action on the queenside. It was the first step of his strategy.

19...♖d6 20 ♔b2 f5

Black admits that his queenside preparations were in vain. Having defended the b6-knight he can finally move the pawns, but to his detriment only. After 20...b4, 21 ♘b1 c4 22 bxc4 ♘xc4+ 23 ♗xc4 ♖xc4 24 ♖c1 exposes the bad position of the rook on d6. Black's idea with the text-move is to prepare ...b4 by first playing ...fxe4, but White's reply nullifies it by making sure that after a subsequent ...b4 the c4-square will be fully covered.

21 ♖c1 ♖f6 22 a4! *(D)*

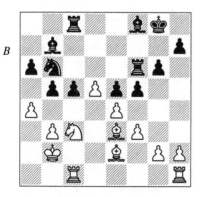

Having immobilized the mass of black pawns, White's last few moves

have prepared the final blow, which undermines the black rampart by opening a breach in it.

22...bxa4 23 bxa4 a5 24 ♔c2 c4 25 ♖b1 ♗b4 26 ♘a2 ♗c5 27 ♗xc5 ♖xc5 28 ♘c3

Some commentators pointed out that 28 f4 worked, but with 28 ♘c3 at his disposal, why should White look for other moves? It belongs perfectly to the general strategy started with 17 b3. The penetration on the b-file is the next step. Note also that the d5-pawn is waiting its time.

28...♗c8 29 ♖b2 ♗d7 30 ♖hb1 ♗xa4+ 31 ♘xa4 ♘xa4 32 ♖b8+ ♔g7

32...♖f8 loses to 33 f4.

33 ♖1b7+ ♖f7 34 d6

The moment has finally arrived. As material is reduced, potential blockading pieces are removed from the board. The passed pawn, which watched the middlegame complications from its protected central position, advances triumphantly at last.

34...♖xb7 35 ♖xb7+ ♔f6 36 ♖xh7 ♖c8 37 d7 ♖d8 38 ♗xc4 ♘c5 39 ♖f7+ ♔g5 40 ♗b5 fxe4 41 fxe4 1-0

The game is a first-class lesson on protected passed pawns. Botvinnik's d-pawn had been waiting in ambush since the opening to be able to crown White's strategy at the very end. It succeeded because there was no blockader to stop it. Thinking of all the games with a passed pawn we always come to that same essential point. In practical terms it is difficult to imagine a successful fight against a passed pawn without there being a reliable blockader. The following games are devoted to the indivisible destiny of passed pawns and their blockaders.

Petrosian – Fischer
USSR – Rest of World,
Belgrade 1970
English Opening

1 c4 g6 2 ♘c3 c5 3 g3 ♗g7 4 ♗g2 ♘c6 5 ♘f3 e6 6 0-0 ♘ge7 7 d3 0-0

The move-order in the English Opening is of great importance. The order chosen by Petrosian allows Black a very flexible structure characterized by the strong fianchettoed bishop.

8 ♗d2 d5 9 a3 b6 10 ♖b1 ♗b7 11 b4

Played in harmony with the preparatory moves ♗d2 and ♖b1, the text-move is an apparently natural attempt at seizing space and initiative on the queenside. However, on closer examination this is precisely the moment when White begins to stray from firm ground.

11...cxb4 12 axb4 dxc4 13 dxc4 ♖c8

This is the first sign that the c4-pawn is vulnerable, but White was still looking optimistically at the position, as his next move confirms.

14 c5?

It is quite obvious that 14 ♕b3 or 14 ♕a4, the moves which somehow belong to this type of position, would be met by 14...♘d4 and in case of 14 ♘e4 Fischer demonstrated 14...♘a5. After the game Petrosian saw the events in it from another angle and proposed the far more cautious 14 ♘b5 in order to protect the c-pawn by ♘a3.

14...bxc5 15 bxc5 *(D)*

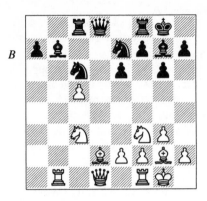

Just at the moment when White felt that the open b-file and advanced passed pawn constituted elements of advantage, Black now demonstrates the opposite by a brilliant positional manoeuvre:

15...♘a5! 16 ♘a4 ♗c6!

The bishop takes on the duty of blockader, while the knight will take its place at b7, starting to exert pressure on the pawn. Notice also the nicely coordinated activity of the black minor pieces, especially the bishops.

17 ♕c2 ♘b7 18 ♖fc1 ♕d7 19 ♘e1

Played in order to meet 19...♗xa4 by 20 ♖xb7.

19...♘d5 20 ♘b2 ♗b5

Fischer's lesson is impressively simple: first, blockade the passed pawn; second, exert pressure on it! And the pressure does get strong, calling for 21 ♘bd3, which seems best here.

21 ♘ed3 ♗d4

The culmination of Black's strategy against the passed pawn: the pawn is doomed.

22 ♕b3 ♘xc5 23 ♘xc5 ♖xc5 24 ♖xc5 ♗xc5 25 ♘d3

25 ♗xd5 fails to 25...♕xd5.

25...♗xd3 26 ♕xd3 ♖d8 27 ♗f3 ♕c7 28 ♗g5 ♗e7 29 ♗xe7 ♕xe7 30 ♕d4

Exchanging the dark-squared bishops does not seem the wisest thing White could do because the exchange favours Black. 30 ♗xd5 would also be good for Black, reminding us of the 34th match-game between Alekhine and Capablanca. However, 30 ♖a1 should be given a chance.

30...e5 *(D)*

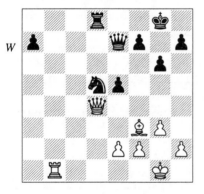

Seeking his chances on both wings is definitely a better policy than relying just on the a7-pawn.

31 ♕c4 ♘b6 32 ♕c2 ♖c8 33 ♕d3 ♖c4 34 ♗g2 ♕c7 35 ♕a3 ♖c3 36 ♕a5 ♖c5 37 ♕a3 a5 38 h4 ♘c4 39 ♕d3 ♘d6 40 ♔h2 ♔g7 41 ♖d1

Black has significantly improved the position of his pieces and the idea of exchanging queens will not bring relief. 41 h5 might at least give Black some uneasy moments.

41...♘e8 42 ♕d7 ♕xd7 43 ♖xd7 ♘f6

43...♘c7 is even stronger.

44 ♖a7 ♘g4+ 45 ♔g1 ♖c1+ 46 ♗f1 ♖a1 47 e4 a4 48 ♔g2 ♖a2 49 ♖xf7+

A losing move, but there is no way out any more. On 49 ♔g1 Black wins by 49...♘xf2 (49...♖xf2 is met by 50 ♗h3) 50 ♗c4 ♘h3+ 51 ♔h1 ♖f2 52 ♗e6 a3 53 ♗xh3 a2, etc.

49...♔xf7 50 ♗c4+ ♔e7 51 ♗xa2 a3 52 ♔f3 ♘f6 53 ♔e3 ♔d6 54 f4 ♘d7 55 ♗b1 ♘c5 56 f5 ♘a6 57 g4 ♘b4 58 fxg6 hxg6 59 h5 gxh5 60 gxh5 ♔e6 61 ♔d2 ♔f6 62 ♔c3 a2 63 ♗xa2 ♘xa2+ 64 ♔b2 ♘b4 65 ♔c3 ♘c6 66 ♔c4 ♘d4 0-1

The blockade of the passed pawn exposed its static weakness, reminding us of the same fate suffered by isolated pawns in similar circumstances.

Bondarevsky – Smyslov
USSR Ch 1946
Ruy Lopez

1 e4 e5 2 ♘f3 ♘c6 3 ♗b5 a6 4 ♗a4 ♘f6 5 0-0 ♗e7 6 ♗xc6 dxc6 7 ♖e1

Having decided to enter this peaceful line, White usually continues 7 ♘c3 or 7 ♕e1 in order to avoid the pin by ...♗g4, which comes into consideration after the text-move.

7...♘d7 8 d4 exd4 9 ♕xd4 0-0 10 ♗f4 ♘c5 11 ♕xd8 ♗xd8 12 ♘c3 f5 13 e5? *(D)*

White has just committed a positional error worth analysing and remembering. Black has preserved his bishop-pair and naturally tries to open the position for his bishops. White refuses to give in, relying on his central passed pawn, at the moment well protected and supported. However, the further course of the game shows that Bondarevsky should have been more careful, and kept the balance by playing 13 ♗g5.

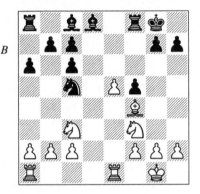

13...♘e6!

Obvious and natural, but so strong that it deserves an exclamation mark. Black could play 13...♗e6, but after 14 b4 followed by 15 ♘d4 White would destroy the blockader. The knight, on the contrary, is much more powerful at e6. White cannot attack it or exchange it, which justifies the conclusion that the square of such a blockader is a strong square. It is protected from frontal attack. At the same time we cannot fail to see that the e6-knight not only blockades the e5-pawn, but that other neighbouring squares come under Black's efficient control.

14 ♗d2 g5 15 ♘e2 c5

Again simple and precise; Black's last two moves secure the privileged position of the blockader.

16 ♗c3 b5 17 b3 ♗b7

Here we start to feel another phenomenon typical for pawn blockade: an efficient blockader is a source of active counterplay. Black has seized a spatial advantage and stands better.

18 ♘g3 g4 19 ♘d2 ♗e7 20 ♘h5 ♔f7 21 ♘f1 ♔g6 22 ♘f6 ♖ad8

Having activated his king, Black could also continue 22...♘d4, but the simplifying process he provokes on the d-file favours him completely.

23 ♖ad1 ♖xd1 24 ♖xd1 ♖d8 25 ♖xd8 ♗xd8 26 ♘e3

Facing the double threat of ...♘f4 and ...♘d4, White should try 26 ♗b2. The text-move worsens his position.

26...f4

Slowly but surely the passed pawn becomes shaky. At the same time the position of white pieces deteriorates.

27 ♘d1

27 ♘ed5 and 27 ♘exg4 lose a piece, while 27 ♘f1 ♗xf6 28 exf6 ♗e4 is hopeless as well.

27...♗xf6 28 exf6 ♗e4

Black's positional advantage has been transformed into a material advantage. The consequences of the powerful blockader on e6, which literally pushed into passivity and paralysed the white pieces, has become obvious.

29 ♗b2 b4

29...♗xc2 30 ♘c3 would change the scene significantly. The c2-pawn is doomed and Black will take it when convenient to him.

30 f3 ♗xc2 31 ♘f2 gxf3 32 gxf3 ♗b1 33 ♘e4 ♗xa2 34 ♘d2 a5 35 ♔f2 ♘d4 36 ♗xd4 cxd4 37 ♔e2 ♔xf6

Finally, the passed pawn meets its destiny.

38 ♔d3 ♔e5 39 ♔c2 a4 40 bxa4 c5 41 a5 c4 42 a6 d3+ 0-1

The lesson we draw is obvious: a mighty blockader is a fatal enemy of passed pawns. The reason is equally obvious: the strength of a passed pawn is in its mobility and when it loses that vital quality, it is doomed to a slow death in the endgame.

The success or failure of passed pawns depends largely on the support of other pieces and the coordination of their activity. In closed positions the support they can muster is more limited, and the success of their mission in doubt. The passed pawn in such circumstances often ends up as a sacrificial lamb; the only question is what compensation we can obtained. Practical comparison will help again.

Marović – Stupica
Yugoslav Ch, Zagreb 1961
King's Indian Defence

1 d4 ♘f6 2 c4 g6 3 ♘c3 ♗g7 4 ♘f3 0-0 5 g3 d6 6 ♗g2 ♘c6 7 0-0 e5 8 d5 ♘e7 9 e4 ♘d7 10 ♗e3

More consistent is 10 b4, seeking action on the queenside, the natural field of White's activity. The textmove was prepared for my opponent, who had misplayed this variation in a previous encounter.

10...f5

This thematic side-blow is sometimes prepared by 10...h6, but 11 ♕d2 ♔h7 12 ♖ad1 f5 13 exf5 gxf5 14 ♘h4 ♘f6 15 ♕c2 reveals its darker side.

11 ♘g5 ♘c5?

11...♘f6!? 12 exf5 gxf5 is correct; then 13 ♘e6 ♗xe6 14 dxe6 c6 15 ♕b3 ♕c8 leaves the passed pawn in the enemy camp in danger.

12 ♗xc5 dxc5 13 ♘e6 ♗xe6 14 dxe6 *(D)*

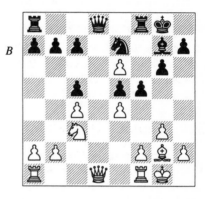

Surrounded behind Black's lines, the passed pawn runs a great risk again. Before entering this position, White had to evaluate clearly what he could get for it.

14...c6 15 ♕d7!

My opponent had missed this move. The exchange of queens will make it more difficult for Black to win the pawn, offering White plenty of time to look for additional motifs, using the open file, the light-square diagonals and his knight.

15...♕xd7 16 exd7 ♖ad8 17 ♖ad1 ♖f7 18 ♖d3

By doubling his rooks, White satisfies his pawn's need for defence, but at the same time he has in mind a later ♖a3, using the third rank to penetrate the closed position.

**18...♔f8 19 ♖fd1 ♘g8 20 ♘a4 b6
21 exf5 gxf5 22 ♗xc6 e4 23 ♖a3 ♘f6
24 ♘c3 ♘xd7 25 ♖xa7**

The collateral action on the a-file came in time.

**25...♗d4 26 ♗xd7 ♖fxd7 27 ♖xd7
♖xd7 28 b3**

The knight is free; the material advantage is decisive.

**28...♔f7 29 a4 e3 30 fxe3 ♗xe3+
31 ♔g2 ♖xd1 32 ♘xd1 ♗d4 33 ♘f2
♗e5 34 ♘d3 ♗c7 35 ♔f3 ♗d6 36
♘f4 ♗xf4 37 ♔xf4 ♔f6 38 ♔e3 ♔e5
39 ♔d3 h6 40 ♔e3 ♔e6 41 ♔f4 1-0**

Some General Observations

In trying to understand the nature of the passed pawn, we watched it in characteristic situations that reveal its best qualities as well as its drawbacks.

Studying its role in the endgame we understood that, contrary to its ancestors, isolated and hanging pawns, the passed pawn is characterized by an essential difference: its power increases in the endgame. We can go so far as to say that the side possessing a passed pawn, especially a distant one, has created the preconditions for victory. When the number of pieces is reduced, it is increasingly difficult to hold up a passed pawn far on the wing, requiring constant watch of a blockader. We could see for ourselves that no 'extenuating circumstances', neither opposite-coloured bishops nor major pieces, helped the weaker side against a distant passed pawn. No matter which piece was given the duty of the blockader, it was at least partly

absorbed by it and so was lost to the rest of the board. Each time it happened, the balance of power was upset.

To make things worse for its adversaries, the passed pawn often takes part in tactical complications. Its position on the seventh rank has inspired numerous clever combinations, adding to its notoriety as a trouble-maker.

Notwithstanding its excellent endgame record, we often associate the passed pawn in our mind with its role played in the centre of the board, where its mobility comes to the fore.

Living in more favourable circumstances, not opposed by the enemy's infantrymen, the passed pawn is a privileged descendant of isolated and hanging pawns. Its strength originates from its mobility and grows through its movement forward. The further it advances, the stronger it gets, accumulating power by its sheer movement. When it reaches the sixth or seventh rank, it is reminiscent of a sharp wedge splitting the board and enemy pieces in two disoriented parts, which lose coordination and the ability to perform.

Its movement is accompanied by tactical surprises of all kinds. The little, modest pawn turns into a nasty monster. On most occasions it takes much more than routine play to stop it.

After each step it makes, its possessor's manoeuvring space widens, while the defender's breathing space gets reduced and the coordination of his pieces feebler. We can say without exaggeration that a far-advanced pawn is like a bone stuck in the throat. Its advance forces passive resistance at best, and in a very large percentage of cases it breaks any meaningful counterplay.

The very existence of the passed pawn in the centre has wider connotations – of spatial advantage, initiative, freedom of manoeuvre and action. Naturally, its active role would not be possible without the active support of other pieces; usually the support of major pieces, propelling the pawn down the file, and minor pieces, which clear its way through exchanges. That support is of critical importance. The moment it fails, the moment the blockading forces overcome its kinetic energy, chances are reversed. A mighty blockader, generally a knight or bishop, can tip the balance of power to its advantage and turn the tables. When that happens, the road to the endgame is a slow process of weakening, regularly irreversible and fatal.

Considering all that, the passed pawn lives an exciting life, but often a highly risky one. Often the by-product of a sacrifice, burdened by high expectations, it has to survive in adverse circumstances. It depends, therefore, on clear judgement and precise calculation and, contrary to other types of pawn situations, one can rely less on general maxims. Each situation, more and deeper than with other central formations, is a specific case to be evaluated on its own merits.

4 Doubled Pawns

The diagram before us represents the pawn-structure of a well-known opening variation.

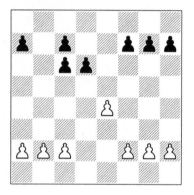

It is characterized by the doubled black pawns on the c-file. A glance at the pawn-formation will give away its little secrets.

On the positive side of the scales we notice that the c6-pawn remains a useful part of the structure by covering the central d5-square, which otherwise would be a strong square for White. We notice also that by retaking at c6 Black has opened the b-file and can use it for counter-pressure on the queenside.

On the negative side, we conclude at once that the block of pawns on c7, c6 and d6, which contains the doubled pawns, can hardly move forward without weakening the squares around it.

Speculating further, we could conclude as well that the chances of improving the pawn-structure are not realistic. Besides, the exchange on c6 left a potentially weak isolated pawn at a7, which, as we can easily imagine, may be exposed to attack.

These are simple thoughts inspired by the diagram position. We shall proceed now to find out how far master practice supports our preliminary views and speculations. Chess wisdom is in chess practice.

Capablanca – Janowski
St Petersburg 1914
Ruy Lopez

1 e4 e5 2 ♘f3 ♘c6 3 ♗b5 a6 4 ♗xc6 dxc6 5 ♘c3 ♗c5 6 d3 ♗g4 7 ♗e3 ♗xe3?! 8 fxe3 *(D)*

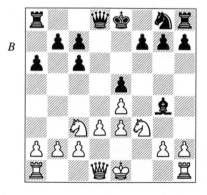

We are very early in the opening, which, seen from the point of view of modern theory, looks somewhat odd. Black's fifth move was quite ambitious and resulted in the exchange on e3. Commentators condemned the exchange, pointing out that it serves White and suggested as better 7...♕e7. In order to judge objectively, we have to notice the changes in the position and evaluate them. We notice that the e3-pawn stands well, covering the squares d4 and f4, which before the exchange were potentially weak. We also notice that the f-file has been opened, and that it is only White who will be able to make use of it. We can, therefore, concur with the critics and favour 7...♕e7.

We shall notice immediately that apart from the doubled e-pawns, there is a pair of doubled pawns in Black's camp. Like the e3-pawn, the c6-pawn has its significance in covering the d5-square. The importance of both pairs of doubled pawns is based on their static value.

8...♕e7 9 0-0 0-0-0?!

In spite of the semi-open f-file, the kingside is a healthier place for Black's king. Either here or on the previous move, a solid plan was to prepare ...0-0 by ...f6 and ...♘h6-f7.

10 ♕e1 ♘h6 11 ♖b1!

Secure in his refuge on g1, White's king can comfortably order an attack on the other wing. The text-move prepares a pawn assault on Black's castled position. At this moment we notice a shortcoming characterizing doubled pawns. When they move, they leave holes around them, which the opponent can exploit. 11...c5 would be quite a useful reply, preventing b4, were it not for the hole on d5.

11...f6 12 b4 ♘f7 13 a4 ♗xf3 14 ♖xf3 b6

Capablanca was right in indicating the text-move as a grave error and pointing out that 14...b5 was the only move that could stop the imminent deterioration of Black's position.

15 b5 cxb5 16 axb5 a5 17 ♘d5 (D)

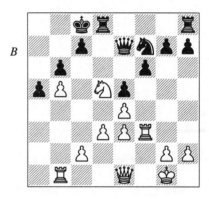

The fact that Black could not hold his ground at c6 influences significantly the course of the game. Do not consider that it happens by chance. The doubled pawns, when they make up part of a larger pawn-mass, can be strong and statically useful, but as soon as they advance they in general become weaker, while new weaknesses arise around them. The d5-square has become an impregnable white stronghold, enabling him to launch an immediate assault.

17...♕c5 18 c4 ♘g5 19 ♖f2 ♘e6 20 ♕c3 ♖d7 21 ♖d1 ♔b7 22 d4

Having protected White's vital dark squares in the centre for a large part of the game, the e3-pawn now supports the final pawn-storm.

22...♕d6 23 ♖c2 exd4 24 exd4 ♘f4 25 c5 ♘xd5 26 exd5 ♕xd5 27 c6+ ♔b8 28 cxd7 ♕xd7 29 d5 ♖e8 30 d6 cxd6 31 ♕c6 1-0

The following game and our discussion of it will corroborate our first impressions about doubled pawns.

Polugaevsky – A. Zaitsev
USSR Ch playoff match (game 2),
Vladimir 1969
Ruy Lopez

1 e4 e5 2 ♘f3 ♘c6 3 ♘c3 d6 4 d4 exd4 5 ♘xd4 ♘f6 6 ♗b5 ♗d7 7 0-0 ♗e7 8 ♗xc6 bxc6 (D)

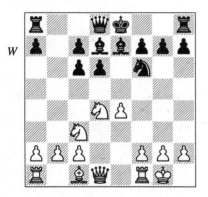

After the initial moves Black has remained with doubled pawns on the c-file, ceding a spatial advantage to his opponent. The c6-pawn, however, is well defended and, besides, usefully placed, keeping the d5-square under control. The problem with the black constellation lies in its limited mobility: when you advance either ...c5 or ...d5, holes are created in the black position.

9 ♕f3

White flirts with the idea of playing e5, which is the only way to increase the pressure on the c6-pawn. More in vogue over the decades has been 9 b3 0-0 10 ♗b2, when we reach a delicate situation which must be played with patience. 10...♖e8 11 ♖e1 ♗f8 12 ♕d3 g6 13 ♖ad1 ♗g7 14 f3 ♕b8, opposing the fianchettoed bishop on b2 and ready to seek counterplay by ...a5-a4, offers Black a good game. Compare this cautious approach, recommended by Dr Lasker, with the impatient reaction started by 10...d5 11 e5 ♘e8 12 ♕d2 c5 13 ♘de2 c6, when Black has moved his pawns a rank up the board, gaining some space. Closer inspection, however, will reveal that the pawns are weaker now than in their initial position. It was difficult to attack the c6-pawn, while the c5-pawn, on the contrary is more vulnerable. Bilkat-O.Bernstein, Ostend 1907 continued 14 ♖ad1 ♕c7 15 ♘f4 ♕b7 (16 ♘xd5 was threatened) 16 ♘a4 (threatening ♗a3) 16...c4 17 ♗d4, when neither 17...♕b5 18 ♕e3 nor 17...cxb3 18 cxb3 could satisfy Black. Moving the pawns forward lost their initial, natural tenacity.

9...0-0 10 ♖e1

10 e5 is not such a threat after all. 10...♘g4 11 exd6 ♗xd6 12 ♗f4 (or 12 g3 ♘xh2) 12...♘xh2 would be quite unpleasant for White.

10...c5 11 ♘f5 ♗xf5 12 ♕xf5

12 exf5 just yields space to Black after 12...d5 13 ♗g5 c6.

12...♘d7 13 ♘d5 ♘b6

Black's 10th move ceded the d5-square to White, but only temporarily. The manoeuvre ...♘d7-b6 takes back what was given. The exchange on d5 would solve all Black's potential difficulties.

14 ♘e3 ♕c8 15 e5?!

Impatiently played, trying to find advantage where there is none.

15...d5 16 ♕xc8 ♖fxc8 17 a4 d4

This time the pawn advance is logical – their movement does not leave weaknesses behind.

18 ♘f5 ♗f8 19 b3 ♖d8 20 a5?!

Polugaevsky himself criticized this move – rightly so, as White chases the knight to a better place and the a5-pawn becomes potentially endangered. 20 ♗d2 was correct, when 20...d3 could be met by 21 c4, leaving the passed pawn well blockaded and the d5-square denied to the b6-knight.

20...♘d5 21 ♗d2 ♖ab8 22 ♖ab1

Now White had to take into consideration ...d3, because his b3-pawn would be vulnerable.

22...♖b5! *(D)*

An excellent reaction. If White intended 23 e6 fxe6 24 ♖xe6, he had to change his mind because of 24...♘b4.

23 ♖e4 g6 24 ♘h4?

An unfortunate decision. 24 ♘g3 ♘b4 25 c3 still keeps White in the game.

24...♘b4 25 c3 dxc3 26 ♗xc3 ♖d3 27 ♖c4 ♘d5 28 ♗e1 ♖bxb3 29 ♖bc1 ♗h6 30 ♖a1 ♖d4 31 ♖aa4

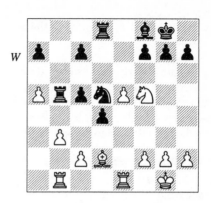

There are no good solutions. 31 ♖xc5 loses to 31...♗f8, while 31 ♖xd4 cxd4 opens the way for the c-pawns, which are finally set free. The text-move irremediably weakens the first rank.

31...♖b1 32 ♘f3 ♗d2 33 ♔f1 ♗xe1 34 ♘xd4 cxd4 35 ♖xd4 ♗c3+ 36 ♔e2 ♗xd4 37 ♖xd4 ♖b5 0-1

The lesson of this game is simple. The doubled pawn is statically strong and useful in its initial position. Therefore, its hasty advance, causing side-weaknesses, may be perilous and needs thorough preparation.

Sutovsky – Morozevich
Pamplona 1998/9
French Defence

1 e4 e6 2 d4 d5 3 ♘c3 ♘f6 4 ♗g5 dxe4 5 ♘xe4 ♗e7 6 ♗xf6 gxf6 7 ♘f3

Here we have another typical case of doubled pawns. The exchange on f6 weakened Black's kingside, but Black sees compensation in the open g-file, while the well-defended f6-pawn performs the useful duty of controlling the e5-square and denying it to the f3-knight.

7...a6

A cautious approach is needed here. 7...f5 8 ♘c3 ♗f6 9 ♕d2 just weakens Black, and does nothing for his development. On the contrary, White is ready to castle queenside and to make a central thrust.

8 ♕d2 b5 9 ♕h6

One would prefer normal development, but it is intriguing to see what can be done against the debilitated kingside. Sutovsky evidently felt the same inquisitive urge.

9...♗b7 10 ♗d3

Here 10 ♕g7 ♖f8 11 ♕xh7 wins a pawn, but after 11...f5 12 ♘ed2 (12 ♘g3? loses after 12...♗xf3! 13 gxf3 ♕xd4) 12...♗f6 the scene is dominated by the bishop-pair.

10...♘d7 11 ♘g3

Two thoughts are behind this move: ♗e4, in order to diminish the pressure on the long light-square diagonal, and ♘h5, to realize some concrete threats and give some meaning to the early queen sally. It is useful to notice that 11 0-0-0 could be met by 11...f5 12 ♘eg5 ♗xg5+ 13 ♘xg5 ♕f6. After thorough preparation the doubled pawn moves forward without negative consequences.

11...f5

At the proper moment Black's f6-pawn advances. It facilitates the defence and at the same time threatens 12...♗xf3.

12 ♘h5 ♗f8 13 ♕e3?!

13 ♘g7+ ♗xg7 14 ♕xg7 ♕f6 15 ♕xf6 ♘xf6 16 ♗e2 was objectively

the best way out, although it is quite pleasant for Black. The retreat is an admission of failure for the whole concept.

13...♘f6 14 ♕e5?

Tempted by the seemingly strong pin, White returns to the quagmire from which he withdrew just a move earlier. Rather than playing for tricks, it was time to think how to save his skin, e.g. 14 ♘xf6+ ♕xf6 15 ♕e2 0-0-0 16 0-0-0.

14...♘xh5 15 ♕xh8 ♗xf3 16 gxf3 ♘f6 *(D)*

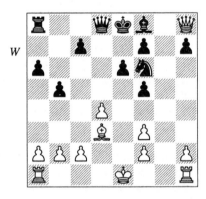

The result of White's faulty strategy is obvious in the diagram. The queen is not only out of play but in danger of never returning: 17...♔e7 followed by 18...♕d5 is an obvious threat, while the clever 17 d5 finds a good response in 17...♕e7, threatening ...0-0-0. If we complete the picture with the damaged pawn-formation and weak light-squared bishop, we can say without exaggeration that White is lost. There follow merely desperate attempts to extricate the queen.

17 Rg1 Wxd4 18 Rg8 ♔e7 19 ♔f1
♗g7 20 Wxg7 Rxg8 21 Wh6 Wxb2 22
Re1 Wc3 23 Wh4 c5 24 Rd1 c4 25
♗xf5 Wxf3 26 Wd4 ♘d5 0-1

27 ♗e4 is punished by 27...♘e3+.

Doubled pawns preserve their static stability and firmness and if not thoughtlessly pushed forward are not an easy prey; nor can the side-weaknesses they leave around them be exploited by violent means. We shall consider several cases characterized by the typical constellation of doubled pawns, in which they play an active, positive role.

Spassky – Korchnoi
Candidates match (game 14),
Belgrade 1978
Vienna Game

1 e4 e5 2 ♘c3 ♘f6 3 g3 d5 4 exd5
♘xd5 5 ♗g2 ♘xc3 6 bxc3 ♗d6 7 ♘f3
0-0 8 0-0 *(D)*

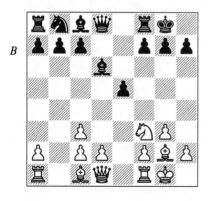

White has accepted doubled c-pawns, finding full compensation for the damaged pawn-structure in the

pressure he can exert on the b-file and the long light-square diagonal, and also in the compact and flexible central pawn-mass.

8...c5 9 d3 ♘c6 10 ♘d2

The pawns cover important central squares and can be used very flexibly, depending on the circumstances. Later on Spassky will carry out d4, but ♘c4-e3 and c4, creating a grip on d5, is also possible.

10...Wd7 11 Wf3

Played to prevent 11...b6. The g2-bishop is stronger if not opposed by a black fianchettoed bishop at b7.

11...Wc7 12 ♘e4 ♗e7 13 ♗e3 c4 14 d4 ♗e6

14...f5 fails to 15 ♘c5, and then 15...♗xc5 16 Wd5+ or 15...e4 16 We2.

15 Rfd1 Rad8 16 We2 ♗d5 17 Rab1 exd4 18 cxd4

The doubled pawn has been advantageously transformed into a passed pawn on a central file.

18...Rfe8 19 ♘c3 *(D)*

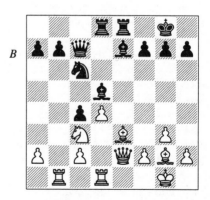

As we have already learnt, the blockaders of the passed pawn should be removed. Simultaneously the c4-pawn will be weakened, forcing the black knight to the edge of the board.

19...♗xg2 20 ♔xg2 ♘a5 21 ♕f3 ♘c6 22 ♕e2 ♘a5 23 a4 b6 24 ♕f3 ♕d7 25 ♖b5 ♘b7 26 ♗f4 ♘d6 27 ♗xd6 ♗xd6 28 ♘e4 ♗e7 29 c3

The passed pawn has now become a protected passed pawn, a valuable asset for the endgame.

29...g6 30 g4!

Thwarting counterplay by ...f5.

30...♖f8 31 ♖db1

White intends a5.

31...a6?

This is bad, but 31...f5 32 gxf5 ♖xf5 33 ♖xf5 ♕xf5 34 ♕xf5 gxf5 fails to 35 ♘g3 ♖f8 36 ♖b5 f4 37 ♘f5, etc.

32 ♖xb6 f5 33 gxf5 ♖xf5 34 ♕e2 ♕xa4 35 ♖b7 ♖e8 36 ♖c7 ♗d6 37 ♖xc4 ♖xe4

Black starts to play weakly in time-trouble.

38 ♖c8+ ♔g7 39 ♕xe4 ♕a2 40 ♖f1 ♕f7

This move makes it easy. Better was 40...♖g5+ 41 ♔h1 ♖h5.

41 f4 ♖h5

41...♗xf4 42 ♔h1 is also hopeless.

42 ♖e8 ♕b3 43 ♖e6 ♕b2+ 44 ♕e2 ♕b8 45 ♕e4 ♕b2+ 46 ♕e2 ♕b8 47 ♖e4 ♖b5 48 ♖f2 ♕b7 49 ♕f3 ♕c8 50 h3 a5 51 ♖e5 ♗xe5 52 fxe5 ♕f5 53 c4 ♖b4 54 ♕e3 ♕c8 55 e6 ♖xc4 56 ♕e5+ ♔h6 57 ♕f4+ ♔g7 58 ♕f6+ ♔h6 59 ♕h4+ 1-0

The metamorphosis of a doubled pawn into a passed pawn does not occur often, but one should be open to such possibilities and make use of them.

Keres – Reshevsky
Los Angeles 1963
Ruy Lopez

1 e4 e5 2 ♘f3 ♘c6 3 ♗b5 a6 4 ♗a4 ♘f6 5 0-0 ♗e7 6 ♖e1 d6 7 ♗xc6+ bxc6

We find doubled pawns most often on c3, c6, f3 and f6, as it is on these squares that bishops are traded for knights. Such pawns form part of the pawn-mass, so they are not considered weak.

8 d4 ♘d7 (D)

After 8...exd4 9 ♘xd4 ♗d7 10 ♘c3 0-0, 11 ♗f4 seems most natural. With ♖e1 already played, notice that 11 b3 can be met by 11...d5 12 e5 ♗b4. One should be ready to exploit such possibilities. Although they look clumsy, doubled pawns are mobile and it is good to keep this in mind.

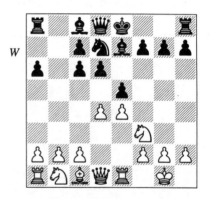

9 ♘bd2 f6 10 ♘c4 ♘b6

In expectation of ♘a5, 10...♘f8 and ...♘e6 seems a better choice.

11 ♘a5 ♗d7 12 ♕d3?!

The idea to harass the c6-pawn was a good one, but the a5-knight should be supported by 12 c4, exploiting the position of the knight on b6. Now we see why the manoeuvre ...♘f8-e6 was preferable: c4 could be met by ...c5. The text-move looks like rather a mild measure against the black pawn-mass.

12...0-0 13 ♗e3 ♔h8 14 ♖ad1 exd4 15 ♘xd4 c5

Black decides to step forward, fighting for space, but he can afford 16 ♘dc6 ♕e8.

16 ♘f5 ♖e8 17 b3 ♗f8 18 ♗c1 ♗e6 19 ♘e3 ♕d7 20 a4 c6

After a couple of hesitant moves by White, Black seizes his opportunity and his doubled, backward pawns advance in the centre, well supported by all the black pieces.

21 ♘ac4 ♘xc4 22 ♘xc4 ♖ad8 23 ♘b6 ♕b7 24 a5 d5 25 ♗f4? (D)

Slowly and clumsily the black pawns have advanced, seizing space and initiative. The text-move misses the threat and the pawns now become vicious. 25 ♗a3 was in order to prevent the worst...

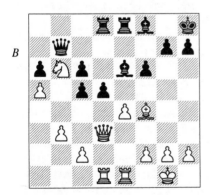

25...c4!

White missed the point: now 26 bxc4 is met by 26...♗b4, while 26 ♕c3 cxb3 27 cxb3 d4 is also good for Black.

26 ♕d2 cxb3 27 cxb3 d4

The doubled pawns have produced a rare fruit – a passed pawn on a central file.

28 b4 ♗b3

It is useful to diminish the pressure on the passed pawn and remove the pieces standing in its way.

29 ♖b1 ♕f7 30 ♗c7 ♕xc7 31 ♖xb3 f5

Together with the passed pawn, and we know it already, tactical chances arise.

32 ♕d3

32 exf5 does not work because of 32...♕f4 33 ♕d1 ♖xe1+ 34 ♕xe1 d3, when the pawn penetrates too far.

32...fxe4 33 ♖xe4 ♖xe4 34 ♕xe4 c5 35 bxc5 ♕xc5 36 g3

36 ♕e1 does not save the pawn in view of 36...d3 37 ♖b2 ♕c2!. The pawn advance has thoroughly changed the situation. Black's material advantage and active pieces will prevail.

36...♕xa5 37 ♕d3 ♕e1+ 38 ♔g2 a5 39 ♕f3 ♕e6 40 ♖b5 ♗b4

40...d3 41 ♘d5 d2 42 ♖xa5 ♕e1 also wins. Pushing the passed pawn as far as possible is usually the best method, but the last few moves were played in time-pressure.

41 ♘d5 ♕d7 42 ♕d3 ♕c6 43 f3 ♗d2 44 ♘e7 ♕e8 45 ♘d5

45 ♘f5 ♗b4 46 ♘xd4 h6 will cost White the pinned knight.

45...a4 46 ♖c5 ♗e3 47 ♕f5 d3

A good defence against the threatened ♘f6.

48 Rc3 Bd4 49 Rxd3 We2+ 50 Kh3 g6 51 We4 Wxe4 52 fxe4 Bb2 53 Nb4 Rxd3 54 Nxd3 Kg7

In spite of Keres's tenacious resistance, Black prevails by fine play. Some little fine points are worth seeing in the minor-piece endgame, in which the black bishop is vastly superior, owing to the outside passed pawn.

55 Kg4 Kf6 56 Kf3 a3 57 Nb4 Ke5 58 Ke3 Bd4+ 59 Kd3 Bc5 60 Na2 Bg1 61 h3 h5 62 Nb4 Bc5 63 Na2 Bf2 64 g4 h4 65 Nb4 Bc5 66 Na2 g5 67 Nc3 Ba7 68 Na2 Kf4 69 Nc3 Bb8 70 Kc2 Be5 71 Nd5+ Kg3 72 Kb3 Kxh3 73 Ne3 Kg3 0-1

It is rare indeed for doubled pawns to yield a passed pawn, but we encounter active doubled pawns more often.

Spassky – Gligorić
Baden-Baden 1980
Vienna Game

1 e4 e5 2 Nc3 Nf6 3 g3 Bc5 4 Bg2 Nc6

At first glance it seems that Black can build a full pawn-centre by 4...c6, but after 5 Nge2 d5 6 exd5 cxd5 7 d4 exd4 8 Nxd4 Black is burdened with a shaky isolated pawn.

5 d3 d6?!

Black was off his guard. 5...a6 should come first in order to preserve the well-posted bishop.

6 Na4 Bg4

6...Bb4+ 7 c3 Ba5 8 b4 is also to White's advantage.

7 f3 Bxg1? (D)

A hasty decision. It was much better to retreat to e6 and allow doubled

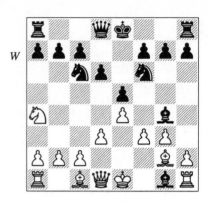

pawns on the c-file without doubling the white g-pawns. The reason will soon be apparent...

8 fxg4 Bc5 9 Nxc5 dxc5 10 g5

We have an instructive example of strong doubled pawns which can be used aggressively. Together with them goes the semi-open f-file and pressure along it. Black probably entered this passive position counting on the fact that the pawn-structure is closed to White's bishop-pair. That was also a wrong evaluation.

10...Nd7 11 Be3 We7 12 0-0 Nf8 13 h4

A natural advance before the bishop takes its place at h3.

13...Ne6 14 Bh3 0-0-0 15 Wh5 Rdf8 16 Rf2 Kb8 17 Raf1 Ncd8 18 Kh2 b6 19 a3! (D)

An excellent strategy: having pressed Black to the maximum, tying all his forces to defence, it is time to switch to the other wing and open the position.

19...a5 20 c3 Wd6 21 Wd1 Re8 22 b4 axb4 23 axb4 cxb4 24 cxb4 Nd4

24...Wxb4 fails to 25 Ra2 followed by 26 Wa1.

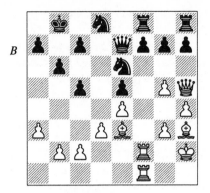

25 ♖a2 ♕c6 26 ♗xd4 exd4 27 ♕a1 ♖e7 28 ♖a7 ♕c2+ 29 ♔h1 ♕xd3 30 ♖c1 ♘c6 31 ♖a8+ ♔b7 32 ♖xh8 ♘b8 33 ♗c8# (1-0)

Do not fail to notice that all this was made possible by the exchange fxg4 and the advance g5. By enabling White to squeeze Black in defence of his major weakness at f7, it changed the situation completely. What followed was conditioned by the favourable pawn-structure dominated by the doubled pawn on g5. Its very existence directed the course of the struggle.

Janowski – Capablanca
New York 1916
Slav Defence

1 d4 d5 2 c4 c6 3 ♘f3 ♘f6 4 ♘c3 ♗f5?!

Today we know that the early development of the queen's bishop is not so good if the knight is already developed on c3. The reason lies in 5 cxd5 cxd5 (or 5...♘xd5 6 ♘d2) 6 ♕b3 winning a pawn or forcing the f5-bishop back to c8.

5 ♕b3?! ♕b6 6 ♕xb6?!

6 c5 is better.

6...axb6 7 cxd5 ♘xd5 8 ♘xd5 cxd5 9 e3 ♘c6 10 ♗d2 ♗d7!! (D)

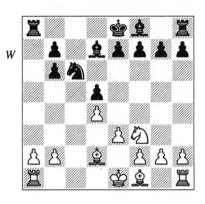

A deep, extraordinary idea. Black withdraws the well-placed bishop to an apparently passive position, but, as we shall see, he has in mind a brilliant strategic plan on the queenside.

11 ♗e2

If White understood what was in the making, he would have continued 11 ♗d3 or 11 ♗b5, followed later by ♔e2.

11...e6 12 0-0 ♗d6 13 ♖fc1 ♔e7 14 ♗c3 ♖hc8 15 a3

If it is not necessary, never move your pawns!

15...♘a5 16 ♘d2 f5

Before he carries out his idea, Black thwarts the possible e4, which would activate White.

17 g3 b5

The seemingly useless doubled pawns on the b-file take the roles of important actors on the queenside.

18 f3 ♘c4 19 ♗xc4

It is better to take with the knight. However, in any case the modest doubled pawn has played its part in bringing about a promising pawn-structure.

19...bxc4 20 e4 ♔f7 21 e5?

The e5-square should be preserved for the white knight by 21 exd5, followed by f4 and ♘f3-e5.

21...♗e7 22 f4 b5 23 ♔f2 ♖a4 24 ♔e3 ♖ca8 25 ♖ab1 h6

Black plays masterfully, engaging his forces on both wings.

26 ♘f3 g5 27 ♘e1 ♖g8 28 ♔f3 gxf4 29 gxf4 ♖aa8 30 ♘g2 ♖g4 31 ♖g1 ♖ag8 32 ♗e1 b4! *(D)*

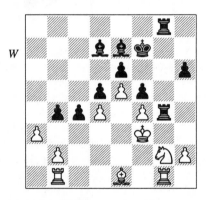

It has fallen upon two humble doubled pawns on the b-file to carry out one of the deepest strategic plans in the whole of chess literature. The first, by advancing to b5 and after the exchange on c4, created a very favourable pawn constellation. The second, by sacrificing itself, will open the way for Black's forces into White's camp.

33 axb4 ♗a4

That's it! The bishop penetrates the blocked stronghold via c2, and 34 ♖c1

cannot prevent it because of the devastating reply 34...♖xf4+.

34 ♖a1 ♗c2 35 ♗g3 ♗e4+ 36 ♔f2 h5 37 ♖a7 ♗xg2 38 ♖xg2 h4 39 ♗xh4 ♖xg2+ 40 ♔f3 ♖xh2 41 ♗xe7

If 41 ♖xe7+ ♔f8 42 ♗f6, then Black plays 42...♖gh8.

41...♖h3+ 42 ♔f2 ♖b3 43 ♗g5+ ♔g6 44 ♖e7 ♖xb2+ 45 ♔f3 ♖a8 46 ♖xe6+ ♔h7 0-1

The doubled pawns, from time to time, get their special opportunities, but on many occasions it takes a great player and an open mind to notice such possibilities. Even among the champions, most would pass by Capablanca's extraordinary idea.

Smyslov – Uhlmann
Mar del Plata 1966
French Defence

1 e4 e6 2 d4 d5 3 ♘c3 ♗b4 4 e5 ♘e7 5 a3 ♗xc3+ 6 bxc3 c5 7 ♘f3 ♗d7 8 a4

In three games of the 1977 candidates final Spassky played 8 dxc5 against Korchnoi. This made possible the manoeuvre ♖b1-b4-g4 with pressure on both wings. Those games again threw light on the importance of the move-order.

8...♕a5 9 ♕d2 ♘bc6 10 ♗e2

On 10 ♗d3 Black has the good reply 10...f6 11 0-0 (or 11 exf6 gxf6 12 dxc5 e5) 11...fxe5 12 ♘xe5 ♘xe5 13 dxe5 0-0.

10...♖c8 *(D)*

One of Uhlmann's innumerable novelties of those days. Black threatens 11...cxd4 12 cxd4 ♕xd2 13 ♗xd2 ♘f5 and since 14 ♗c3 is not available,

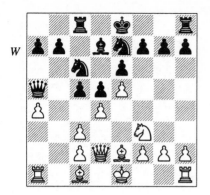

W

White must play 14 c3, allowing the reply 14...♘a5.

11 dxc5!?

White gives himself three isolated pawns on the c-file and leaves the e5-pawn seriously weakened! However, Smyslov will prove that the apparently shaky pawns on the c-file will have their role.

11...♘g6 12 0-0

If White plays 12 ♕e3, then Black continues 12...d4 with enough counterplay.

12...0-0?!

A couple of years later, the tireless champion of the French Defence, Wolfgang Uhlmann, improved on this by 12...♘gxe5.

13 ♕e3 ♕c7 14 ♘d4!

Smyslov shows a deep evaluation of the position: in spite of his seemingly compromised pawn-structure, White will have a better endgame. An extraordinary decision indeed!

14...♕xe5 15 ♘b5 ♕xe3 16 ♗xe3 a6 17 ♘d6 ♖c7 18 a5

Taking away an important square from the c6-knight.

18...e5 19 ♖fb1 ♘d8 20 ♖d1 ♗c6 21 ♗g4 ♘e6 22 ♖ab1 ♘e7 23 g3 f5 24 ♗h3 g6 25 f4 d4

Both 25...exf4 and 25...e4 leave Black in a passive position; his choice is certainly better.

26 cxd4 ♘d5 27 ♗f2 exd4

27...♘c3? loses to 28 fxe5.

28 ♗xd4 ♘xd4 29 ♖xd4 ♖e7 30 ♔f2 ♘c3?

Activating the other rook by means of 30...♖f6 was correct.

31 ♖e1 ♖xe1 32 ♔xe1 ♘e4 33 ♘xe4 ♗xe4 34 c3 ♖f6

It is important that 34...♖c8 and 34...♖f7 both fail to 35 ♖xe4. The apparently out-of-play h3-bishop has preserved unusual activity.

35 ♖d8+ ♔g7 36 ♖d7+ ♖f7?

The ensuing endgame unequivocally shows that the rooks should be kept on the board.

37 ♖xf7+ ♔xf7 38 ♔d2 ♔e6 39 c4 ♔d7 40 ♔e3 ♔c6 41 ♔d4 ♔d7 42 ♔e5 ♗f3

Otherwise 43 g4 decides.

43 ♔f6 ♔c6 44 ♔g7 ♔xc5 45 ♔xh7 ♗h5 46 ♗f1 ♔b4 47 ♗g2 ♔xa5

47...♔xc4 loses to 48 ♗xb7 ♔b5 49 ♔h6 ♔xa5 50 ♔g5 ♔b6 51 ♗xa6 ♔xa6 52 h3, etc.

48 ♗xb7 ♔b6 49 ♗c8 a5 50 ♗d7 ♔c5 51 h3 ♗f3 52 ♔xg6 ♗c6 53 ♗xf5 a4 54 ♗b1 a3 55 f5 ♗e4 56 ♗a2 ♗d3 57 h4 ♔d4 58 h5 ♔e5 59 g4 ♔f4 60 ♔g7 1-0

Even in endgames, doubled pawns are not as helpless as it is popularly believed. With harmonious minor-piece activity, and, of course, in the hands of a strong player, doubled pawns can fully participate in general strategy. In this game the c2- and c3-pawns covered important central squares, and the c5-pawn supported a knight invasion on d6, which thwarted any counterplay. Like Spassky's g5-pawn in his game versus Gligorić, Smyslov's oddly-arranged infantrymen dictated the course of the battle.

However, we have to be aware that such pawns are not so common in the endgame and that negative examples largely prevail; but we shall speak on the subject later in the text. Having analysed the doubled pawn in favourable circumstances, we shall pay now attention to its drawbacks.

Tarrasch – Rubinstein
Mährisch Ostrau 1923
Four Knights Game

1 e4 e5 2 ♘f3 ♘c6 3 ♘c3 ♘f6 4 ♗b5 ♗b4 5 0-0 0-0 6 d3 d6 7 ♗g5 ♗xc3 8 bxc3 ♕e7 9 ♖e1 ♘d8 10 d4 ♗g4

This is a well-known theoretical position, played and explored thoroughly in the first few decades of the 20th century. The recommended continuation is 10...♘e6 11 ♗c1 c5, confronting White in the centre and keeping the position closed and unfavourable to the white bishops. This response is possible because 12 dxe5 dxe5 13 ♘xe5 would lose to 13...♘c7.

11 h3 ♗h5 12 g4 ♗g6 13 d5 *(D)*
13...c6 14 ♗c4?

In conjunction with this move, the blockade by 13 d5 loses its sense. As a consequence the doubled pawns on the c-file remain isolated while the

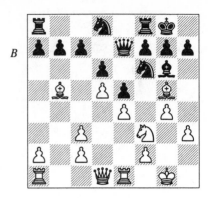

B

d8-knight is presented with the exit e6. White's play can be justified only if the knight is kept out of play, and 14 ♗d3 is correct. Spassky-Gligorić, Sarajevo 1986 continued 14...cxd5 15 exd5 e4 16 ♗xe4 (16 ♗f1 is inadequate in view of 16...♘e6) 16...♗xe4 17 ♕d4 ♘e6 18 ♕xe4 and Black was lost. Gligorić concluded that taking at d5 was dubious and that Black could safely keep the position closed; after 14...h6 15 ♗h4, he could play 15...♖c8 16 c4 ♖e8. It is even possible to exchange on d5 here: 15...cxd5 16 exd5 ♖c8 17 c4 e4 18 ♗xe4 ♗xe4 19 ♕d4 g5 (if 19...♖e8 then 20 ♘d2) 20 ♗g3 ♘e6 21 dxe6 ♗xf3 22 ♗xd6 ♖fd8 23 ♗xe7 ♖xd4 24 ♗xf6 ♖f4 25 e7 ♖e8, etc.

14...♖c8 15 dxc6 bxc6

There was no solution other than to exchange pawns on c6, but the present pawn-structure is worse for White than the previous one. The doubled isolated pawns are significantly weaker than the doubled pawns that constituted part of the central pawn-mass. At move 8, immediately after the exchange on c3, we had a compact pawn-mass, not so mobile, but firm. By playing 10 d4, White sought the initiative in the centre. His pawn-formation was not so solid any more, but the doubled pawns were still together and their clumsiness could not be exploited in any foreseeable way. At that moment they were still playing an active role, supporting the tension in the centre. After the exchange at c6 they have no role whatever, apart from the passive fight for existence.

16 ♗d3 ♘e6 17 ♗c1 ♘c5 18 ♘d2
18 ♗a3 fails to 18...♘cxe4 19 ♗xe4 ♘xe4 20 ♖xe4 ♗xe4 21 ♗xd6 ♕d8 22 ♗xf8 ♕xd1+ 23 ♖xd1 ♗xf3, etc.
18...h5
While White is engaged in passive defence of his pawns, Black strikes at the white king's weakened defences.
19 ♗a3 ♘e6 20 ♘c4 c5
White's bishops have no luck in their search for good diagonals: the pawn-structure continues to tell against them.
21 ♗c1 hxg4 22 hxg4 ♘h7 23 ♔g2 ♘hg5 24 f3 ♖cd8 25 ♘b2 d5! (D)

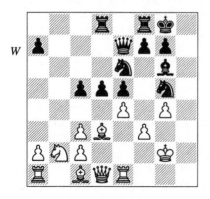

White is given no time to play the intended ♗c4. Black opens the game, which is in full harmony with the fact that his pieces are more active.
26 exd5 ♖xd5 27 c4 ♖d4 28 ♗e3
28 ♖xe5 does not work due to 28...♕f6 29 ♖e1 ♘f4+ 30 ♗xf4 ♖xf4, etc.
28...♖d6 29 ♕e2 e4
The breakthrough in the centre at move 25 yielded a pawn-majority on the kingside, which is now used to shatter the last protection of the white king.
30 fxe4 ♘xe4 31 ♕f3 ♘4g5 32 ♕g3 ♕b7+ 33 ♔f1 ♖b6 34 ♘a4 ♗xd3+ 35 cxd3 f5 36 ♗xg5 fxg4+ 37 ♔g1 ♘xg5 38 ♘xb6 ♘f3+ 39 ♔f2 ♘xe1+ 0-1
White's nightmare began with 14 ♗c4?.

Unless well prepared and in specific favourable circumstances, the advance of the doubled pawns is regularly accompanied by risks. As we could witness in the previous example, moving forward debilitates the squares around them, sometimes even the whole files. On the second and third rank such pawns are less exposed to pressure. A doubled pawn at c3 or f6, for instance, is more secure and stable than a doubled pawn on the fourth or fifth rank. The following games will give us a chance to compare.

Portisch – Fischer
Santa Monica 1966
Nimzo-Indian Defence

1 d4 ♘f6 2 c4 e6 3 ♘c3 ♗b4 4 e3 b6 5 ♘e2 ♗a6

Bronstein's move, or more precisely, the move David Bronstein liked and popularized.

6 ♘g3?!

This is inconsistent. After the natural move 6 a3, 6...♗xc3+ 7 ♘xc3 keeps White's pawn-structure healthy, while 6...♗e7 is met by 7 ♘f4 d5 8 cxd5 ♗xf1 9 ♔xf1 exd5 10 g4 seizing space and the initiative, as in the well-known game Botvinnik-Smyslov, World Ch match (game 2), Moscow 1954.

6...♗xc3+ 7 bxc3 d5 *(D)*

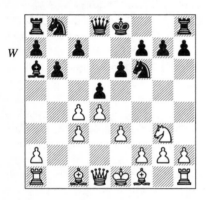

White's 6 ♘g3 has been countered correctly: having damaged White's pawn-formation, Black now provokes the c4-pawn into exchanging on d5, which should lead to a balanced position due to White's loss of castling rights. White, however, wants more.

8 ♕f3 0-0 9 e4

Portisch expects too much of this advance. That he is ready to sacrifice the c4-pawn is understandable, given the full pawn-centre and tactical threats he would get in return, but he underrates the line played in the game...

9...dxe4 10 ♘xe4 ♘xe4 11 ♕xe4 ♕d7!

A little, subtle point which probably escaped White's attention. By being ready to trade his rooks for the white queen, Black makes possible the active ...♘c6.

12 ♗a3 ♖e8 13 ♗d3 f5 14 ♕xa8 ♘c6 15 ♕xe8+ ♕xe8 16 0-0 ♘a5 *(D)*

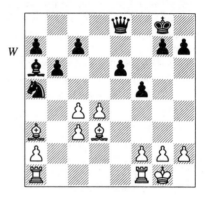

At the end of complications Black returns to the c4-pawn. The trouble with pawn weaknesses lies in the fact that they remain weak through all the vicissitudes of the game and in the end are doomed. Their weakness is lasting. White's pawn-structure was damaged on move 6 and after just ten more moves, when the complications have passed, the handicapped c4-pawn is about to fall.

17 ♖ae1 ♗xc4

17...♕a4 is even stronger. Then 18 ♗b4 ♗xc4 19 ♗xc4 ♘xc4 20 ♖xe6 a5 21 ♗e7 ♘d2 22 ♖fe1 ♘e4 is most unpleasant for White.

18 ♗xc4 ♘xc4 19 ♗c1 c5 20 dxc5 bxc5 21 ♗f4 h6

The decisive counter-action comes on the kingside.

22 ♖e2

White cannot thwart the pawn advance by 22 h4 due to 22...e5 23 ♗xe5 ♘xe5 24 f4 ♘f3+ 25 gxf3 ♕a4, etc.

22...g5 23 ♗e5 ♕d8 24 ♖fe1

In case of 24 f4 there is 24...♘d2 followed by 25...♘e4.

24...♔f7 25 h3 f4 26 ♔h2 a6 27 ♖e4 ♕d5 28 h4 ♘e3

The final solution.

29 ♖4xe3 fxe3 30 ♖xe3 ♕xa2 31 ♖f3+ ♔e8 32 ♗g7 ♕c4 33 hxg5 hxg5 34 ♖f8+ ♔d7 35 ♖a8 ♔c6 0-1

Nimzowitsch – H. Johner
Bern 1931
Nimzowitsch's Opening

1 ♘f3 ♘f6 2 b3 d5 3 ♗b2 c5 4 e3 ♘c6?! 5 ♗b5 ♗g4 6 ♗xc6+ bxc6 7 h3 ♗xf3 8 ♕xf3 ♕c7 9 d3 e6 10 ♘c3 *(D)*

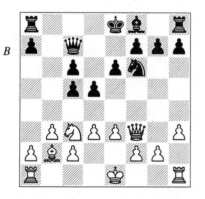

Black has played the opening phase superficially. By developing his queen's knight too early, he allowed the lasting weakness of doubled pawns on the c-file. His next decision was to offer a pawn sacrifice, which White rejected on principle. Having designated the c5-pawn as its future target, he manoeuvres his knight to a4 at once.

10...♗d6 11 ♘a4 ♗e5

Black believes that the reduction of material will ease his burden. As a matter of fact, his conception begun by 8...♕c7 is a result of some basic misunderstanding. In general, all pawn weaknesses, doubled pawns included, become more serious with the reduction of material.

12 ♗xe5 ♕xe5 13 0-0 ♘d7 14 ♕e2!

A subtle move. The idea is not to free the f2-pawn for action, but to move the queen to the other wing, increasing the pressure on the c5-pawn. Its final destination is a5.

14...0-0 15 ♕d2 f5

In view of White's threat, this move seems rather careless, but Johner believed he had a tactical solution in defence of the c5-pawn.

16 ♕a5 ♖fb8 *(D)*

This does not defend the pawn as Black hoped, but, it is true, 16...♕d6 also leaves Black in a passive, unsatisfactory position.

17 ♘xc5! ♖b5 18 ♘xd7 ♕xa1

This was meant as punishment, but Nimzowitsch had looked a little farther.

19 ♕c7 ♕c3 20 a4

A subtle, decisive point based on the loss of coordination of the black rooks.

20...♖b4

If 20...♖a5, then 21 ♕d6 ♖e8 22 ♘e5.

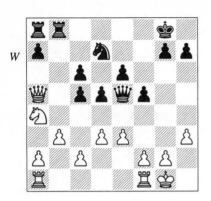

21 ♘e5 ♖f8?! 22 ♘xc6 ♔h8 23 ♕d6 1-0

A nice short game, based entirely on the weakness of the doubled pawns. A black doubled pawn on the fifth rank is quite an easy target and therefore vulnerable.

The fact that doubled pawns lose their natural strength when they advance tempts us to conclude that a good strategy against doubled pawns should be based on provoking their advance. And indeed, sometimes that strategy works well. However, it is not the only method that yields results against doubled pawns. Many a time we have to do just the opposite – to blockade the pawns, immobilize them and make use of their weakness later on when the circumstances allow it.

Staunton – Bristol Chess Club
Correspondence game 1844-5
Bird's Opening

**1 f4 d5 2 ♘f3 c5 3 e3 ♘c6 4 ♗b5 a6?
5 ♗xc6+ bxc6**

Black's pawn-structure has suffered early damage, without any compensating factors. The early development of the queen's knight cannot be recommended. Today, more conscious of opening nuances, every good player would prefer 2...♘f6 or 2...g6, avoiding the pin by ♗b5. Of course, 4...a6 is a serious error, losing time and inviting long-term problems with the pawn-formation.

6 0-0 e6 7 c4! (D)

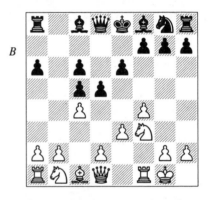

Some 80 years later Nimzowitsch was to recommend that one blockade doubled pawns before attacking them. It is to Staunton's credit that he understood the position fully and found this natural move.

7...♘h6

Expecting b3 and ♗b2, Black selects this extravagant move, planning a later ...f6. Natural was 7...♘f6 followed by ...♘d7.

8 ♕e2 ♗d6 9 ♘c3 ♕e7 10 b3

Introducing not only the fianchetto, but also the typical manoeuvre ♗a3 and ♘a4, if the opportunity presents itself.

10...f6 11 d3 0-0 12 e4 dxe4?

Annotating on this game in his book on Staunton, Raymond Keene was perfectly right: "A positional blunder which removes all the flexibility from Black's pawn-structure. Just as bad would have been 12...d4 13 ♘a4, eyeing the front c-pawn. The only playable move at this point is 12...♗b7!, holding firm in the centre, but such positional necessities were not generally understood until Nimzowitsch explained them in his books *My System* and *Chess Praxis*."

I could only warn of the well-known fact that the doubled pawns are much more vulnerable if they are cut off from the pawn-mass and isolated.

13 dxe4 e5 14 f5

Not only closing the way out to the light-squared bishop, but opening attacking prospects on the kingside.

14...♘f7 15 ♘h4

For the time being White leaves the doubled pawns in peace. He could increase the pressure on them by ♗e3, ♕f2 and ♘a4, but Black would move his knight to b7 and hold out. The prospects on the kingside are bright, while the c5-pawn cannot escape – simple, logical reasoning!

15...♗d7 16 ♖f3 ♖fd8 17 ♗e3 ♗e8 18 ♖af1 ♘g5 19 ♖g3 h6 20 ♕g4 ♖d7 21 ♘f3

White has finally found the key to Black's lock.

21...♔f8 22 ♘xg5 hxg5 23 h4 (D)

23...♗f7

This will lose without a fight. Analysing, I was attracted by the following variation: 23...gxh4 24 ♕xh4 ♔g8

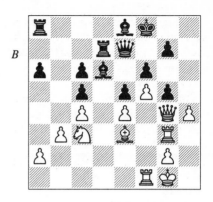

(or 24...♗f7 25 ♕h8+ ♔g8 26 ♗h6) 25 ♖h3 ♕f8 26 ♘a4 ♖ad8 27 ♕f2 and the c5-pawn falls. That such possibilities arise cannot be ascribed to chance. Certain types of weaknesses grow ripe in the course of the game and after some time you just have to pick them. It is typical of doubled pawns, too.

24 hxg5 ♔e8 25 g6 ♗g8 26 ♖h3 ♔d8 27 ♕e2 ♗c7 28 ♘a4 ♖dd8 29 ♕f2 ♔b7 30 g4 ♕c7 31 ♗xc5 ♗xc5 32 ♘xc5+ ♔c8 33 ♖d3 ♖xd3 34 ♘xd3 ♕d6 35 ♖d1 ♔c7 36 ♖d2 ♕d4 37 ♕xd4 exd4 38 ♔f2 ♖d8 39 ♔f3

After a couple more moves Black resigned. Stuck at c5, the pawn was eventually lost.

Geller – Smyslov
Candidates tournament,
Zurich/Neuhausen 1953
Nimzo-Indian Defence

1 d4 ♘f6 2 c4 e6 3 ♘c3 ♗b4 4 e3 c5 5 ♗d3 0-0 6 a3 ♗xc3+ 7 bxc3 ♘c6 8 ♘e2 b6 9 0-0 ♗a6

The Sämisch Variation of the Nimzo-Indian is characterized by the early exchange and doubled pawns on the c-file. As soon as they are blockaded, Black prepares to exert as much pressure on them as possible.

10 e4 ♘e8

Before proceeding with the conceived plan, Black must make sure he can thwart White's action on the kingside. Now 11 f4 would be met by 11...f5. However, it looks a more logical continuation than the one chosen by Geller.

11 ♕a4?! ♕c8!

A good defensive solution: 12 dxc5 would now be punished by 12...♘e5. At the same time the pressure exerted on c4 grows.

12 ♗e3 d6 13 ♖ad1 ♘a5 14 dxc5 dxc5 *(D)*

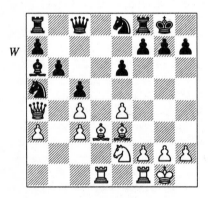

Confronted with a difficult choice, White has chosen to accept a pair of doubled isolated pawns, whose future is dubious. The lesson of our next game is that a blockaded position has other drawbacks for the player with the doubled pawns, but generally speaking it is a better option than allowing

the pawns to become isolated. For the time being White gets rid of the direct pressure on the c4-pawn, but it is a temporary solution, which will be called into question sooner or later.

15 e5 ♕c6 16 ♕c2 f5 17 ♕a2?

This is desperately passive. White should have sought his chances in the continuation 17 exf6 ♘xf6 18 ♗g5, although 18...♗xc4 19 ♗xf6 ♗xd3 20 ♖xd3 ♖xf6 21 ♖fd1 ♕e8 is in Black's favour.

17...♕a4 18 ♘f4 ♘c7 19 ♗c2 ♕e8

The unnecessary 19...♕xc4 would just complicate things. Black leaves the pawns in their predicament, preparing to open a new front on the kingside.

20 ♗b3 g5 21 ♘h3 h6 22 f3 ♕e7 23 ♘f2 ♖ad8 24 ♘d3 ♕g7 25 f4 ♖d7 26 ♘c1 ♖fd8 27 ♖xd7 ♖xd7 28 ♕e2 *(D)*

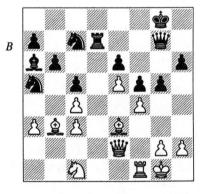

White has had to spend many tempi with his knight in order to free his queen, but in the struggle to maintain the material balance, he has hopelessly lost the coordination of his pieces. As if that were not enough, Black now uses the pin on the a6-f1 diagonal to bring his reserves onto the battlefield:

28...♘d5 29 ♗d2 ♘xf4 30 ♗xf4 gxf4 31 ♖xf4 ♕g5 32 g3 ♔h7 33 ♔f2 ♕d8 34 ♕h5 ♖g7 35 ♕e2 ♖d7 36 ♕h5 ♕g5 37 ♕e8 ♕e7 38 ♕xe7+ ♖xe7 39 ♗a2 ♖d7 40 ♔e2 ♗b7

The players were now out of time-trouble, during which White did not manage to improve his situation. Nothing can be done about the shattered pawn-formation and the sick pawn on c4.

41 ♗b1 ♔g8 42 g4 fxg4 43 ♖xg4+ ♖g7 44 ♖h4 ♖g1 45 ♔d2 ♔g7 46 ♗d3 ♗f3 47 ♖f4 ♗h5 48 ♘e2 ♖g2 49 ♔e3 ♖g5 50 h4 ♖xe5+ 51 ♔d2 ♘b3+ 52 ♔d1 ♖e3 53 ♔c2 e5 54 ♖f2 e4 0-1

It is curious that three years later, again in the Candidates tournament, the same players met and Geller had to endure the same hard lesson.

Geller – Smyslov
Candidates tournament,
Amsterdam 1956
Nimzo-Indian Defence

1 d4 ♘f6 2 c4 e6 3 ♘c3 ♗b4 4 a3 ♗xc3+ 5 bxc3 c5 6 e3 b6

A logical reaction: the potentially vulnerable c4-pawn is blocked, which will enable Black to exert some pressure on it later. At the same time, the light-squared bishop is developed naturally.

7 ♘e2

The great Candidates tournament of 1953 was not lucky for Geller's Sämisch Variation. As we have seen,

he lost without a fight against Smyslov, and also suffered a famous loss against Euwe, which continued 7 ♗d3 ♗b7 8 f3 ♘c6 9 ♘e2 0-0 10 0-0 ♘a5 11 e4 ♘e8 12 ♘g3 cxd4 13 cxd4 ♖c8 and White was facing material loss very early in the game (14 ♕a4 would be met by 14...♗a6), for which he did not quite achieve enough compensation.

7...♘c6 8 ♘g3 0-0

The manoeuvre ♘e2-g3 is not much of an improvement in comparison with the previous game. By castling immediately, Black is ready to meet the threat of e4 by ...♘e8 with a balanced position.

9 ♗d3 ♗a6 10 e4 ♘e8

Black could not grab the pawn to his advantage by 10...cxd4 11 cxd4 ♘xd4 because 12 ♗b2 yields a strong initiative.

11 ♗e3

Black evaluated correctly that after 11 d5 ♘a5 12 ♕e2 neither 12...♕h4 13 0-0 ♘d6 14 e5 ♘dxc4 15 ♘e4 nor 12...♘d6 13 e5 ♖e8 14 exd6 exd5 15 ♗e3 d4 16 ♕h5 would satisfy him; instead he planned to continue 12...f6, followed by 13...♘d6 with better play.

11...♘a5 12 ♕e2 ♖c8! *(D)*

A typical procedure: after the blockade comes the pressure. Note that after 12...♘d6 13 e5 ♘dxc4 14 ♕h5 g6 15 ♕h6 (with the devastating threat 16 ♘h5) 15...f5 16 ♗g5 White has a dangerous attack.

13 d5

The pressure Black is exerting forces White to parry the immediate threats by blocking the centre. At first,

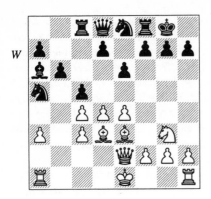

commentators believed that White should have kept tension by 13 罝c1, but Grandmaster Taimanov looked further and proposed 13...心d6 14 e5 cxd4 15 cxd4 (if 15 奧xd4 then 15...心f5) 15...心dxc4 16 豐h5 g6 17 豐h6 心xe3 18 心h5 罝xc1+ 19 曾d2 心f5 20 奧xf5 心b3+ 21 曾e3 罝c3+ 22 曾f4 豐h4+, winning. Geller's choice annuls the tension, but his central pawn-mass becomes less flexible and mobile.

13...豐h4 14 0-0 心d6 15 罝ad1 f5!

An instructive moment. Smyslov knows well that the immobile c4-pawn will remain as weak as it is now and he does not hurry to capture it. Before that Black finds it urgent to limit the activity of the bishop-pair and thwart any initiative on the kingside.

16 dxe6 dxe6 17 exf5 exf5 18 豐f3 奧b7 19 豐f4 豐f6 20 奧b1 心e4 21 罝d7

After 21 心xe4 fxe4 22 豐xf6 罝xf6 23 罝d7 罝f7 24 罝fd1 奧c6 the endgame remains characterized by the unhappy doubled pawns.

21...豐c6 22 罝xb7

Or 22 罝e7 心xc3, etc.

22...豐xb7 23 心xf5 罝ce8 24 豐g4 曾h8 25 心g3 心xg3 26 hxg3 豐f7 27 豐h4 h6 28 奧d3 豐f6 29 豐h5 罝d8 30 奧e2 豐f5 31 豐h4 豐f6 32 豐h5 心c6 33 g4 豐f7 34 豐h4 心e7 35 豐h3 心g6 36 豐h2

36 g5 would be met by 36...心f4, and 36 g3 by 36...曾g8.

36...心f4 37 奧f3 豐xc4

With the threats to his king removed, the time has come to capture the pawn. It took a lot of patience and practical wisdom to wait for this moment.

38 g5 罝d6 39 罝c1 罝g6 40 gxh6 罝xh6 41 豐g3 豐e4!! *(D)*

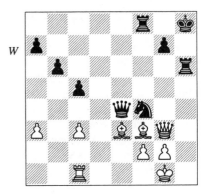

Simple, logical and beautiful! By threatening 42...豐h7, Black forces exchanges, and this simplifies his task.

42 奧xf4

After 42 豐g4 豐h7 43 g3 Black wins by 43...心e2+.

42...罝xf4 43 豐xf4 罝xf4 44 罝e1 罝a4 45 罝e8+ 曾h7 46 奧e4+ g6 47 g4 罝xa3 48 罝e6 罝xc3 49 曾g2 b5 50 f3 b4 51 g5 罝h4 52 奧xg6+ 曾g7 53 曾g3 罝d4 54 奧e8 b3 55 g6 罝d8 0-1

White overstepped the time-limit.

In spite of their positive values, doubled pawns are more often than not a liability. There is a type of doubled pawns which is a critical case of the species. I refer to doubled isolated pawns, such as those by which Geller's position was burdened. A couple of illustrative games will help the reader to see clearly the reasons behind their weakness in various circumstances.

Rukavina – Karpov
Interzonal tournament,
Leningrad 1973
English Opening

1 c4 ♘f6 2 ♘c3 e6 3 ♘f3 c5 4 d4 cxd4 5 ♘xd4 ♗b4 6 ♘c2 ♗xc3+ 7 bxc3 (D)

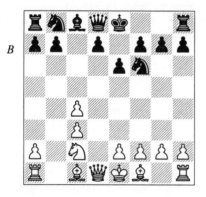

White has accepted doubled isolated pawns on the c-file, relying on the strength of his dark-squared bishop, which is ready to take its place on a3.

7...♕a5 8 ♘b4?

Inconsistent and unnatural. In the game Ivkov-Fischer, Vinkovci 1968,

White continued 8 ♕d3 ♘c6 9 ♗a3, sticking to his initial idea. After 9...b6 10 ♗d6 he even obtained an advantage, stifling realistic counterchances, but the correct 9...d5 10 e3 e5, with the idea of 11...♗e6, would have offered Black good play.

8...0-0 9 e3 b6 10 ♗e2 ♗b7 11 0-0 ♖c8

It is already obvious that White has no compensation for his weaknesses on the c-file.

12 f3 ♘c6 13 ♕b3 ♕e5 14 ♘xc6 ♖xc6 15 ♗d2

White is compelled to defend passively.

15...♕c7 16 ♕a4 a5 17 ♖fb1 ♗a6

We are hardly out of the opening and the doubled pawn is lost.

18 ♖b2 ♗xc4 19 ♗xc4 ♖xc4 20 ♕b5 ♖c6 21 e4 d6

Black finds the simplest and most convincing way to realize his material advantage. The f6-knight travels via d7 and e5 to c4, its unassailable stronghold, from where it controls all the important squares around.

22 ♕g5 ♘d7 23 ♕e7 ♘e5 24 ♕xc7 ♖xc7 25 ♖b5 ♘c4 26 ♗c1 ♖ac8 27 ♖ab1 ♖c5

We can now use the famous formula: further comment is not necessary.

28 ♔f1 ♔f8 29 ♔e2 ♔e7 30 ♖5b3 ♔d7 31 a4 ♔c7 32 ♗f4 ♔b7 33 ♗e3 ♖5c6 34 ♗d4 f6 35 ♖d1 ♖d8 36 f4 d5 37 ♗f2 ♖cd6 38 ♗c5 ♖c6 39 ♗f2 ♖dd6 40 exd5 ♖xd5 41 ♖xd5 exd5 42 ♖b5 ♖e6+ 43 ♔d3 ♔c6 44 g3 ♖e7 45 ♖b1 ♖b7 46 ♖b5 ♘d6 47 ♖b2 b5 48 axb5+ ♖xb5 0-1

It is true that this is one of the worst scenarios that can befall doubled isolated pawns, but it is a reality they are often forced to endure. The very fact that due to their immobility they are especially endangered in the endgame is a relevant fact about doubled pawns of which one should never lose sight. The following game is an impressive warning.

Boleslavsky – Smyslov
USSR Team Ch 1948
Ruy Lopez

1 e4 e5 2 ♘f3 ♘c6 3 ♗b5 a6 4 ♗a4 d6 5 c4 ♗g4 6 ♘c3 ♘f6 7 h3 ♗xf3 8 ♕xf3 ♗e7 9 ♘e2 0-0 10 ♗xc6 bxc6 11 d4 *(D)*

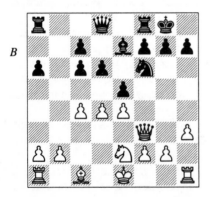

In the continuation characterized by 5 c4, which Duras popularized, White succeeds in carrying out d4, but at an unfortunate moment – when his king is still in the centre. Smyslov's reply will be energetic...

11...d5! 12 dxe5 ♗b4+ 13 ♘c3 ♘xe4 14 0-0 ♗xc3 15 bxc3 ♕e7 16

cxd5 cxd5 17 c4 ♕xe5 18 ♗f4 ♕c3 19 cxd5 ♕xf3 20 gxf3 ♘f6 21 ♗xc7 ♘xd5 22 ♗g3 ♖fc8 *(D)*

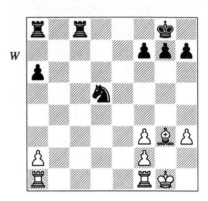

After a practically forced series of moves we enter this simple endgame. White's pawn-structure is lastingly damaged, but with reduced material it does not seem relevant. However, it is indeed relevant!

23 ♖fd1 ♖c5 24 ♖d2 h6

The most precise. 24...f6 opens the seventh rank, which is not wise when all the rooks are on the board. 24...g6 is even less recommendable in view of the existence of the dark-squared bishop.

25 ♖e1 ♖ac8 26 ♗d6?!

White underrates the potential danger. It is preferable to keep both rooks; Black's chances increase when one pair of rooks is exchanged. 26 ♔g2 was better.

26...♖c1 27 ♖xc1 ♖xc1+ 28 ♔g2 ♘b6 29 ♗g3 ♖c6 30 ♔f1?

While the exchange of one pair of rooks favoured Black, the exchange of all the rooks diminishes Black's active possibilities. In Smyslov's opinion, 30 ♖d6 was better.

30...f6 31 ♔e2 ♔f7 32 ♔d3 ♖c5

The rook moves to a5, where it stands actively in view of the backward a2-pawn and its free movement on the a-file.

33 ♖b2 ♘d7 34 ♔d4 ♖a5 35 ♖c2 ♔e6 36 ♖c6+ ♔f5 37 ♖c7 ♘e5 38 ♖c5

If 38 ♖xg7, then Black wins material by 38...♘xf3+ 39 ♔e3 ♖a3+ 40 ♔e2 ♘d4+, etc.

With the text-move, in expectation of 38...♖a4+, White has in mind 39 ♔c3 ♖a3+ 40 ♔b4 ♖xf3 41 a4 with chances on the queenside. However, Black has other ideas...

38...♖a3! *(D)*

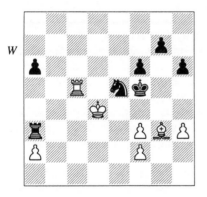

A cunning reply. By threatening mate, Black forces his opponent into a difficult rook ending.

39 ♗xe5 ♖a4+ 40 ♖c4

40 ♔e3 offers better resistance, although after 40...fxe5 41 ♖c2 ♖a3+ 42 ♔e2 a5 43 ♖d2 g6 44 ♖c2 h5 45 ♖b2 ♖c3, the threat ...♔f4 wins a pawn.

40...fxe5+ 41 ♔d3 ♖xa2 42 ♖g4 g5 0-1

In the end it is the immobile doubled isolated pawns which become the prey. Boleslavsky's loss is disheartening indeed!

The trouble with such a passive, isolated unit is connected with their inability to transform into more favourable pawn-formations. Even when that happens, it is an inferior endgame in the best of cases.

Spassky – Petrosian
World Ch match (game 23),
Moscow 1966
French Defence

1 e4 e6 2 d4 d5 3 ♘c3 ♘f6 4 ♗g5 dxe4 5 ♘xe4 ♗e7 6 ♗xf6 ♗xf6 7 ♘f3 ♗d7?!

Petrosian probably had in mind 8 ♗d3 ♗c6 9 c3 ♘d7 10 ♕e2 ♗e7 with satisfactory play. That, however, is not White's only option.

8 ♕d2 ♗c6 9 ♘xf6+ ♕xf6

9...gxf6 10 ♕f4 is also advantageous to White, but recapturing with the pawn would deny White the e5-square, which the white knight occupies at once.

10 ♘e5 0-0 11 0-0-0

Long castling keeps active options on the kingside.

11...♘d7

In case of 11...♖d8, with the idea of 12...♗e8 and ...♘c6, White reacts by 12 h4.

12 ♘xc6 bxc6

Black allowed the damage to his pawn-structure in view of White's inability to prevent ...c5, getting rid of the doubled c-pawn. He must have taken into consideration as well that the open b-file can be used for counter-pressure on the b2-pawn.

13 h4!

The quickest way to activate the king's rook. On the third rank it can be used against Black's pawn weaknesses.

13...Rab8 14 Rh3 c5

Saddled by the doubled pawn, one naturally tries to get rid of it. Unfortunately for Black, although the text-move seems to be a perfect way to do so, he will have to pay high price in the process.

15 Wg5! (D)

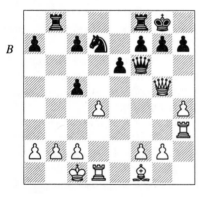

An extraordinary move.

15...cxd4

Since 15...Wxf2?? loses to 16 Rf3, Black must accept the exchange of queens and together with it a difficult endgame.

16 Wxf6 Nxf6 17 Rxd4

Doubled pawns are no longer a concern for Black, but the consequences remain in the form of two isolated

pawns. To make things worse, White's rooks are more active and his long-range bishop is superior to the black knight.

17...Rb7

Petrosian thought later that 17...c5 was more tenacious. It may be so, but it would not change the essential characteristics of the position.

18 Rb3

With his superior pawn-structure, it is useful for White to exchange a pair of rooks. Black would do best to reply 18...Rb6, avoiding it.

18...Rxb3 19 axb3 Ra8 20 Rc4 Ne8 21 Ra4

In view of the plan of 22 g3 and 23 Bg2, the a7-pawn cannot be defended.

21...Nd6 22 g3 Kf8 23 Bg2 Rc8 24 Rxa7 Ke7 25 Kd2 h6 26 c4 g5 27 hxg5 hxg5 28 Kc3 Kd7 29 b4 Rh8 30 b5 Rh2 31 Bc6+ Kd8 1-0

Not waiting for the obvious 32 c5.

The doubled pawns left behind a hopeless endgame. The trouble is that the doubled pawn is not the only weakness in the position. The pawns around them are debilitated at the same time and represent a lasting weakness.

Petrosian – W. Schmidt
Olympiad, Skopje 1972
English Opening

1 c4 Nf6 2 Nc3 d5 3 cxd5 Nxd5 4 g3 g6 5 Bg2 Nb6 6 d3 Bg7 7 Be3 Nc6?! (D)

As a witty grandmaster noted, mistakes are waiting in ambush to be committed and when playing chess we can commit them as early as this.

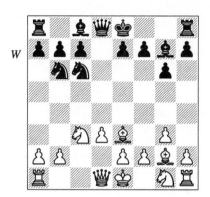

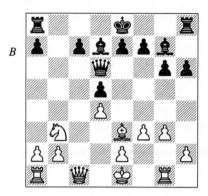

8 ♗xc6+!? bxc6 9 ♕c1

White's fianchettoed light-squared bishop is a strong piece on the important diagonal and many players would hesitate to exchange it for a piece of lesser importance. Petrosian, however, knows that bishops are strong among other reasons exactly because they can often be exchanged favourably. Having broken Black's pawn-structure, White prepares to meet 9...0-0 with 10 ♗h6, denying Black the bishop-pair.

9...h6

This move has been criticized. The h6-pawn is under attack, but on the other hand 9...h5 allows a later ♘g5, which does not suit Black, who is planning ...♗h3.

10 ♘f3 ♗h3 11 ♖g1 ♗g4

Chasing the knight to a better place.

12 ♘d2 ♘d5 13 ♘xd5 cxd5 14 ♘b3 ♕d6 15 f3 ♗d7 16 d4 *(D)*

Black has been successful in getting rid of the doubled c6-pawn through exchanges (just like Petrosian was against Spassky), but is soon obliged to enter an inferior endgame characterized by the backward c7-pawn and

general weakness on the c-file. Note also that the central pawn-formation favours knight plus bishop versus Black's two bishops.

16...♖b8?!

Commentators proposed as stronger 16...h5 17 ♔f2 e5. The text-move does little to generate compensation for the inferior pawn-structure and passive bishops.

17 ♔f2 h5 18 ♗f4 e5 19 dxe5 ♗xe5 20 ♕e3 f6 21 ♕xa7 *(D)*

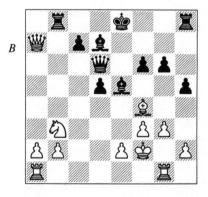

The typical process is at the end: the weakness of the doubled pawns has been transformed into a lastingly damaged queenside pawn-formation. Now White's positional advantage becomes a material advantage.

21...0-0 22 ♖ac1 ♖fe8 23 ♗xe5 ♕xe5 24 ♖ge1 ♖a8 25 ♕xc7 ♕e3+ 26 ♔g2 ♖a7 27 ♕d6 h4 28 gxh4 ♗e6 29 ♖c3 ♕h6 30 a3 ♖d7 31 ♕g3 d4 32 ♖d3 ♗xb3 33 ♖xb3 ♕d2 34 ♔f1 ♔h7 35 ♖b8 ♖e5 36 ♕g4 f5 37 ♕g5 ♖e3 38 ♕f6 1-0

What is fundamentally wrong, says an old Latin proverb, by passage of time cannot be rectified. When weak doubled pawns are transformed into some other formation, their weakness stays with it.

Some General Observations

As our survey demonstrates, doubled pawns are of two natures, sharing that intriguing, relative quality with other types of pawns we have studied. Depending on the circumstances, they are either useful stones on which the pawn rampart is built or, when irrevocably damaged, a sick part of its tissue.

As mentioned earlier, c3, c6, f3 and f6 are the most common places for the birth of doubled pawns for the obvious reason that in numerous opening variations bishops are exchanged for knights on these squares. Respecting the principle of recapturing towards the centre, on such occasions the b- and g-files are opened for counterplay, while the doubled pawns become part of the central pawn-mass, doing their duty in covering the all-important squares in the centre.

We have seen that in their initial position doubled pawns cannot in general be successfully attacked and that they fulfil their duties in cooperation with the other pawns to which they are attached. In certain situations, cautiously and after thorough preparation, they can even play an active part in the overall plans.

However, we have also learnt that when moving forward they weaken squares around them and themselves become more exposed to pressure. We have to keep in mind that only on rare occasions can doubled pawns be transformed into more positive formations and that it is even rarer for them to produce a passed pawn. Therefore, generally speaking, the further they advance, the more sensitive their situation gets. When a doubled pawn reaches its fourth rank, its destiny already becomes very uncertain, simply because the pawns are so easily attacked. On such occasions they tie other pieces to their defence, often leading to a general passivity and a lack of activity.

The most critical type of doubled pawns arises when the pair is isolated from other pawns, losing all flexibility and hope of improvement. Then they are weak indeed! As a rule, the possibilities of defence of doubled isolated pawns get reduced in parallel with the reduction of material on the board, often culminating in the simplest endgames.

The characteristics we have traced suggest how to deal with doubled pawns. Quite often good results are achieved by provoking their advance, which is in harmony with their dynamic weakness. In majority of cases, however, success is achieved by means of blockade. Sometimes it is a precondition for early middlegame pressure, but more often for a long-term, slow process of reducing the means of defence.

When possessing doubled pawns, unless we are talking of some unusual circumstances, one should stick to two golden rules:

a) Do not advance doubled pawns thoughtlessly, without a specific reason and a good plan;

b) Take care not to isolate doubled pawns from the pawn-mass. For their strength is of a static nature, coming to the fore in the compact pawn-structures of which they make part.

5 Backward Pawns

Backward pawns are either isolated pawns or the last pawns in a chain of pawns. We generally find them on their second rank or just a square forward on their third rank. It is their position on the board which tells against them and their very name implies a positional weakness.

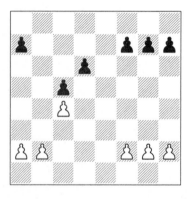

Our diagram represents a typical case of a backward pawn. Placed at d6, it is under pressure. It cannot advance and it cannot be sacrificed for some counterplay. Therefore it must be defended. The defence ties Black's forces in the passive effort to keep the material balance. An additional shortcoming is the weak d5-square, White's strong square, a regular occurrence with backward pawns. So all the black forces are tied in defence on a narrow part of the board, causing passivity and lack of counterplay. In general, that is the negative image of backward pawns we come across so often, but we shall learn that backward pawns in harmony with minor pieces can play a useful, positive role. It is our aim to see its face and the reverse. In order to understand and distinguish between their drawbacks and their qualities we shall consider examples from the rich master experience.

Karpov – Andersson
Madrid 1973
Bogo-Indian Defence

1 d4 ♞f6 2 c4 e6 3 ♞f3 b6 4 g3 ♝b4+ 5 ♞bd2 ♝b7 6 ♝g2 0-0 7 0-0 c5?! 8 a3 ♝xd2 9 ♝xd2 cxd4 10 ♝b4 ♜e8 11 ♝d6 (D)

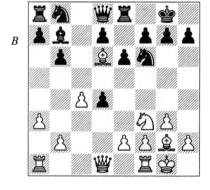

Black's opening is not an example of good play. By ceding the bishop-pair and capturing on d4 he made possible the manoeuvre ♗b4-d6. The dark-squared bishop blocks the d7-pawn in its initial position, preventing Black from freeing his game. The d7-pawn will remain backward as long as the blockade on d6 exists.

11...♘e4?! 12 ♕xd4 ♘a6 13 b4 ♖c8 14 ♖ac1 ♘xd6 15 ♕xd6

In entering this continuation, Black probably relied on the possibility of removing the bishop from d6, but a new blockader has taken the bishop's place at d6. It is true that the queen in most cases is too valuable to be used as a blockader, but combined with the subsequent ♖fd1 its role on the d-file is natural.

15...♘c7

Black could continue 15...♕c7, but then his knight would remain out of play. The d7-pawn is threatened and Andersson, an excellent master of defence, conjures up a hidden defence: the knight moves to e8 in order to chase the queen and get some breathing space. The trouble with backward pawns is often not just their own weakness, but the lack of room to manoeuvre that is a consequence of their position on the board.

16 ♖fd1 ♖e7 17 ♕d3 ♗xf3

17...d5 does not work because of 18 e4, while 18 ♘g5 hangs in the air. Black is forced to enter an endgame in which White's bishop will be superior to Black's passive knight.

18 ♗xf3 ♘e8 19 ♗b7 ♖c7 20 ♗a6! (D)

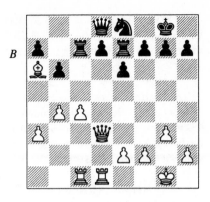

Not many players would find this deep manoeuvre. If Black had been counting on playing ...d6, then he now had to think again, as ♗b5 would win the backward pawn. He will be forced to live in a very restricted space.

20...♖c6 21 ♕b3 ♕b8 22 ♕a4 ♖c7

The threat was 23 ♗xd7.

23 ♕b5 ♘f6 24 f3 d5

Black finally manages to advance his backward pawn, but only to face other serious problems. The manoeuvre ♗b7-a6, coupled with a deep strategic decision to transfer the queen to b5, will produce a pawn-majority on the queenside...

25 c5 h5 26 a4 ♖e8 27 cxb6 axb6 28 a5

The queenside pawn-majority is now transformed into a passed pawn, which proves to be White's decisive weapon.

28...♖xc1 29 ♖xc1 ♕e5

Since 29...bxa5 30 ♕xb8 ♖xb8 31 bxa5 ♖a8 32 ♖c8+ and other types of endgame are lost as well, Black tries to improvise counterplay on the king-side, which is futile and soon fails...

30 ♕xb6 d4 31 ♔h1 ♕e3 32 ♖f1
e5 33 ♗d3 h4 34 gxh4 ♕f4 35 ♖g1
♕xh4 36 a6 g6 37 a7 ♔g7 38 ♗xg6
1-0

38...fxg6 39 a8♕ leaves no hope.

The entire course of the game was
influenced by the backward pawn at
d7, and its blockade. The consequences
for Black were a lack of manoeuvring
space and general passivity.

Karpov – Svidler
Dos Hermanas 1999
Grünfeld Defence

1 d4 ♘f6 2 c4 g6 3 ♘c3 d5 4 ♘f3
♗g7 5 ♕b3 dxc4 6 ♕xc4 0-0 7 e4 a6
8 e5 b5 9 ♕b3 ♘fd7 10 e6 fxe6 11
♗e3!

White has damaged his opponent's
pawn-structure, but with no intention
of trying to make use of it at once by
11 ♕xe6+ or 11 ♘g5, continuations
which had failed in earlier games to
produce positive results in the face of
Black's strong counterplay.

11...♘f6

Earlier, in Wijk aan Zee 1999, Svidler defended this same position against
Kasparov and continued 11...♘b6,
when 12 h4 ♘c6 13 h5 led to an attack
for White.

12 a4 bxa4 13 ♖xa4 (D)
13...♘c6

Svidler has accepted the pawn sacrifice, but at the cost of a lastingly damaged pawn-formation: broken pawn-
islands containing several backward
pawns. In order to compensate for the
weaknesses, he hopes to use the b-file
and to generate counter-pressure on it.

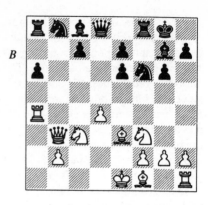

The alternative was 13...♘d5, intending to meet 14 ♗c4 by 14...c6, pinning
his hopes to his firm albeit passive position. However, that move does little
to develop the queenside and also exposes Black's kingside to attack by
h4-h5.

**14 ♗c4 ♖b8 15 ♗xe6+ ♔h8 16
♕c4 ♗xe6 17 ♕xe6 ♕d6**

This is how Black hoped to settle
the issue: after 18 ♕xd6 the weak a6-
pawn would be balanced by the weak
b2-pawn.

18 ♘g5 ♖xb2 19 0-0

Black was not afraid of 19 ♘f7+,
when he had a strong reply in 19...♖xf7
20 ♕xf7 e5. With the text-move, White
finishes his development and renews
the threat ♖xa6, which forces further
events.

19...♘d8 20 ♕h3 ♕d7

Threatened by 21 ♘ce4, Black enters an endgame in which material balance is maintained, but Black remains
burdened by two backward pawns on
c7 and e7.

**21 ♕xd7 ♘xd7 22 ♖xa6 ♘b6 23
h4 ♖c2**

On 23...♘c4 there is 24 ♘d5.
24 ♘ce4 h6 25 ♘f3 ♘c6 26 ♖aa1!
(D)

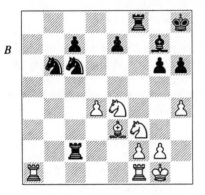

Simple and strong. White plans to exchange a pair of rooks, when he will be able to press more strongly against the backward c7-pawn, the more exposed of the two passive black pawns.

26...♘b4 27 ♖fc1 ♖xc1+ 28 ♖xc1 ♘4d5 29 ♘c5 ♖f6

The difficulties Black has been experiencing in the game are the consequence of two backward pawns 'adorning' his pawn-structure. The c7-pawn and the e7-pawn are in need of constant defence. Besides, do not fail to notice that the squares in front of them, c6 and e6, are weak and can be exploited by white pieces, which is quite a common case with backward pawns.

30 ♗d2

The pressure on d4 is feeble and does not require the bishop to remain on e3. White will now be able to increase the pressure on the e-file by ♖e1 at any moment.

30...♖d6 31 ♘b7 ♖f6

31...♖d7 obviously loses to 32 ♘e5, and 31...♖e6 32 ♘d8 ♖e4 33 ♖c6 ♔h7 34 ♘e6 is hopeless.

32 ♘e5 ♔h7 33 g3 ♖f8 34 ♘c5 ♖a8 35 ♖c2

White is in no hurry, as the pawn weaknesses are lasting; Black cannot get rid of them. So White can afford a tempo to cover his second rank against the intended 35...♖a2.

35...♖d8 36 ♔g2 ♗xe5

When a player resorts to such exchanges, then his position must be desperate indeed. Of course, the question is what else there is to do.

37 dxe5 ♘d7 38 ♘xd7 ♖xd7 39 ♖c6 ♘b6 40 ♗c1 ♖d5 41 ♖e6 ♘c8

Or 41...♖d7 42 h5.

42 h5 gxh5 43 ♖xh6+ ♔g7 44 ♖xh5 c5 45 ♔f3 c4 46 ♗e3 e6 47 ♖h4 ♘e7 48 ♖xc4 ♘g6 49 ♗d4 1-0

The backward pawns on the seventh rank proved very sensitive, especially when exposed to the perfect technique of a great positional player like Karpov. The lack of space made an organized defence difficult.

Euwe – Capablanca
Amsterdam AVRO 1938
Queen's Indian Defence

1 d4 ♘f6 2 c4 e6 3 ♘f3 b6 4 g3 ♗b7 5 ♗g2 ♗e7 6 0-0 0-0 7 ♘c3 d5 8 ♘e5 ♘e4?!

On 8...♘bd7 the c6-square remains weakened after 9 cxd5 exd5 10 ♕a4, which causes unpleasant difficulties to Black. 8...c6 9 e4 is rather passive and since the text-move also fails, it seems that the patient 8...♕c8 was the best choice.

9 cxd5 exd5 10 ♘xe4 dxe4 11 ♕c2! *(D)*

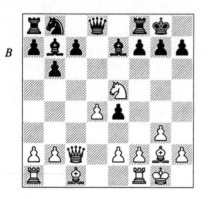

An excellent continuation. Excluding 11...f6 by 12 ♗xe4 and 11...♕xd4 by 12 ♕xc7, the queen makes it difficult for Black to develop his queenside in a normal manner, while targeting the backward c7-pawn.

11...f5 12 ♗e3 ♘a6

In view of the pressure on the c-file, Black's development has become questionable, and he must resort to unnatural solutions. On a6, the knight defends the c7-pawn, but the c6-square is now available to White's knight.

13 ♖ac1 ♕d5 14 ♘c6

By provoking exchanges, White accentuates the weakness of the backward pawn and the c6-square in front of it; this is a typical phenomenon for pawn weaknesses in general.

14...♗xc6 15 ♕xc6 ♕xc6 16 ♖xc6 ♖f6 17 ♖fc1 ♖xc6 18 ♖xc6 ♗d6 19 a3

By placing the b4-square under control, White keeps the a6-knight out

of play. In defence of backward pawns, pieces are often forced into unnatural positions, when coordination between them is disrupted.

19...♖e8 20 ♗f4

The exchange of the dark-squared bishops will remove the key defender of the c7-pawn. At first glance it seems questionable because the bishop is shut in on g2, but it is easy to foresee its liberation.

20...♗xf4?!

On 20...♖d8 White intended 21 e3 followed by 22 f3. Stronger resistance was offered by 20...♘b8 21 ♖c3 ♗xf4 22 gxf4 c6 although again 23 e3 and 24 f3 keeps an advantage.

21 gxf4 ♔f7 22 e3 ♖e6 23 ♖c4

The trouble with backward pawns lies in their immobility. Now 23...c5 would lose to 24 ♖a4 b5 25 ♖a5 cxd4 26 exd4, when the threat 27 ♗f1 is fatal. So, threatened by 24 ♖a4, Black must weaken his pawn-formation further...

23...b5 24 ♖c3 c6 25 f3 g6

25...exf3 26 ♗xf3 ♘b8 loses to 27 d5.

26 fxe4 fxe4 27 a4!

This is lethal.

27...bxa4

27...b4 28 ♖b3 opens the way for 29 ♗f1, while 27...♘c7 28 axb5 ♘xb5 29 ♖c5 threatens 30 ♗h3, whereupon Black's position, with several pawn-islands and weak pawns, cannot be held.

28 ♖c4 ♔f6 29 ♖xa4 c5 30 ♗f1

The move has been hanging in the air for some time. The advantage accumulated by the constant, concentrated pressure on the backward pawn has been transformed into a superior endgame of bishop versus knight, which soon yields a material advantage and victory.

30...cxd4 31 ♖xa6 dxe3 32 ♖xe6+ ♔xe6 33 ♗h3+ ♔d5 34 ♔f1 ♔c4 35 ♔e2 ♔b3 36 ♗e6+ ♔xb2 37 ♗g8 a5 38 ♗xh7 a4 39 ♗xg6 1-0

Analysing this game we find it was shaped by the same positional characteristics which we saw in the two victories by Karpov: a backward pawn on its second rank, a weak square in front of it, lasting pressure on the file, and an inferior endgame as the result. We could feel that pawns on their second rank are in an exceptionally difficult situation because no coordinated defensive effort is possible due to the shortage of space. A pair of backward pawns, on their second and third ranks, is susceptible to the same worries.

Tal – Kupreichik
Sochi 1970
Sicilian Defence

1 e4 c5 2 ♘f3 g6 3 d4 cxd4 4 ♘xd4 ♗g7 5 c4 ♘c6 6 ♗e3 ♘h6?! 7 ♗e2 d6 8 ♘c3 0-0 9 0-0 f5?!

The Maroczy Bind is characterized by White's powerful centre. Since his superiority in that sector thwarts any serious counterplay, Black prepares and carries out side-blows.

10 exf5 ♘xd4 11 ♗xd4 ♗xd4 12 ♕xd4 ♘xf5 13 ♕d2 *(D)*

Black has succeeded in simplifying the position through a series of exchanges but White has kept his spatial

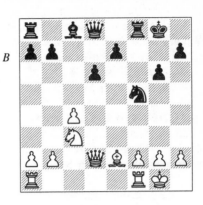

advantage. The d5-square is an important square which can be used by minor pieces, while the central files will be used to exert powerful pressure on the pair of pawns on d6 and e7. The pair is linked in its passive inability to advance. If the e7-pawn advances, then the d6-pawn becomes backward. Besides, there are the usual weak squares in front of them – d5 and e6. These factors all aggravate Black's defence.

13...♗d7 14 ♗f3 ♗c6 15 ♗d5+!

The strong squares are there to be used at will.

15...♔g7

After 15...♗xd5 16 cxd5, Black's poor e7-pawn remains tragically debilitated.

16 ♖fe1 e5

The d6-pawn is now potentially weak, argues Black, but a subsequent ...♘d4 will cover it sufficiently. However, with such shaky pawns one should always consider tactical blows.

17 c5! dxc5 18 ♖xe5 ♖e8 19 ♖ae1 ♕d6 20 ♖e6 ♖xe6 21 ♖xe6 ♕d7 22 ♕f4

It is as simple as that, in spite of White's weak back rank. The unprotected black king makes it possible.

22...♗xd5 23 ♕e5+ ♔f7

If 23...♔h6 then 24 ♘xd5 ♖d8 25 ♘e3.

24 ♖f6+ ♔g8 25 ♘xd5 ♕a4

25...♖d8 and 25...♖e8 both lose to 26 ♖xg6+! hxg6 27 ♘f6+, etc.

26 h3 ♖d8? 27 ♖xf5 1-0

Szabo – Larsen
Vinkovci 1970
Sicilian Defence

1 ♘f3 c5 2 c4 ♘c6 3 d4 cxd4 4 ♘xd4 g6 5 e4 ♗g7 6 ♗e3 d6 7 ♘c3 ♘h6?!

Black intends ...f5. He can try this idea in various different sequences, but it has regularly failed to provide Black with satisfactory results. Either the temporary tactical complications pass, leaving behind a prospectless pawn-structure, or the pawn-formation proves vulnerable to tactics. One idea is for Black to play, on his previous move, 6...♘h6 7 ♘c3 0-0 8 ♗e2 f5 9 exf5, and then to continue 9...♗xd4 10 ♗xh6 ♖xf5 11 0-0 ♕b6, but this neglects his development. After 12 ♘d5 ♗xf2+ 13 ♔h1 ♕d4 it looks as if Black might get away with it, but 14 ♗g4 ♕xd1 15 ♖axd1 ♖f7 16 ♘xe7+ ♘xe7 17 ♗e6 turns out to be a clean refutation.

8 ♗e2 0-0 9 0-0 f5?! 10 exf5 gxf5

10...♘xf5 11 ♘xf5 ♗xf5 12 c5 dxc5 13 ♗xc5 b6 14 ♕b3+ ♔h8 15 ♖ad1 ♕c8 16 ♗e3 e5 17 ♕a4, as in Kovačević-Barcza, Zagreb 1972, again proves that White has various tactical devices

to seize the initiative. Here White is threatening 18 ♗f3 and the intended 17...♘d4 would fail to 18 ♗xd4 exd4 19 ♖xd4.

11 f4 ♗d7

11...♕b6 had also been tried, but then 12 ♘xf5 ♕xb2 13 ♘xh6+ ♗xh6 14 ♘d5 is advantageous to White. Larsen, therefore, decides to avoid exchanges.

12 ♕d2 ♘g4 (D)

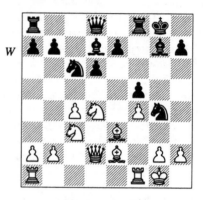

Black's problem in all similar positions stems from Black's vitally weakened central pawn-formation, which cannot be improved whatever he tries. Using the semi-open central files, the strong d5-square and his active bishops, White will stifle his opponent unless some counterplay can help Black. Larsen understands this perfectly.

13 ♗xg4 fxg4 14 ♘d5

The best squares belong to White's centralized pieces, leaving Black but a narrow choice: either respond by 14...e6, which permanently weakens the d6-pawn, or wait, which proves an equally suspect policy...

14...♖f7 15 f5! ♔h8

This move is bad, but the position offers only bad moves. For example: 15...♘xd4 16 ♗xd4 ♗xf5 17 ♗xg7 ♔xg7 18 ♕g5+ ♗g6 19 ♖xf7+ ♔xf7 20 ♖f1+ ♔g7 21 ♕xg4.

16 ♘e6 ♕g8 17 ♘xg7 ♕xg7 (D)

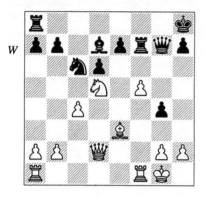

18 ♘xe7

It is not by chance that such sacrifices work. Strong centralized pieces set against passive pawn-formations often produce tactical solutions.

18...♘xe7 19 f6 ♕g6 20 fxe7 ♖xe7 21 ♗d4+ ♔g8 22 ♖f6 ♕h5 23 ♖af1 g3 24 hxg3 ♗e6 25 ♕f4 ♖f7 26 g4 1-0

Réti – Colle
Hastings 1926
Queen's Indian Defence

1 ♘f3 ♘f6 2 c4 e6 3 g3 b6 4 ♗g2 ♗b7 5 0-0 ♗e7 6 d3 0-0 7 ♘c3 c5 8 e4 ♘c6 9 d4 ♘xd4 10 ♘xd4 cxd4 11 ♕xd4 ♗c5?!

Black plays optimistically. The text-move and the subsequent knight manoeuvre are asking for trouble.

12 ♕d3 ♘g4 13 h3 ♘e5 14 ♕e2 ♖c8 15 b3 f5

This move is more than the position can stand.

16 exf5 ♗xg2 17 ♔xg2 ♗d4 18 ♗b2 ♖xf5 19 f4 ♘c6

Black's central pawn-structure is by now quite familiar to us.

20 ♖ad1 ♕e7 21 ♘b5 ♗xb2 (D)

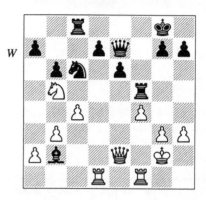

22 ♘d6!

This brilliant tactical stroke decides the game at once. As I stressed earlier, an irreparably passive pawn-structure often invites a tactical solution.

22...♗a3 23 ♘xc8 ♕f8 24 ♖xd7 ♖f6 25 ♘xa7 1-0

Be they isolated backward pawns or pairs of backward pawns (one on its second rank and the other on its third rank), they remain symbols of inactivity. Quite often they are dealt with in the manner Réti demonstrated masterfully in this short game.

Backward pawns, however, arise more often on their third rank. Sometimes they arise by mistake and rarely survive, but sometimes they form part of the general strategic plan; indeed this is a feature of many modern opening variations. Being a rank further forward, they are generally better supported, and the pieces behind them command more space, which makes possible better coordination. We shall devote attention to both situations in turn.

Tarrasch – Lasker
World Ch match (game 10),
Munich 1908
Ruy Lopez

1 e4 e5 2 ♘f3 ♘c6 3 ♗b5 ♘f6 4 0-0 ♘xe4 5 d4 ♗e7 6 ♕e2

White has been successful with 6 dxe5 as well as with 6 ♖e1, but the move applied by Tarrasch became the most popular choice. It pushes Black into a resilient but rather passive position, burdened early on with doubled pawns.

6...♘d6 7 ♗xc6 bxc6 8 dxe5 ♘b7

The b7-knight is temporarily out of play, but it will return via c5. Tarrasch-Taubenhaus, Monte Carlo 1903 continued instead 8...♘f5, but after 9 ♕e4 g6 10 ♘d4 ♘xd4 11 ♕xd4 0-0 12 ♗h6 ♖e8 13 ♘c3 Black had the worse of it. When he continued 13...♗g5?, he was punished by the decisive 14 ♗xg5 ♕xg5 15 ♘e4 ♕xe5 16 ♘f6+, etc.

9 ♘c3 0-0 10 ♖e1 ♘c5 11 ♘d4 ♘e6 12 ♗e3 ♘xd4

Perhaps 12...♖b8 is more appropriate. When you try to break out from a passive position, it is in general the

more active side that gains the advantage.

13 ♗xd4 c5 14 ♗e3 d5 15 exd6 ♗xd6 16 ♘e4!

In the eighth game of the same match, 16 ♕h5 was met by 16...♗b7, the c5-pawn being indirectly defended by 17...g6. The text-move, however, is much stronger. It is available due to the fact that 16...♗xh2+ 17 ♔xh2 ♕h4+ 18 ♔g1 ♕xe4 19 ♗xc5 ♕xe2 20 ♖xe2 gives Black an inferior endgame.

16...♗b7 17 ♘xd6 cxd6 18 ♖ad1 *(D)*

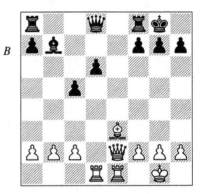

Black has got rid of his doubled pawn, but there remains a backward pawn at d6, and it is exposed to pressure from White's major pieces on the d-file and from the dark-squared bishop. The subsequent battle will revolve around it.

18...♕f6 19 c4

The classical treatment of pawn weaknesses starts with fixing them. In later decades the alternative 19 f3 ♖ae8 20 ♕d2 ♖e6 21 ♗f2 was discovered.

19...♖fe8 20 ♕g4

Since the b2-pawn is taboo, White takes the opportunity to activate his queen, threatening 21 ♕d7.

20...♗c6?!

Black could instead prevent White's threat by 20...♖e6, as suggested by Paul Keres.

21 ♖e2

White's 20th move eliminated potential threats to g2, and at the same time vacated e2 for the rook manoeuvre, doubling rooks and increasing pressure on the d6-pawn. It is crucial that 21...♖e4 22 ♕g3 ♖xc4 23 ♖xd6 ♖d8 24 ♖xd8+ ♕xd8 25 h3 would now leave Black in still deeper trouble. It is not surprising that Lasker spent a whole hour looking for a reply.

21...♖e4 22 ♕g3 ♕e6 23 h3

23 ♕xd6 would be answered by 23...♖g4. With the text-move, White takes the opportunity to give his king a flight-square.

23...♖d8

23...♕xc4 24 ♗h6 g6 25 ♖xe4 ♕xe4 26 ♖xd6 offers White better chances in view of his better-protected king.

24 ♖ed2 ♖e5 25 ♗h6! *(D)*

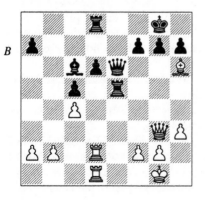

An instructive moment! As 25...g6 weakens the black kingside for good and 25...♕xh6 loses to 26 ♕xe5, the d6-pawn is finally doomed. When pieces are tied to the defence of weak points, tactical solutions are a common and logical consequence.

25...♕g6 26 ♗f4 ♖e6 27 ♗xd6 ♕h5 28 ♕g4 ♕xg4 29 hxg4 ♖e4 30 ♗xc5 ♖xd2 31 ♖xd2 h5 32 ♖d6 1-0

A good lesson: backward pawns require defence and that in turn leads into passivity, which has further consequences.

Fischer – Trifunović
Bled 1961
Ruy Lopez

1 e4 e5 2 ♘f3 ♘c6 3 ♗b5 a6 4 ♗a4 ♘f6 5 0-0 ♘xe4 6 d4 b5 7 ♗b3 exd4

We know today that 7...d5 is indispensable, but Trifunović, the king of draws, was relying on some old analysis of his.

8 ♖e1 d5 9 ♘c3 ♗e6

After 9...dxc3 10 ♗xd5 ♗b7 11 ♗xe4 ♗e7 12 ♕e2 Black cannot castle.

10 ♘xe4 dxe4 11 ♖xe4 ♗e7 12 ♗xe6 fxe6 13 ♘xd4! *(D)*

This was a novelty at the time. In old times they used to continue 13 ♖xe6, when 13...♕d5 or 13...♕d7 followed by ...0-0-0 enables Black to escape.

Fischer correctly prefers to take on d4 and deal with the e6-pawn later, rather than taking on e6 and having to live with a pawn on d4.

13...0-0

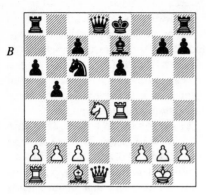

Now 13...♕d5 would be met by 14 ♕g4.

14 ♕g4 ♘xd4 15 ♖xd4 ♕c8 16 ♖e4

Having given Black a backward pawn on the e-file, White starts to increase the pressure on e6.

16...♖f6 17 ♗e3

After the game Fischer pointed out a hidden trap: 17 ♗g5? ♖g6 18 h4 h6 19 ♕h5 ♕e8 and White loses.

17...♕d7 18 ♖d1 ♕c6 19 ♗d4 ♖g6 20 ♕e2 ♖d8 21 g3 ♕d5 22 ♖e1

Like Tarrasch in the previous game, Fischer follows the simplest method: increasing the pressure on the backward pawn to the maximum. This causes a loss of coordination in Black's pieces, which are tied to the defence of the e6-pawn.

22...c5

22...♕xa2 would fail to 23 b3, as the queen has strayed out of play. This idea is relevant in the following moves as well.

23 ♗c3 ♖d6 24 ♗e5 ♖d8 25 ♗f4 c4

Black could defend his weakness by 25...♔f7, but then after 26 b3 he could only wait and despair. When defending backward pawns you often reach the point of decision: either stubborn defence, which leads to total passivity with normally a fatal outcome sooner or later, or a material sacrifice that gives some compensation and hope. Trifunović decides upon the latter course of action.

26 ♖xe6 ♖xe6 27 ♕xe6+ ♕xe6 28 ♖xe6 ♗f6 29 ♖xa6 ♖d1+ 30 ♔g2 *(D)*

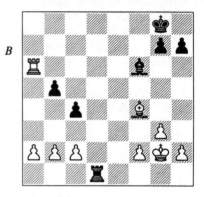

30...♗xb2

30...♖b1 is interesting, but 31 a4 ♖xb2 (if 31...b4 then 32 ♖c6) 32 axb5 ♖xb5 33 ♖c6 c3 34 ♖e6 ♔f7 35 ♖e2 offers White a simple plan: to move the king to the queenside, and after the exchange of the bishops the c3-pawn will fall.

31 ♖b6 ♖a1 32 ♖xb5 ♖xa2 33 ♖c5 ♖a4

After 33...c3 Black would be vulnerable at g7.

34 ♗e5 ♗xe5 35 ♖xe5 ♖a2 36 ♖e2

Black must face the grim reality: his king is cut off and his c4-pawn shaky – quite enough to lose the game.

36...♔f7 37 ♔f3 ♔f6 38 ♔e4 g5 39
♔d4 ♔f5 40 f3 c3 41 ♖f2 ♖a3 42 ♔c4
h5 43 ♔b4 ♖a8 44 f4 ♔e4 45 fxg5
♔e3 46 ♖g2 ♔d4 47 ♖e2 ♖b8+ 48
♔a4 ♖g8 49 h4 ♖f8 50 ♖e7 ♖f3 51
♖d7+ ♔c4 52 ♖c7+ ♔d4 53 ♖d7+
♔c4 54 ♖c7+ ♔d4 55 ♔b3 ♖xg3 56
♖d7+ ♔e4 57 ♖h7 ♔d4 58 ♖xh5 ♖g1
59 ♖h8 ♖b1+ 60 ♔a4 ♖a1+ 61 ♔b5
♖b1+ 62 ♔c6 ♖g1 63 ♖d8+ ♔c4 64
♖e8 ♔b4 65 ♔d5 ♖d1+ 66 ♔e6 ♖e1+
67 ♔f7 ♖f1+ 68 ♔g6 ♖f2 69 h5 ♖xc2
70 h6 ♖h2 71 h7 c2 72 ♖c8 ♔b3 73
♔g7 1-0

Karpov – Hort
Budapest 1973
French Defence

1 e4 e6 2 d4 d5 3 ♘d2 ♘f6 4 e5 ♘fd7
5 c3 c5 6 ♗d3 ♘c6 7 ♘e2 ♕b6 8 ♘f3
cxd4 9 cxd4 f6 10 exf6 ♘xf6 11 0-0
♗d6 *(D)*

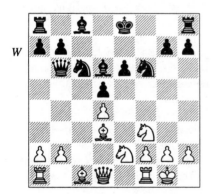

By exerting strong pressure on the
base pawn on d4 and the wedge at e5,
Black has broken up White's pawn-
chain. This has given Black more space

and enabled him to finish his development by bringing his minor pieces to
their natural positions. The price he
paid is the backward e6-pawn, the last
pawn of the central pawn-unit. For the
time being it is well protected, as is the
potentially weak square in front of it.

12 ♘c3

In the 1950s and early 1960s there
was a strong feeling that 12 ♗f4 caused
serious problems for Black. It is natural to weaken Black's control of the e5-
square and after 12...♗xf4 (12...♕c7
fails to the patient 13 ♗g3) 13 ♘xf4,
13...0-0 14 ♕d2 leaves White ready to
increase the pressure on the e6-pawn.
However, 13...♕xb2 14 ♖e1 0-0 denies White much more than equality.

12...0-0 13 ♗e3

Quite often one cannot make immediate use of potential pawn weakness.
On such occasions, experienced players know that patience is their best
weapon, keeping in mind that pawn
weaknesses are of a lasting nature.
The firm centre makes it possible to
seize space on the queenside by playing a3 followed by b4 or ♘a4, or to
take advantage of the position of the
black queen on b6 to act in the centre
by ♘e5.

The text-move, developing White's
last piece, is based on the tactical point
13...♕xb2 14 ♘b5 ♗e7 15 ♖b1 ♕xa2
16 ♖a1 ♕b2 17 ♖a4, trapping the
queen.

13...♕d8?!

13...♗d7 is considered more flexible. In that case 14 ♘e5 is met by
14...♗xe5 15 dxe5 ♕xb2.

14 ♗g5 ♗d7 15 ♖e1 ♕b8 16 ♗h4

White is ready to play ♗g3, which is the point of the bishop's manoeuvre. The exchange of the dark-squared bishops will strengthen White's control of the e5-square, when the e6-pawn will feel more exposed.

16...a6 17 ♖c1 b5?!

Played to thwart ♘a4 and seize space on the queenside, but it also represents a substantial weakening of the c-file.

18 ♗b1 ♗f4 19 ♗g3 ♗xg3 20 hxg3

It is clearer now that White has achieved his aims. He has obvious pressure on the c- and e-files, a spatial plus and more freedom to manoeuvre.

20...♕b6 21 ♘e2

After White's 18th move one could expect 21 ♕d3 with 22 ♘e5 in mind, but the text-move is also good. ♘f4 and perhaps ♘d3 are tempting ideas.

21...♖ae8 22 ♘f4 ♘xd4

Seeing that further waiting in a position where he is burdened by weaknesses on the central squares c5 and e5 can only worsen his situation, Hort decides to seek chances in tactical counterplay.

23 ♕xd4

Karpov pointed out after the game that 23 ♘xd4 e5 24 ♘xd5 ♕xd4 (or 24...♘xd5 25 ♘f3) 25 ♘xf6+ ♖xf6 26 ♕xd4 exd4 27 ♖xe8+ ♗xe8 28 ♖c8 ♔f7 29 ♖d8 wins material.

23...♕xd4 24 ♘xd4 e5 25 ♘fe6 ♗xe6 26 ♖xe5 ♗d7 27 ♖xe8 ♖xe8 28 f3 (D)

Black has finally rid himself of the backward pawn, but on the other hand he now has a blockaded isolated pawn,

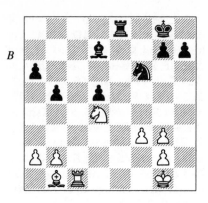

and thus a dubious endgame. The lesson here is that weak pawns tend to remain weak even when transformed into some other type of pawn.

28...♖c8 29 ♖xc8+ ♗xc8 30 ♔f2 ♔f7 31 ♔e3 ♔e7 32 b4

White secures his strong square c5, and at the same time fixes a new weakness at a6.

32...g6 33 g4 ♘d7 34 f4 ♘f8

With all his pawns on light squares, the colour of the white bishop, the intended knight exchange cannot be good, but 34...♘b6 fails to 35 ♘c6+ ♔d6 36 ♘e5 ♘c4+ 37 ♔d4. 34...♔d6 seems the only move coming into consideration.

35 g5 ♔d6 36 ♔f3

White is ready to set his kingside pawn-majority in motion.

36...♘e6 37 ♘xe6 ♗xe6 38 ♔e3

The centralized king will force Black into zugzwang.

38...♗g4 39 ♗d3 ♗e6 40 ♔d4 ♗g4 41 ♗c2 ♗e6 42 ♗b3 ♗f7 43 ♗d1 ♗e6 44 ♗f3 ♗f7 45 ♗g4 1-0

The backward a6-pawn is at the mercy of White's bishop.

Smyslov – Boleslavsky
'Absolute' USSR Ch,
Leningrad/Moscow 1941
French Defence

1 e4 e6 2 d4 d5 3 ᐁc3 ᘔb4 4 e5 c5 5 a3 ᘔxc3+ 6 bxc3 ᐁe7 7 a4 ᘑa5 8 ᘑd2 ᐁbc6 9 ᐁf3 c4?

Blocking the position at this moment plays into White's hands. The c1-bishop is presented with a nice post at a3 and an open diagonal to work on.

10 g3

When fianchettoed, the light-squared bishop will keep in check any counter-action in the centre.

10...0-0 11 ᘔg2 f6 12 exf6 ᘉxf6 (D)

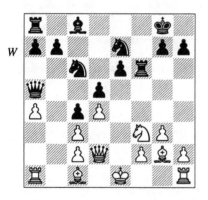

By trying to find some counterplay, Black gives himself long-term difficulties. The e6-pawn will remain backward, and e5 will be a strong square for White.

13 0-0 ᘔd7 14 ᘔa3 ᘉe8 15 ᐁh4 ᐁc8

White has prepared f4 in order to fix Black's weakness at e6. Rather than

allowing himself to be squeezed into his back two ranks, Black would do better to offer the exchange of a pair of knights by 15...ᐁf5.

16 f4 ᐁ6e7 17 ᘉfb1!

Grand strategy! Before he undertakes any action on the kingside, White wants to block any counter-action on the other wing.

17...ᘑc7 18 a5 ᘔc6 19 ᐁf3 ᐁg6 20 ᐁe5!

White provokes the exchange in order to open the f-file for attacking purposes.

20...ᐁce7

20...ᐁxe5 21 fxe5 ᘉf7 22 ᘉf1 ᘉxf1+ 23 ᘉxf1 ᘑxa5 24 ᘔb4 ᘑc7 25 ᘑf4 h6 26 ᘔf3, followed by ᘔh5, gives White a penetrating attack.

21 ᘔc5 a6

Now it is time to turn to the kingside. Black is innocuous on the queenside, while the e6-pawn waits to be exploited.

22 ᐁg4 ᘉf7 23 ᘉe1 ᐁf5 24 ᘉe2 h6 25 ᘉae1 ᘑc8 26 ᘔf3

The preparations are slow, but thorough and meaningful. The g2-square is vacated for the rook; the pawn advance is in the air.

26...ᖴh7 27 ᘉf1 ᘑc7 28 ᘑe1 ᐁf8

If 28...ᘑd7 there is 29 ᐁf2 ᐁf8 30 ᘔh5 g6 31 ᘔf3 threatening 32 ᐁg4 or in case of 31...h5 then 32 ᐁh3, slowly provoking new weaknesses.

29 ᐁe5 ᘉf6 30 g4 ᐁd6 31 ᘑg3 ᐁf7

31...ᐁe4 fails to 32 ᘔxe4+ dxe4 33 ᐁxc4 ᘔb5 34 ᐁd6.

32 g5 ᐁxe5 33 gxf6 ᐁxf3+ 34 ᘉxf3 gxf6 35 f5

Forcing the exchange of queens. White will decide the issue on the g-file.

35...♕xg3+ 36 ♖xg3 e5 37 ♖eg2 ♘d7 38 ♖g7+ ♔h8 39 ♖7g6 ♔h7 40 ♗a3 exd4 41 ♖c1 1-0

Fixed weaknesses on Black's third rank combined with other disadvantages are a bad omen. In our game it was White's large spatial advantage, strong dark-squared bishop and concentrated forces on the kingside that could not be parried. The e6-pawn, although not itself in danger, and even more the weak e5-square in front of it, were the basic motive for White's strategic plan and the cause of its success.

Given that backward pawns are so often potentially weak, one frequently sees players deliberately provoking their appearance. This task is usually performed by a knight, which occupies one of the dominant central squares. The opponent must then decide how to deal with this problem. If exchanging off the knight is not appealing, then he can use a pawn to chase it away, but this may mean accepting a pawn weakness on the neighbouring file. The device is often used and it is worth devoting some attention to it.

Romanishin – G. Kuzmin
Tashkent 1980
Sicilian Defence

1 ♘f3 g6 2 d4 ♗g7 3 c4 c5 4 e4 cxd4 5 ♘xd4 ♘c6 6 ♗e3 ♘f6 7 ♘c3 0-0 8 ♗e2 d6 9 0-0 ♗d7

The Maroczy Bind can be reached via various move-orders. In my personal opinion none of them is quite satisfactory for Black, because too much is given to White in the early phase. His power in the centre is considerable and his spatial advantage evident.

10 ♖c1 ♘xd4 11 ♗xd4 ♗c6 12 ♕d3 a5

After the manoeuvre ...♗d7-c6, it is necessary to prevent White's expansion on the queenside. After 12...♘d7 13 ♗xg7 ♔xg7 14 b4 ♘f6 15 ♔h1 a5 16 b5 ♗d7 17 f4 White has the advantage. The text-move, however, weakens Black's queenside.

13 ♘d5! (D)

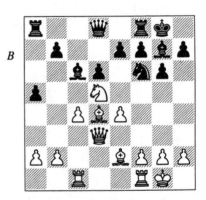

White provokes Black's e-pawn forward, making use of the weakness of b6 and fully aware that the position after the exchange on d5 would favour him.

13...e6 14 ♘c3 a4 15 ♖fd1

White's provocation has yielded a weakness in the form of the backward d6-pawn, offering White a good target.

15...♕a5 16 a3 ♖fd8 17 ♕e3 ♖d7!

Ingenious defence: Kuzmin plans to meet 18 ♗b6 by 18...♗h6. This requires further manoeuvring from White, but it does not change the fact that the d6-pawn is weak for good.

18 ♖c2 ♕d8 19 ♗b6 ♕f8 20 ♕f4 ♖c8 21 ♗e3 ♘e8 22 ♕h4

The d6-pawn, being there and needing protection, has forced Black into passive defence in restricted space. 22 ♘d5 would have made Black's position even more difficult, as pointed out by Romanishin in his analysis after the game.

22...f5 23 exf5 gxf5 24 f3 ♗e5 25 ♖cd2

Black has obtained some breathing space, but at a price. Now he has two backward pawns on his third rank, both stuck there: whichever advances leaves a hole in the position.

25...♕g7 26 ♘d5 ♖f7 27 ♗h6 ♕g6 28 ♘f4 ♗xf4 29 ♕xf4 ♖f6 30 ♕g5

The exchange of queens will eliminate Black's counterplay on the kingside, whereupon the white bishop-pair and the black pawn weaknesses will be emphasized.

30...♔f7 31 ♕xg6+ ♖xg6 32 ♗e3 e5 33 ♔f2

33 ♔f1, planning g3 and f4, is more precise. This plan is not possible with the king on f2 because of ...♘f6.

33...♔e7 *(D)*
34 ♗b6?!

Unfortunately, White starts to play superficially in time-trouble, ruining his good work. 34 c5 is correct, when 34...dxc5 35 ♗xc5+ opens the position to the benefit of White's bishops, while 34...d5 35 ♖xd5 ♗xd5 36 ♖xd5 ♖e6 (or 36...♔f6 37 f4) 37 ♗g5+ ♘f6 38 ♗b5 is no more pleasant for Black.

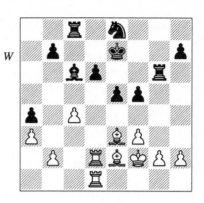

34...♘c7 35 ♗d3 ♗d7 36 g4 ♖h6 37 gxf5 ♘e8 38 ♖g1 ♖xh2+ 39 ♔e3 ♖xd2 40 ♔xd2 ♔f6 ½-½

This game was in the end spoilt by time-trouble, but the provocative 13 ♘d5 and its consequences remain a good lesson.

Spassky – Donner
Leiden 1970
French Defence

1 e4 e6 2 d4 d5 3 ♘c3 ♘f6 4 ♗g5 dxe4 5 ♘xe4 ♗e7 6 ♗xf6 ♗xf6 7 ♘f3 ♗d7?! 8 ♕d2 ♗c6 9 ♘xf6+ ♕xf6 10 ♘e5 0-0 11 0-0-0

When discussing doubled pawns we analysed one of the match-games between Spassky and Petrosian that reached this position.

11...♖d8

Donner tries to improve on Petrosian's 11...♘d7.

12 ♕e3 ♗e8 13 g3 ♘d7 14 ♗g2 c6 15 f4

Donner has avoided doubled pawns but at the cost of several tempi and a suspiciously passive position. He faces two problems: on the one hand, he cannot reduce the material by 15...♘xe5 because after 16 dxe5 ♕e7 17 ♖xd8 he either loses the a7-pawn or must cede the open file to White; on the other, he must bring his buried e8-bishop to life, but that will cost as well.

15...♕e7 16 h4 f6

The centralized knight has played its role: it has provoked Black's f-pawn forward, which leaves a backward pawn at e6.

17 ♘f3 ♗h5 18 ♗h3 ♗xf3 19 ♕xf3 ♘f8 20 ♖he1 ♕f7 21 ♗f1! (D)

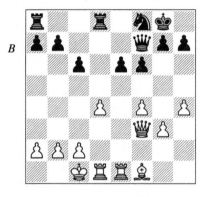

The bishop is looking for a better view at the e6-pawn. Black's problems are not just with the backward pawn; he has White's superior bishop versus his passive knight and the general instability of his vulnerable kingside to worry about.

21...♖d6 22 ♗c4 ♖ad8

If 22...f5, then 23 g4 g6 24 h5 totally opens up the black king's defences.

23 f5 ♖xd4 24 fxe6 ♖xd1+

24...♕e7 25 ♕a3 c5 26 ♕xa7 wins.

25 ♖xd1 ♖xd1+ 26 ♕xd1 1-0

26...♕e7 would be punished by 27 ♕d8 – the same motif again.

Numerous games confirm that provoking backward pawns is a frequent device and quite often rewarding. It often happens on the central files, very much like in our game, and sometimes it is the only subtle way to weaken the enemy position.

However, there is more to backward pawns than the label of weakness, regularly attached to them, suggests. In a number of important variations from various openings Black voluntarily accepts backward pawns and, in spite of their apparent sensitivity, builds his plans on them. The role played by the d6-pawn is exceptional and worthy of thorough attention.

Gutman – Suetin
USSR 1972
King's Indian Defence

1 d4 ♘f6 2 c4 c5 3 d5 d6 4 ♘c3 g6 5 e4 ♗g7 6 ♗e2 e6 7 ♘f3 0-0 8 0-0 ♖e8 9 dxe6 ♗xe6 (D)

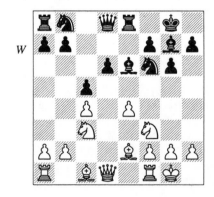

10 h3

In the first decades after the Second World War the King's Indian Defence was explored extensively in all its ramifications. Encouraged by a great deal of experience in lines in which the potentially weak d6-pawn successfully survived all the plans and tricks used against it, Black embarked on more courageous projects. One of them was the position in front of us, in which the backward d6-pawn looks to be left at White's mercy. But when Suetin entered this variation against Gutman, the dedicated connoisseurs of the King's Indian already knew that 10 ♗f4 ♘c6 11 ♗xd6 (11 ♕xd6 ♕a5 is worse) 11...♘d4 offers Black excellent counterplay. Then 12 e5 (12 ♗xc5 fails to 12...♘xe2+ 13 ♕xe2 ♕c8, and 12 ♘xd4 cxd4 13 ♕xd4 to 13...♘xe4, when Black has the initiative) 12...♘d7 13 ♘xd4 cxd4 14 ♕xd4 ♘e5 15 ♗xe5 ♕xd4 16 ♗xd4 ♗xd4 gives Black enough compensation for the sacrificed pawn – one can find the details in any good text on the system today.

With the text-move, aware of the above continuation, White prepares ♗e3, in order to establish full control over the d4-square, and hopes to be able to build pressure on the d6-pawn in better circumstances after finishing his development – the backward pawn is there to stay for some time.

10...♘c6 11 ♗e3 ♕b6 12 ♖b1

Defending the pawn – White would like to make use of the pin on the g1-a7 diagonal and has in mind a later b4.

12...♘d7!

Again the pawn is offered, but 13 ♕xd6 ♘d4 cannot be attractive to White: 14 ♕xb6 ♘xe2+ 15 ♘xe2 axb6 changes the scene dramatically.

13 ♘b5

13 ♘g5 is a better option, but the d6-pawn looks so vulnerable that White cannot resist the temptation. Strangely enough, Black continues to reply cold-bloodedly...

13...♘de5 14 b4

Since neither 14 ♕xd6 nor 14 ♘xd6 works, the additional pin finally threatens to eliminate the obstinate pawn. However...

14...♘xf3+ 15 ♗xf3 ♖ed8

It is as simple as that. The pin is invalidated.

16 ♕c1 ♘d4

The d6-pawn proved a hard nut to crack; Black now seizes the initiative.

17 ♗xd4

17 ♗d1 ♕c6 is not attractive for White, but the exchange brings about a central passed pawn in a position in which Black's bishop-pair will play its role.

17...cxd4 18 a4 ♖dc8 19 a5 ♕d8 20 ♗e2 a6 21 ♘a3 ♕h4 22 ♕d2 ♖c7 23 ♗d3 ♖e8 24 ♖b3 ♖ce7 25 b5 ♗c8 26 ♘c2 ♖e5 27 f4 ♖c5 28 bxa6 bxa6 29 ♖b8 g5! *(D)*

When White was forced to relinquish his pressure on the d6-pawn, the scene changed all of a sudden. The clever move Black has just played demonstrates how vulnerable White has become on the dark squares. The d6-pawn secures the strong squares c5 and e5, and is now free and under no pressure, enabling it to fulfil a positive

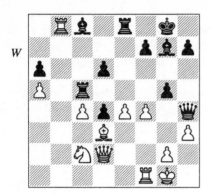

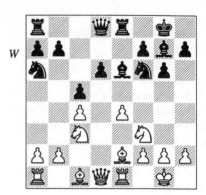

task. White is burdened with too many pawn-islands and his pieces are uncoordinated. Gutman's position will collapse soon.

30 ♘b4 gxf4 31 ♖xf4 ♕g5 32 ♘d5 ♖f8 33 ♕f2 ♗e6 34 h4 ♕e5 35 ♘e7+ ♔h8 36 ♖xf8+ ♗xf8 37 ♘f5 ♖xa5 38 ♘xd4

38 ♕xd4 only prolongs White's suffering after, e.g., 38...♖a4.

38...♖a1+ 39 ♗f1 ♗xc4 40 ♕e3 ♗h6 41 ♕c3 ♗xf4 0-1

Despite appearances, the backward pawn on the d-file was not so weak after all!

Kraidman – Vasiukov
Manila 1974
King's Indian Defence

1 d4 ♘f6 2 c4 c5 3 d5 d6 4 ♘c3 g6 5 e4 ♗g7 6 ♘f3 0-0 7 ♗e2 e6 8 0-0 ♖e8 9 ♖e1 ♘a6 10 dxe6 ♗xe6 *(D)*

Trying to make use of the seemingly dramatic weakness at d6, White resorted to all his imagination and cunning and no continuation was left unturned. With his 9th move, a useful

waiting move, he provoked the only useful waiting reply, before giving Black a backward d-pawn. White now hopes to exert pressure on the d6-pawn in a new situation in which ...♘c6-d4 is impossible.

11 ♗g5 h6 12 ♗f4 ♕b6 13 b3 ♗g4

Black defends actively: he leaves the d6-pawn *en prise* but threatens to take the e4-pawn.

14 h3 ♗d7!

Black is patient. The pressure on the e4-pawn is still there and can be further increased by 15...♗c6. At the same time his temporarily wayward knight on a6 is not without prospects – the manoeuvre ...♘c7-e6 awaits it, with d4 as an eventual target.

15 e5?!

White could protect the e4-pawn by 15 ♗d3 for instance, but then he relinquishes his hold on the backward pawn. The pressure disappears and Black gets precious time to improve the position of his pieces. Still, the text-move asks for trouble.

15...dxe5 16 ♘xe5 ♖ad8 17 ♕c1 ♗f5

Black has seized the initiative. The obvious lack of coordination in White's camp will work against him.

18 ♗g4 ♗xg4 19 hxg4 ♘b4 20 ♖e3 ♖d4 21 ♖f3

21 g5 is met by 21...♖xf4 (21...♘h5 22 gxh6, or 21...hxg5 22 ♗xg5 ♖xe5 23 ♖xe5 ♘d3 24 ♕e3 ♘xe5 25 ♕xe5) 22 gxf6 (22 ♘d7!? is critical) 22...♖xe5 23 fxg7 (or 23 ♖xe5 ♕xf6 24 ♖e8+ ♔h7) 23...♕f6, when Black has the advantage:

a) 24 ♖xe5 ♕xe5 25 g3 fails to the obvious 25...♖xf2.

b) 24 a3 is met by the hidden resource 24...♖h4, with the points 25 g3 ♖h2, 25 ♖xe5 ♕xe5 26 axb4?! ♕h5 and 25 axb4 ♖eh5 26 ♖h3 ♖xh3 27 gxh3 ♕f3.

21...♕e6 22 ♗g3 ♘xg4 23 ♘xg4 ♖xg4 24 ♖b1 h5 25 a3 ♘c6 26 ♘d5 ♘d4 27 ♘c7? ♘xf3+ 28 gxf3 ♖xg3+ 29 fxg3 ♕h3 0-1

The seemingly helpless d6-pawn survived again. If it could survive or be sacrificed with compensation, then, Black concluded, we should look again at numerous other positions characterized by backward pawns and see if their value should be re-assessed. We owe to the late 1960s and 1970s a new look at some old variations...

Ribli – Planinc
Amsterdam 1973
King's Indian Defence

1 ♘f3 g6 2 d4 ♗g7 3 c4 ♘f6 4 g3 0-0 5 ♗g2 d6 6 ♘c3 ♘bd7 7 0-0 e5 8 e4 ♖e8 9 h3 exd4 10 ♘xd4 ♘c5 11 ♖e1 a5 12 ♖b1 c6 *(D)*

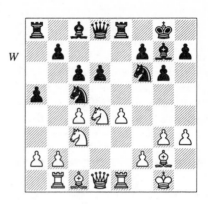

Today many such positions are taken on without a second thought. Often players are not aware of how much effort was invested in order to find the best move-orders, to correct old prejudices, to discover and distinguish subtle nuances. The d6-pawn in the Fianchetto Variation had been considered very sensitive for years and Black's whole concept therefore dubious. To make things more difficult for Black, White was constantly introducing new ideas. Ribli's 12 ♖b1 was a useful, waiting move. Sooner or later the rook will support the advance of the b-pawn, while the bishop waited for Black to play 12...c6, ready to endanger the backward pawn as soon as it appears on the board.

13 ♗f4 a4

Black needs space and he seizes it on the queenside. For the time being he does not worry about the d6-pawn because after 14 ♘c2 he can parry the direct threat by an elegant reply – 14...♘fd7, when neither 15 ♕xd6 nor 15 ♗xd6 works because of the response 15...a3.

14 b4

That is why the rook took its place on b1. The advance of the b-pawn will thwart Black's counter-chances on the queenside and chase away the c5-knight, seizing a significant spatial advantage. 14 ♕d2 was proposed as a good alternative, when White is in a better situation to attack the d6-pawn. Black could reply 14...♘h5 15 ♗e3 ♘f6, lifting the siege, but if I remember well our analysis after the game, Planinc, true to himself, was considering 14...♕a5 (but not 14...♕b6 15 ♗xd6 ♖d8 16 e5 ♘e8 17 ♘xc6 bxc6 18 ♗xc5) 15 ♗xd6 ♖d8 16 e5 ♘e8, seeking complications.

14...axb3 15 axb3 h6!?

Black could again resort to 15...♘h5 16 ♗e3 and exert counter-pressure by 16...♖a3. Then 17 ♕c2 could be met by the hidden tactical blow 17...f5. However, Planinc always gave preference to original ideas.

16 b4

Petrosian proposed as an improvement 16 ♕c2, setting a trap: 16...♘fxe4 17 ♘xe4 ♗xd4 18 ♘xd6 ♖xe1+ 19 ♖xe1, when 19...♖a1 loses material to 20 ♖xa1 ♗xa1 21 ♕a2 ♗f6 22 ♕a8. Black can put up more resistance by 19...♘e6 20 ♘xc8 ♘xf4 21 ♘e7+ ♔g7 22 gxf4 ♖a1 23 ♖xa1 ♗xa1 24 ♘xc6 bxc6 25 ♗xc6 ♕d6, but there is no fun in defending such a position. Instead, Black can resort to one of the routine King's Indian manoeuvres – 16...♘g4, when 17 ♖ed1 ♘e5 18 ♗e3 prepares f4, securing a spatial advantage, but not more than that.

16...♘e6 17 ♘xe6

When your opponent is short of space, it is better to avoid exchanges like this, but on 17 ♗e3 Black replies 17...♘g5 and White has to part with his dark-squared bishop; this is the point of 15...h6.

17...♗xe6 18 ♗xd6 ♗xc4

In the end the backward pawn has fallen but in exchange for the valuable c-pawn. The position is balanced.

19 e5 ♘d7

In his comments Petrosian showed a hidden possibility: 19...♖e6 20 ♕d4 (or 20 f4 ♘h5 21 ♔h2 ♖xd6 22 ♕xd6 ♕xd6 23 exd6 ♗xc3 24 ♖ec1 ♗a2) 20...♘d5 and now 21 ♘xd5 ♗xd5 22 ♗xd5 ♕xd6, but White, of course, can choose 21 ♕xc4, with a level position.

20 f4 f6! 21 b5 fxe5 22 bxc6 bxc6 23 ♗xc6 ♖a6 24 ♕f3? *(D)*

24 ♗d5+ was necessary in order to keep the balance, but White misses a tactical reply...

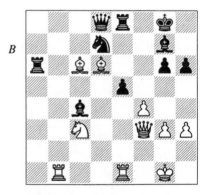

B

24...e4 25 ♗xd7?

Petrosian analysed 25 ♘xe4 ♗d4+ 26 ♘f2 ♗xf2+ 27 ♔xf2 ♖a2+ 28 ♔g1

♕b6+ 29 ♔h1 ♖ee2, when Black wins nicely, and 25 ♖xe4 ♖xc6 26 ♖xe8+ ♕xe8 27 ♕xc6 ♕e3+ 28 ♔h2 ♕xc3, when White can resist but can hardly hope to save the game.

25...♗d4+

Ribli was evidently anticipating 25...♖xd6 26 ♖xe4, but missed this intermediary check, which decides the game quickly.

26 ♔h2 ♖xd6 27 ♘xe4 ♖xd7 28 f5 gxf5 29 ♕xf5 ♖f8 30 ♕h5 ♗g7 31 h4 ♗d3 32 ♖bd1 ♗xe4 0-1

Smejkal – Planinc
Ljubljana 1973
King's Indian Defence

1 ♘f3 ♘f6 2 c4 g6 3 g3 ♗g7 4 ♗g2 0-0 5 0-0 d6 6 d4 ♘bd7 7 ♘c3 e5 8 e4 ♖e8 9 h3 exd4 10 ♘xd4 ♘c5 11 ♖e1 a5 12 ♕c2 c6 *(D)*

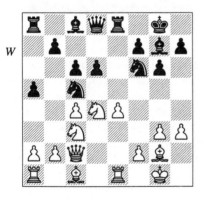

The more that direct attempts against the backward pawn failed, the more White turned to quiet solutions, planning to seize a spatial advantage, push his opponent into passive defence, and only then try to grab the d6-pawn. Since then c2 has become the queen's favourite place.

13 ♗e3

On 13 ♗f4, Black defends his sensitive point by 13...♘fd7 14 ♖ad1 ♘e5.

13...a4 14 ♖ab1

Expecting 14...♕a5, White prepares in reply 15 b4 axb3 16 axb3 ♕b4 17 ♗d2 ♕b6 18 ♘de2, when he will gradually push his opponent into passive defence. If he succeeds in doing so, then the d6-pawn will become more vulnerable. The alternative, 14 ♖ad1, intending to endanger the d6-pawn as soon as possible, at first failed to produce results. After 14...♕a5, 15 ♘de2 was tried, but Black found a clever reply in defence of his weakened pawn: 15...♘fd7 16 ♖xd6 ♘e5 and Black will recapture the pawn because 17 b3 is met by 17...♗xh3. However, later the much stronger 15 ♗f4 ♗f8 (whenever this move is necessary, there is something wrong with the position!) 16 ♘f3 was found. Confronted by these new problems, Black resorted to 14...♘fd7 15 ♖e2 ♕a5 16 ♖ed2 and at the moment when the threat to the d6-pawn becomes real, Black has a tactical solution: 16...♕b4 17 ♘b1 ♘f6 18 f3 d5 and 16...♘e5 17 ♗f1 a3 18 b3 ♘f3+ 19 ♘xf3 ♗xc3 20 ♖xd6 ♘xe4, when the backward pawn has been exchanged and the balance maintained.

14...♗d7!?

This is typical of the sort of surprising moves Planinc used to pull out of his hat. Not willing to commit his queen to either a5 or e7 (if 14...♕e7, then 15 ♖bd1 at once), Black waits for his opponent to play his hand. The alternative is 14...♘fd7 15 b4 axb3 16 axb3 ♘e5 17 ♖ed1 ♕e7 18 f4 ♘ed7 19 ♗f2 ♘f6 20 ♖e1 ♘h5 21 ♖bd1 ♖a3, when White has a spatial advantage, but Black is not without counterplay.

15 b4 axb3 16 axb3 ♕e7 17 ♖bd1?! (D)

A routine procedure, good and valid in routine positions, but Planinc has taken care to change the essentials of it. The reply proves that 17 f3 was indispensable.

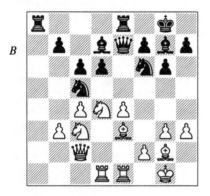

B

17...♘fxe4

This seemingly impossible move works. The key move to make it possible was 14...♗d7. In the King's Indian Defence, the d6-pawn looks most compromised, but as a matter of fact the e4-pawn and especially the c4-pawn are also vulnerable targets in many positions.

18 ♗f4 f5 19 ♘xe4

19 f3 does not work because of 19...♗xd4+ 20 ♖xd4 ♕f6.

19...♘xe4 20 f3 g5!

Smejkal had probably missed this crucial response.

21 ♗c1 ♗xd4+ 22 ♖xd4 ♕e5

22...♕g7, seeking to avoid the problem mentioned in the next note, can be met by 23 ♗b2.

23 ♗b2?

According to Gligorić White preserves better hopes after 23 ♖dd1 ♕c3 24 ♖e2 ♘xg3 25 ♖xe8+ ♗xe8 26 ♕xc3 ♘e2+ 27 ♔f2 ♘xc3 28 ♖d3 ♘a2 29 ♗xg5 d5 30 f4, which is true, because after the text-move the building collapses...

23...♖a2 24 ♕c1 ♕xg3 25 ♖e2 c5 26 ♖d1 f4 27 fxe4 f3 28 ♖d3 ♖f8 29 ♖f2

29 ♕c3 loses to 29...f2+ followed by 30...♕xg2+.

29...♗xh3 30 ♖dd2 ♖f4 31 ♕c3 ♖xb2 32 ♖xb2 ♗xg2 33 ♖xg2 f2+ 34 ♖bxf2 ♕xc3 35 ♖xf4 h6 36 ♖f5 ♕xb3 37 ♖d5 ♕xc4 38 ♖xd6 ♕c1+ 0-1

In this game, the d6-pawn remained just a potential weakness. Its real weakness remained hidden behind Black's active piece-play. We shall see the backward d6-pawn in similar surroundings in various lines of the Sicilian Defence and Ruy Lopez – weak by its position on the board, but firm and tenacious in the midst of active pieces.

Adams – Salov
Dortmund 1992
Sicilian Defence

1 e4 c5 2 ♘f3 ♘c6 3 d4 cxd4 4 ♘xd4 ♘f6 5 ♘c3 e5 6 ♘db5 d6 7 ♗g5 a6 8 ♘a3 b5 9 ♗xf6 gxf6 (D)

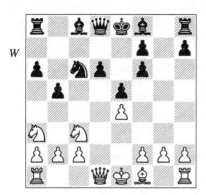

We have reached a standard battle-ground in modern opening theory. To an inexperienced eye, it seems that Black has overstepped the limits of caution. His damaged pawn-structure, with two backward pawns at d6 and f6 and the hole on d5, suggest that all of White's opening desires have been satisfied. However, the further course of the game demonstrates that not all is seen at first glance.

10 ♘d5 f5 11 c3

Having installed his knight on the strong central square, White is planning to transfer his other knight to e3 via c2, so increasing his power on the vital light squares. At the same time the c3-pawn controls two important squares, b4 and d4, denying the c6-knight the central square and setting the scene for later action on the queen-side, based on a4 to break up Black's pawn-structure, or perhaps b4.

Let us note in passing that 11 ♗d3 does little for the general plan if met by 11...♗e6.

11...♗g7 12 exf5 ♗xf5 13 ♘c2 0-0 14 ♘ce3 ♗e6

Both players have achieved their short-term goals. White has strengthened his dominant d5-knight, block-ading the backward d6-pawn, while Black has got rid of his doubled f-pawn and is ready to advance the f7-pawn, with the idea of lifting White's grip in the centre. His d6-pawn re-mains potentially weak, but White is behind in development, and pressure on the d6-pawn does not concern Black at the moment.

However, if White succeeds in fin-ishing his development and can, by exchanging some minor pieces, reach a position with reduced material, then Black's potential weakness on the d-file and his somewhat exposed queen-side pawns may become a real prob-lem. Fearing such an outcome, some partisans of the Sveshnikov Variation believe that Black should himself try to reduce material before the fianchettoed g2-bishop further strengthens White's grip on the central light squares. There-fore, on the previous move, 13...♘e7 has been applied at once in order to meet 14 ♘xe7 by 14...♗xc2 and 14 ♘ce3 by 14...♗e6, when 15 ♘xe7 ♛xe7 16 g3 is met by 16...d5 (if 17 ♘xd5 then 17...♛b7). In case of 15 g3 Black replies 15...♘xd5 16 ♘xd5 0-0 17 ♗g2 a5 18 0-0 f5. In comparison with our game, exchanging a pair of knights suits Black well.

15 g3 ♘e7

15...♖b8 16 ♗g2 is an alternative line. In Timoshenko-Luther, Linares 1998, an attempt was made to win the d4-square for Black's knight by 16...f5 17 ♛h5 b4, but after 18 0-0 bxc3 19 bxc3, White kept the enemy knight out of his camp, refusing to relinquish his hold on the centre. If Black wanted to loosen White's central grip, he should have done it at once. 16...a5 17 0-0 f5 seems to me to be the proper course.

16 ♗g2 ♖b8 17 0-0 ♘xd5

17...♕d7 comes into consideration.

18 ♗xd5

That makes the difference: White is ready to exchange the light-squared bishops, when his powerful knight will be superior to Black's dark-squared bishop.

18...♔h8 19 a4 ♗h6

This is Black's natural reaction: to diminish the pressure by eliminating the e3-knight.

20 axb5 axb5? (D)

The d5-bishop and e3-knight stifle Black's chances of counterplay. Unfortunately, Black misses his opportunity. Correct is 20...♗xe3 21 fxe3 ♗xd5 22 ♕xd5 ♖xb5 23 ♕d2 a5, although White still preserves an advantage.

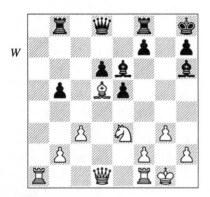

21 ♘c2!

There will be no exchange any more. The knight can reach the d5-square via b4. At the same time the b5-pawn is blocked. The position is unfavourable to Black's bishops and Black, burdened with three pawn-islands, is already facing serious problems.

21...♕d7 22 ♖a6

For the first time we feel that the d6-pawn is vulnerable. The long and slow process of building positional pressure yields results.

22...♗h3 23 ♖e1 ♗g5

This bishop missed the target, and it is transferred now to a more active place.

24 ♘b4 ♗d8 25 ♗e4 ♗b6

25...♖b6 does not work on account of 26 ♕h5 f6 27 ♕h6 ♖f7 28 ♖xb6 ♗xb6 29 ♗xh7, etc.

26 ♘d5

26 ♕h5 was appealing as well.

26...f5 27 ♘xb6 ♕d8 28 ♘d7 ♕xd7 29 ♖xd6 ♕e7 30 ♖d7 ♕g5 31 ♗c2

By continuing to target the h7-pawn, White thwarts any counterplay with ...f4.

31...e4

Even after the stronger 31...♖be8 32 f4 the position is still hopeless.

32 ♕d4+ ♕f6 33 ♕a7 ♕h6 34 ♖a1 b4 35 ♕d4+ ♕f6 36 ♖aa7 ♕xd4 37 cxd4 1-0

The siege of the backward pawn was long and patient. It brought success owing to a series of small errors by which Black neglected his counterplay and after erroneous exchanges emphasized the negative sides of the black pawn-formation.

Anand – Kramnik
Linares 1998
Sicilian Defence

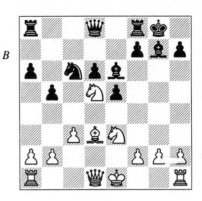

B

**1 e4 c5 2 ♘f3 ♘c6 3 d4 cxd4 4 ♘xd4
♘f6 5 ♘c3 e5 6 ♘db5 d6 7 ♗g5 a6 8
♘a3 b5 9 ♗xf6 gxf6 10 ♘d5 f5 11 c3
♗g7 12 exf5 ♗xf5 13 ♘c2 0-0**

Instead 13...♗e6 allows White to
finish his development without spend-
ing a tempo on ♘ce3. Apart from that,
if the knight stays on c2, it can take
part in queenside actions. After 14 g3
0-0 15 ♗g2 a5 16 0-0, Topalov-Lau-
tier, Tilburg 1998 continued 16...f5 17
♕e2 ♖b8 18 ♖fd1 ♔h8 19 ♘a3, and
following 19...b4?! (correct is 19...♘a7,
keeping the a3-knight out of play, and
with ...b4 followed by ...♘b5 in mind)
20 ♘b5 bxc3 21 bxc3 the backward
d6-pawn was in danger. After 16...♖b8
White can exert direct pressure on the
d6-pawn by 17 ♕d2 ♕d7 18 ♖ad1 f5
19 ♘de3, but Black can organize his
defence successfully: 19...♖bd8 20
♗d5 ♘e7 21 ♗xe6+ ♕xe6 22 ♘d5,
when 22...f4 keeps the c2-knight further from the d5-square and seeks
counterplay on the kingside, as in Tiv-
iakov-McShane, Kilkenny 1998. So
the backward pawn survives various
schemes used against it.

14 ♘ce3 ♗e6 15 ♗d3 *(D)*

If fianchettoed, the light-squared
bishop strengthens the stronghold on
d5, but developed at d3 it is well posi-
tioned against Black's king and also
against Black's kingside counterplay.
Besides, from d3 a short manoeuvre
can transfer the bishop to b3 – another
privileged place for it.

15...f5 16 0-0

On 16 ♕h5 in Adams-Beliavsky,
European Team Ch, Debrecen 1992,
Black replied 16...e4 17 ♗c2 ♘e7 18
♗b3 ♘xd5 19 ♘xd5 a5, preventing
attempts to reach some sort of favourable ending.

In connection with the backward
d-pawn, 16 ♗c2 seems more meaningful. In principle Black should generate
counterplay with his pieces to compensate for his potential weakness, but
always keeping in mind that d6 remains a sensitive point. After 16...♗h6
17 0-0 ♖a7 18 f4 ♕h4 19 g3 ♖g7
Black's optimistic play in Topalov-
Illescas, Linares 1995, was punished
by a brilliant tactical blow – 20 ♘c7!,
when 20...exf4 21 ♘g2 ♕h3 22 ♖xf4
♗xf4 23 ♘xf4 ♖xg3+ 24 ♔h1 led to
victory for White. This idea worked
because at the critical moment the d6-
pawn was left defenceless. The game
Wang Pin-B.Lalić, Linares 1998 continued 16...f4, and then 17 ♕h5 ♖f7
18 ♗xh7+ ♔f8 19 ♗f5 ♕e8 20 ♗xe6
♕xe6 21 ♕g4 ♕h6 22 ♘f5 ♕e6 23
♘fe3 led to a repetition of moves.

16...e4

16...♖a7 has been quite popular in recent years, but exposes Black to the undermining 17 a4 (17 ♕h5 causes fewer difficulties to Black, who calmly replies 17...♖af7 18 f4 ♘e7). The game Zelčić-Sermek, Belišće 1999 continued 17...♘e7 18 ♘xe7+ ♖xe7 19 axb5 axb5 20 ♖a6 d5 21 ♖xe6 ♖xe6 22 ♘xf5 with an initiative for White. 17...b4, offering a pawn to secure a comfortable place at d4, creates a better impression.

17 ♘f4 ♗f7 18 ♗c2 ♗e5 19 ♘fd5

By centralizing the bishop at e5, Black has temporarily got rid of any possible pressures on the backward pawn, but his central formation remains exposed to the undermining move f3.

19...♕g5 20 f4 exf3 21 ♕xf3

In Topalov-Van Wely, Wijk aan Zee 1999, White sought to improve with 21 ♖xf3 ♗h5 22 ♘c7, but 22...♗f4 (22...♖ac8 is also satisfactory) kept the game in the balance.

21...♗h5 22 ♕f2?!

This passive move causes some difficulties for White. After 22 ♕h3 f4 23 ♕d7 (after 23 ♘c7 fxe3 24 ♘xa8 ♖xf1+ 25 ♖xf1 e2, the passed pawn is powerful) 23...♖a7 the game is level.

22...f4 23 h4

23 ♘c7 fails due to 23...♖ac8 24 ♘e6 ♕h6 25 ♘xf8 fxe3.

23...♕d8 24 ♘f5 ♗g6 25 ♘d4 ♘xd4 26 cxd4 ♗xc2 27 dxe5 dxe5 28 ♕c5 ♖f7 ½-½

It is Black who stands better now.

The lesson is straightforward: backward pawns succumb easily in passive positions, but are kept alive and healthy among active pieces whose counterplay hides their positional weakness. The backward pawn which occurs regularly in the Najdorf and Scheveningen Variations of the Sicilian Defence shares that dual nature. It is shaky and it is firm. Which case will prevail depends on the overall activity of Black's pieces, as the following games witness...

Karpov – Polugaevsky
Candidates match (game 8),
Moscow 1974
Sicilian Defence

1 e4 c5 2 ♘f3 d6 3 d4 cxd4 4 ♘xd4 ♘f6 5 ♘c3 a6 6 ♗e2 e5

Opočensky, a Czech master of the older generation, used to play this line and years ago we called it after him. Later it became popular in the games of Miguel Najdorf. In playing 6...e5, Black weakens the d5-square and creates a backward pawn at d6, but seizes space in the centre, chases away White's centralized knight, and will use his minor pieces to cover the potential weakness at d5.

7 ♘b3 ♗e7 8 0-0 ♗e6 9 f4 ♕c7 10 a4

With this and the previous move, White squeezes Black.

10...♘bd7 11 ♔h1 0-0 12 ♗e3 exf4 13 ♖xf4 ♘e5 (D)

Seeking more breathing space, Black has created an ideal place for his knight on e5. However, in doing so, he also cedes the important central d4-square to White's pieces.

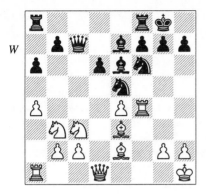

14 a5

White seizes space. The b6-square will be available to the dark-squared bishop, and the queen's rook will be able to enter the play on the fourth rank.

14...♖fe8

In the sixth game of the same match Polugaevsky covered the weakness on b6 by 14...♘fd7, but this loosened his control of the d5-square. After 15 ♖f1 ♗f6 16 ♘d5 ♗xd5 17 ♕xd5 ♕xc2 18 ♘d4 ♕xb2 19 ♖ab1 ♕c3 20 ♘f5 White had excellent compensation for the sacrificed material in the form of active play and the initiative.

15 ♗b6 ♕d7 16 ♖a4

White's advantage lies in spatial control, which broadens the possibilities for him to manoeuvre. The rook will move to d4 to enhance the pressure on the semi-open file.

16...♖ac8

Considering the problems discussed in the next three notes, Botvinnik thought that 16...♘c6 was in order, to prevent ♖d4.

17 ♖d4 ♕c6?

When playing his previous move, Polugaevsky had in mind 17...♖xc3 but he reluctantly gave up the idea considering the consequences of 18 bxc3 ♕c6 19 ♕e1.

18 ♖d2!

This rook manoeuvre is well justified. White enhances the pressure and threatens ♘d4, squeezing Black further. With the c2-pawn defended, ♘d5 will also be possible.

18...♗xb3

18...♗c4 19 ♘d4 ♕d7 20 ♘f5 ♗xe2 21 ♖xe2 would definitely weaken the d5-square and, of course, the backward pawn as well.

With his possibilities of active play not working out, Black decides he must eliminate the b3-knight, which means weakening the d5-square and ceding his opponent a dangerous pawn-majority on the queenside.

19 cxb3 ♘fd7 20 ♗g1 ♗g5?!

In expectation of the relentless b4-b5 Black decides to act, but the exchange of the queen for two rooks won't bring relief, because the same threat remains in the position...

21 ♖xd6 ♗xf4 22 ♖xc6 ♖xc6 23 b4! (D)

The pawn-majority can be turned into a passed pawn supported by the bishops. That threat cannot be parried in any satisfactory way. Note the typical transformation of advantages. There is no backward pawn on the d-file and no pressure on it, but instead Black must face a mobile pawn-majority.

23...♘f6

Polugaevsky was critical of this choice and proposed the alternative

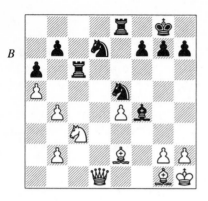

23...罩cc8 as better, but 24 b5 comes all the same with force.

24 b5 罩ce6 25 bxa6 bxa6 26 g3 鱼g5 27 h4 鱼h6 28 鱼b6

The a6-pawn is the natural target.

28...包ed7 29 鱼c4 罩e5

If 29...罩6e7 then 30 鱼f2.

30 豐b3 罩b8 31 鱼xf7+ 曹h8 32 豐c4

An effective solution.

32...鱼d2

32...包xb6 33 axb6 罩e7 loses to 34 e5 罩xe5 35 b7.

33 鱼c7 罩c5 34 豐xc5 包xc5 35 鱼xb8 鱼xc3 36 bxc3 包fxe4 37 c4 包d7 38 鱼c7 g6 39 鱼e6 包ec5 40 鱼xd7 包xd7 41 鱼d6 1-0

The c4-pawn is costly.

Tal – Vogt
Tallinn 1981
Sicilian Defence

1 e4 c5 2 包f3 e6 3 d4 cxd4 4 包xd4 包f6 5 包c3 d6 6 鱼e2 鱼e7 7 0-0 0-0 8 f4 包c6 9 鱼e3 e5

It is in the nature of the 'small centre', such as Black had here, to seek freedom by sudden thrusts in the centre. It is either ...d5 or ...e5 that Black relies on.

10 包b3 (D)

Having explored other continuations White opts for the quiet retreat. 10 包f5 does not produce much after 10...鱼xf5 11 exf5 exf4 12 罩xf4 d5 13 曹h1 罩e8 14 鱼g1 鱼d6 15 罩f3 鱼e5. White also achieves little by 10 fxe5 dxe5 11 包f5 鱼xf5 12 罩xf5 g6 13 罩f1 包d4.

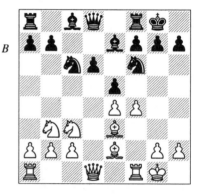

10...exf4 11 罩xf4

Black accepts the backward pawn in return for an attractive central square for his knight. The weakness of the d5-square will be protected by ...鱼e6. After 11 鱼xf4 鱼e6 Black is ready to free his game by 12...d5, which he carries out successfully after 12 曹h1 – 12...d5 13 e5 包e4 14 鱼d3 f5 15 exf6 鱼xf6 16 包xe4 dxe4 and now 17 鱼xe4 豐xd1 18 罩axd1 鱼xb2 or 17 包c5 exd3 18 包xe6 dxc2 19 豐xc2 包d4, etc. The freeing ...d5 can be stopped by 12 鱼f3 but 12...鱼c4 followed by 13...包e5 is not appealing to White.

11...♗e6 12 ♕e1

In expectation of ...d5, White vacates d1 for the rook. 12 ♘d5 would stop it as well, but then after 12...♗xd5 13 exd5 ♘e5 the formidable knight dominates the scene. The same thing happens after 12 ♘d4 ♘xd4 13 ♗xd4 ♘d7 – again Black's knight will be the czar of the centre.

12...♘d7 13 ♖f1 ♘de5 14 ♘d5

On 14 ♖d1 Tal demonstrated that 14...♘c4 15 ♗c1 ♗h4 16 g3 ♗f6 gives Black excellent piece-play, making it unlikely that the weakness of the d6-pawn will be felt.

14...♗g5 15 ♕d2 ♗xe3+ 16 ♘xe3

Now White cannot allow ...♗xd5.

16...♕h4?

In Tal's opinion this was a crucial error. 16...♕g5 is correct, as 17 ♖ad1 g6 will cover the f5-square and the subsequent 18...♖ad8 will solve in straightforward fashion the defence of the d6-pawn.

17 ♘f5 ♗xf5

Perhaps 17...♕xe4 18 ♘xd6 ♕b4 offers better chances than the dismal position to which this move leads.

18 exf5 ♕f6 19 ♖ad1 ♖ad8 20 c4 (D)

Black's sally to h4 has finished badly. The d6-pawn has been blocked as a lasting weakness, and the d5-square is in White's control.

20...♖fe8 21 ♖f2 h6 22 ♕f4 ♕g5 23 g3 f6 24 h4! ♕xf4 25 gxf4 ♘f7 26 ♗f3

The idea of exchanging queens, and especially the weakness on the light squares left by 23...f6, will give White an advantageous endgame with rooks

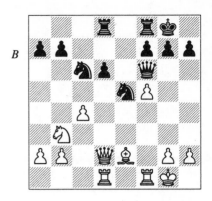

and minor-pieces. A position with so many weak light squares to attack is heaven for the f3-bishop. The d6-pawn is lastingly debilitated, while even the doubled f-pawns play a useful role.

26...♖e3 27 ♔g2 ♔f8

On 27...♘b4 White planned 28 ♖fd2 ♘xa2 29 ♘a5.

28 ♖fd2 ♖de8 29 ♔f2 h5 30 c5!

Active pieces always have at their disposal some decisive solution.

30...d5

Black makes a desperate pawn sacrifice, but 30...dxc5 lets the knight in and is equally desperate.

31 ♖xd5 ♘e7 32 ♔xe3 ♘xd5+ 33 ♔f2 ♘xf4 34 ♖d4 ♘h3+ 35 ♔g2 ♖e3 36 ♗xb7 ♘h6 37 c6 1-0

In this game and the last we saw White laying siege to the backward d-pawn and accumulating small errors and, through the skilful exchange of pieces, turning imperceptible advantages into victory. By including these games in our survey I wanted to show what small differences can separate a successful defence of a backward pawn from a lost endgame. However, in most cases the backward pawn in the Sicilian Scheveningen and Najdorf represents a tough nut that can rarely be cracked.

Spassky – Kavalek
match (game 5), Solingen 1977
Sicilian Defence

1 e4 c5 2 ♘f3 d6 3 d4 cxd4 4 ♘xd4 ♘f6 5 ♘c3 e6 6 ♗e2 ♗e7 7 0-0 0-0 8 f4 a6 9 ♗e3 ♕c7 10 ♕e1 ♘c6 11 a4

One of the innumerable move-orders in the Scheveningen. Having thwarted Black's expansion on the queenside, White transfers his queen to the kingside. From g3 it will keep an eye on the centre and support action against the black king.

11...♘xd4 12 ♗xd4 e5 13 ♗e3

The pin by 13 fxe5 dxe5 14 ♕g3 is met cold-bloodedly by 14...♖e8 15 ♔h1 ♗d8.

13...exf4 (D)

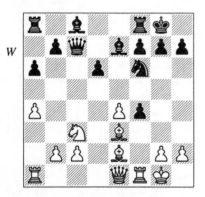

In a slightly different version from what we saw in Tal-Vogt, Black again enters a position characterized by a backward pawn. He plans to use his light-squared bishop to cover the d5-square and move the knight to e5. These are routine Scheveningen manoeuvres which will be smoothly carried out after White's reply.

14 ♖xf4

White can cause more difficulties by 14 ♗xf4 ♗e6 (14...♕b6+ 15 ♔h1 ♕xb2 cannot be recommended due to 16 ♕g3) 15 ♕g3 ♘d7 16 ♗h6. In Solozhenkin-Hjartarson, Linares open 1995, Black defended in the best manner: 16...♕c5+ 17 ♔h1 ♕e5 18 ♗f4 ♕c5 19 ♘d5 ♗xd5 20 exd5 (or 20 ♗h6 ♕d4) 20...♘e5 (by sacrificing a pawn, Black activates his forces, blocks the passed pawn and seizes the initiative) 21 ♗xe5 dxe5 22 ♕xe5 ♗d6 23 ♕f5 ♖ae8 24 ♗d3 g6 25 ♕f3 ♖e3 26 ♕f2 ♕d4 with good play for Black. It is instructive to see various versions of defence with a backward d6-pawn, including its sacrifice.

14...♗e6 15 ♕g3 ♘d7 16 ♖af1 ♘e5 17 ♖f5

Facing a tough defence which has no obvious way of being broken down, White transfers his rook to the h-file. At the moment the idea is possible because 17...♗xf5 would be punished by 18 ♘d5 ♕d8 19 exf5, but against Black's solid fortifications it looks somewhat strange.

17...♖fe8 18 ♖h5 g6 19 ♔h1 ♗f8 20 ♗h6 ♗xh6 21 ♖xh6 ♕e7 22 ♖h4 ♕f8 23 ♖hf4

The repentant rook comes back to the f-file.

23...♖ac8 24 ♖d1 ♖c6 25 ♕e3 ♖ec8 26 ♖df1 ♕d8 27 h3 ♕b6 28 ♕c1

Judging from the useless manoeuvres by the white rooks, it is obvious that the initiative has passed to Black. The centralized knight is powerful and by its very position on the board thwarts any kind of action, while the pressure on the c-file paralyses White's queenside. It goes without saying that in such a situation the backward pawn plays its quiet supportive role in good health.

28...Xxc3?!

Aware of his superiority, Black decides he can sacrifice an exchange. No doubt he can, but there was no need to hurry. 28...♛a5, for instance, would open other options. When your opponent falls into a passive position, your threats are more difficult to meet.

29 bxc3 Xxc3 30 ♛d2 ♛c5 31 ♗d3 ♛d4 32 Xf6 ♘xd3 33 Xxe6!

White's rooks have finally found a productive role. The somewhat exposed position of the black king helps White. Instead 33 cxd3 Xxd3 34 ♛f4 would have failed after 34...Xd1.

33...fxe6 34 cxd3 Xxd3??

Confused by the sudden change of events, Black commits suicide. He had to play 34...♛g7.

35 ♛g5 Xxh3+

After 35...♔g7 White forces mate by 36 ♛f4.

36 gxh3 ♛xe4+ 37 ♔h2 ♛c2+ 38 ♔g1 1-0

Time-trouble spoilt this game. Black used a routine Scheveningen device whereby he obtained a backward pawn that provided excellent support for a centralized knight. He should have triumphed instructively.

Robatsch – Fischer
Capablanca memorial, Havana 1965
Sicilian Defence

1 e4 c5 2 ♘f3 d6 3 d4 cxd4 4 ♘xd4 ♘f6 5 ♘c3 a6 6 ♗c4 e6 *(D)*

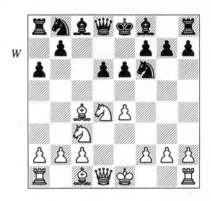

7 a3

In the Sozin Attack, White's light-squared bishop is developed on c4 in spite of Black's firm central formation. However, its aggressive posture is connected with the planned advance f4-f5, which aims to force ...e5 and thus open a gate in Black's pawn-wall on d5. 7 a3 furthers White's plan by preventing ...b5-b4, which would diminish White's pressure in the centre. Unfortunately, in the tense position that arises, each tempo has its special weight. Therefore White generally tries to do without a3, and in the 1960s explored 7 ♗b3 b5 8 f4 ♗b7 (8...b4 9 ♘a4 ♘xe4 10 0-0 highlights a serious delay in Black's development) 9 f5 e5 10 ♘de2, which succeeds in weakening Black on the d5-square, which is no longer controlled by the pawn. If he could establish a lasting dominance on d5, then the backward d6-pawn would be debilitated too, as well as the queen-side pawns. In theory this is nicely planned, but in practice it does not work, because the control of d5 can be substituted by pieces. After 10...♘bd7 11 ♗g5 ♗e7 12 ♘g3 ♖c8, 13 0-0 was refuted in R.Byrne-Fischer, Interzonal tournament, Sousse 1967 by the excellent 13...h5 14 h4 b4, when Black's counter-pressure proved irresistible. Later 13 ♗xf6 ♘xf6 14 ♕d3 ♕c7 15 0-0-0 0-0 did not endanger Black – the d5-square was controlled enough. At the critical moment there was always ...b4 spoiling the conceived plan and thus it is easy to understand why White tried 7 a3.

7...♗e7 8 0-0 0-0 9 ♗a2 b5 10 f4 ♗b7 11 f5 e5 12 ♘de2 ♘bd7

The e4-pawn is safe. 12...♘xe4 13 ♘xe4 ♗xe4 14 ♘g3 ♗b7 15 f6 ♗xf6 16 ♘h5 would give White a strong attack.

13 ♘g3 ♖c8 14 ♗e3

If White became carried away by the idea of diminishing Black's influence in the centre through exchanges after 14 ♘h5, he would be struck on the e-file: 14...♘xh5 15 ♕xh5 ♖xc3 16 bxc3 ♘f6 with excellent compensation.

14...♘b6

Having covered d5 again, Black is ready to play 15...♘c4, shutting off the a2-bishop. This forces events:

15 ♗xb6 ♕xb6+ 16 ♔h1

At first sight, it seems that White has preserved his influence on the critical d5-square. However...

16...♕e3!

This move comes all the more as a surprise because White could reply 17 ♖f3, transferring the rook to d3 in order to strengthen his claim on d5. However, after 17...♕g5 White has to count with ...♖xc3 or ...♖c5, doubling rooks on the c-file. Nevertheless, this would be consistent with White's previous play, which we cannot say of his actual choice.

17 ♘d5?! ♗xd5 18 ♗xd5 ♗d8! (D)

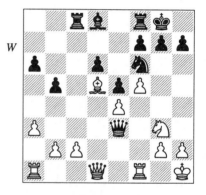

Since 19 ♗b7 can be answered by 19...♖b8, Black seizes the opportunity to activate his bishop on the g1-a7 diagonal. His plan cannot be thwarted by 19 ♖f3 ♕h6 20 ♗b3 because of 20...♘g4 21 h3 ♗b6.

19 a4 ♗b6 20 axb5

If 20 ♗b7 then 20...♖c4 follows, and 20 ♖a3 ♕g5 just adds the threat of 21...♘g4.

20...axb5 21 ♖a6 b4 22 ♘h5

Note that 22 ♖f3 fails to 22...♘g4, emphasizing the strength of the b6-bishop. The attempt to attack Black's king will not work either. White's position is already compromised.

22...♘xd5 23 ♕g4 g6 24 exd5 ♖xc2 25 fxg6 hxg6 26 ♘f6+ ♔g7 27 ♘h5+ ♔h6 28 ♘f6 ♖f2 29 ♖aa1 ♖a8 30 ♕xb4 ♔g7 31 ♕xd6 ♕e2 32 ♘e8+ ♖xe8 33 ♖fe1 ♕g4 0-1

Sax – I. Sokolov
Lugano 1987
Sicilian Defence

1 e4 c5 2 ♘f3 e6 3 d4 cxd4 4 ♘xd4 ♘f6 5 ♘c3 d6 6 ♗e3 ♘c6 7 f4 e5 *(D)*

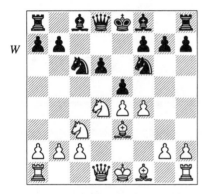

Black acts in the centre at a very early stage in order to thwart White's plan of 8 ♕f3 followed by queenside castling. He concedes a potential weakness on the d-file, relying on his pieces to generate active counterplay.

8 ♘f3

8 fxe5 is met by 8...♘g4, when the king's knight would reach its ideal position by a short-cut.

8...♘g4 9 ♗d2?!

White can afford this move because 9...♕b6 could now be parried by 10

♕e2 ♕xb2 (otherwise 0-0-0, etc.) 11 ♖b1 ♕a3 (or 11...♕xc2 12 ♕b5) 12 ♘b5.

However, 9 ♕d2 is rightly considered a better choice in spite of the exchange of the dark-squared bishop. For instance: 9...♘xe3 10 ♕xe3 exf4 11 ♕xf4 ♗e7 12 0-0-0 ♗e6 13 ♘d5 ♗xd5 14 ♖xd5 with a minimal advantage.

9...exf4 10 ♗xf4 ♗e7 11 ♕d2 ♗e6 12 0-0-0 0-0 13 ♔b1

The d6-pawn is indirectly protected by ...♘f2 and 13 ♘d5 ♗xd5 14 exd5 ♘ce5 causes no problems.

13...♖c8 14 h3 ♘ge5 15 ♘d5 ♖e8

This calm reply is possible since White is threatening nothing.

16 ♗b5 a6!

Another calm answer, which works because 17 ♗xc6 fails to 17...♘c4. The team of black knights perform a first-class job controlling all the relevant squares in the central part of the board.

17 ♗e2 ♗f8 18 ♗g5 ♕a5 19 ♕xa5 ♘xa5 20 b3 ♘ac6 21 ♗c1 ♘d7

The knight moves to c5 to exert counter-pressure on the e4-pawn. In parallel, the d6-pawn will feel better and the whole position becomes quite comfortable.

22 ♘f4 ♘c5 23 ♗d3 ♘b4 24 ♖he1 *(D)*

24 ♘d4 is better. The text-move allows Black to free his game fully.

24...♘cxd3 25 cxd3 d5 26 ♘xe6

On 26 e5 there is 26...♘c2 27 ♖e2 ♘a3+ with good play.

26...♖xe6 27 ♘d4 ♖g6 28 g4 dxe4 29 dxe4 ♖d6 30 ♗f4 ♖dd8 31 a3?

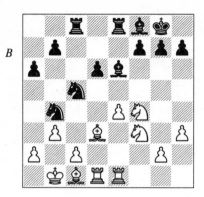

B

By playing ...d5 Black has achieved his aims and now a time-trouble error turns the battle in his favour. A quick, nervous and faulty ending follows, leading to a victory for Black...

31...♗c5 32 ♘f5 ♘d3 33 ♗d6 ♗xd6 34 ♖xd3 ♗xa3 35 ♖ed1 ♖xd3 36 ♖xd3 g6 37 ♘e3 ♖e8 38 ♘d5 ♗e7 39 ♖c3 ♗g5 40 ♖c4 b5 41 ♖d4 ♖c8 42 ♖d1 ♔g7 43 ♖f1 ♖c6 44 ♖e1 a5 45 ♔b2 ♖c5 46 ♖f1 ♗h4 47 ♖f3 ♖c6 48 ♖e3 ♗f6+ 49 ♔b1 ♗e5 50 ♖e1 a4 51 bxa4 bxa4 52 ♔a2 ♖c4 53 ♔a3 ♖d4 54 h4 ♗g3 0-1

Generally speaking, the backward pawns of the Sicilian remain hale and hearty.

Analysing patiently this series of games throwing light on backward pawns, we learn that more often than not they stand their ground. However, it is rare, but not unknown, that backward pawns can play an active role by moving forward or being transformed into a more active type of pawn. We shall now devote some attention to such occasions and such pawns.

Ivkov – Keres
Beverwijk 1964
Ruy Lopez

1 e4 e5 2 ♘f3 ♘c6 3 ♗b5 a6 4 ♗a4 ♘f6 5 0-0 ♗e7 6 ♖e1 b5 7 ♗b3 0-0 8 c3 d6 9 h3 ♘a5 10 ♗c2 c5 11 d4 ♘d7 12 ♘bd2 cxd4 13 cxd4 ♘c6 14 ♘f1?!

In later years White, not satisfied with the course of events, gave preference to 14 ♘b3 a5 15 ♗e3 a4 16 ♘bd2 exd4 17 ♘xd4 ♘xd4 18 ♗xd4 ♘e5 19 ♘f1, followed by ♘e3, with better control of the centre than in our game.

14...exd4 *(D)*

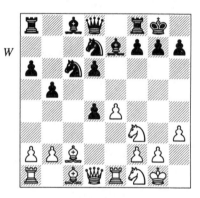

W

Keres found this idea when preparing for the Candidates tournament of 1962, and the idea became popular in the 1960s. By exchanging on d4 Black accepts a backward pawn on the d-file, but in return his dark-squared bishop gets an open diagonal and his knight obtains a fine central post at e5.

15 ♘xd4 ♘xd4 16 ♕xd4 ♘e5 17 ♕d1

Threatened by ...♗xh3, White retreats the queen. The aggressive 17 f4 achieves negative results after 17...♘c6 18 ♕f2 ♗h4 19 g3 ♗f6 20 ♖d1 ♕c7 21 ♔h2 ♗b7.

17...♗f6 18 ♘e3 ♗e6

18...♘c4 is also good, but the text-move, covering the weak d5-square, is more natural.

19 ♘d5

19 ♗b3 would be met by 19...♘c4. White instead decides to gain the bishop-pair.

19...♗xd5 20 ♕xd5?!

How deceptive chess positions can be! Taking with the queen looks natural: the d6-pawn remains backward and if White could transfer his bishop from b3 to d5, or the position could somehow be opened, then the white bishops would dominate the scene. However, looking deeper we come to the conclusion that the position does not favour White's bishops and that humble 20 exd5 was a wiser choice.

20...♖c8 21 ♗b3 ♘c4 22 ♖e2 ♖c5 23 ♕d1 d5! *(D)*

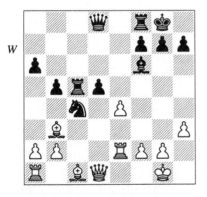

Black's excellent strategy has led to this point, when the backward pawn advances supported by active pieces. Black has seized the initiative at a moment when his opponent still has not finished his development.

24 exd5 ♖xd5 25 ♕e1 ♖d4 26 ♖b1 ♕d6 27 ♗e3 ♘xe3 28 ♖xe3 g6 29 ♖e2 ♔g7 30 ♖d1 ♖c8 31 ♖c1 ♖xc1 32 ♕xc1

White has managed to reduce material and the opposite-coloured bishops give him some hope of survival, but his game is still inferior.

32...h5 *(D)*

32...a5 would cause White more trouble.

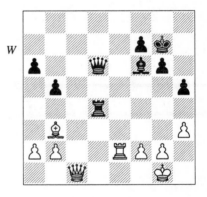

33 ♖e1 a5 34 ♖d1 a4 35 ♗c2 ♖xd1+ 36 ♗xd1?

In time-trouble, White tried to keep the material balance but misses the strong reply. 36 ♕xd1 was essential.

36...♕e6 37 ♕c2 ♕e1+ 38 ♔h2 ♗e5+ 39 g3 h4 40 ♔g2 hxg3 41 ♗f3 gxf2 42 ♕xf2 ♕c1 43 b3

Although pressed by time, Ivkov finds the 'only' moves. Unfortunately for him 43 ♗d5 does not work in view of 43...♕g5+ 44 ♔h1 ♗f6.

43...axb3 44 axb3 ♕f4! 45 ♔f1

Keres pointed out 45 ♗g4 ♕h2+ 46 ♔f1 ♕h1+ 47 ♔e2 ♕e4+, when after 48 ♔f1 ♗c3 another pawn falls. The same happens after 48 ♕e3 ♕c2+ followed by 49...♗c3.

45...♗d4 46 ♕e2 ♕f5 47 ♕e4 ♕xh3+ 48 ♔e2 ♕d7 49 b4 ♗c3 50 ♕c6 ♕d2+ 51 ♔f1 ♕e1+ 52 ♔g2 ♗d4 0-1

Keres – Flohr
Semmering/Baden 1937
Grünfeld Defence

1 d4 ♘f6 2 c4 g6 3 ♘f3 ♗g7 4 g3 c6 5 ♗g2 d5 6 cxd5 ♘xd5?! 7 0-0 0-0 8 ♘c3 ♘xc3 9 bxc3 c5 10 ♗a3 cxd4 11 ♘xd4! *(D)*

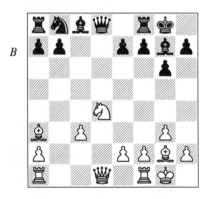

When, on move 6, Black used his knight to recapture on d5, it was both provocative and risky. The idea employed in reply by Keres is at first glance surprising and then, when we understand it fully, inspiring. White is ready to accept some damage to his pawn-structure – and a backward

pawn at c3 – in order to thwart Black's normal development. The powerful knight at d4 will see to this. The c3-pawn supports the knight, and so contributes to the general activity of White's minor pieces.

11...♕c7 12 ♕b3 ♗f6

12...♘c6 13 ♘xc6 bxc6 14 ♕a4 is quite unfavourable for Black, so to prepare ...♘d7 he must invest a tempo defending the e7-pawn.

13 ♖fd1 ♘d7 14 c4

Played in expectation of the evidently planned manoeuvre ...♘b6-c4.

14...♘c5 15 ♕b4 ♘e6

After 15...♘a6 White keeps pressure by 16 ♕b5 and squeezes his opponent by 17 c5, but the text-move worsens Black's position even more.

16 ♘b5 ♕e5 17 ♖ac1! *(D)*

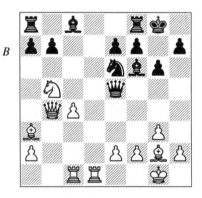

Leaving the e2-pawn *en prise*, White is well aware of the excellent compensation he would get after 17...♕xe2 18 ♘c3 ♕e5 (or 18...♗xc3 19 ♕xc3) 19 ♘d5 with a strong initiative and a large spatial superiority.

17...♖d8 18 ♖d5 ♖xd5

Again 18...♛xe2 19 ♘c3 ♝xc3 20 ♛xc3 hardly comes into consideration. Black is constrained to exchange on d5, which further improves White's pawn.

19 cxd5 a6

This is where Black saw his chance: 20 dxe6 ♛xb5 or 20 ♘c3 ♘d4 awakens hope. But the opened c-file can now be used to break Black's resistance.

20 ♘a7! ♘d4 21 ♖xc8+ ♖xc8 22 ♘xc8 ♛xe2 23 h4 ♘f5 24 ♛e4 1-0

The 'backward' c3-pawn played the key role in Keres's deep strategic plan.

Kupreichik – Kasparov

USSR Team Ch, Kislovodsk 1982
Sicilian Defence

1 e4 c5 2 ♘f3 e6 3 d4 cxd4 4 ♘xd4 ♘c6 5 ♘c3 d6 6 ♝e2 ♘f6 7 ♝e3 ♝e7 8 f4 0-0 9 ♛d2 e5

White has just prepared to castle queenside, but before he can do so, Black strikes in the centre, forcing the knight to retreat.

10 ♘f3

10 ♘xc6 bxc6 11 0-0-0 would have no sense now, because the c6-pawn covers the critical d5-square, while the semi-open b-file can be used for counter-attack. 10 ♘f5 ♝xf5 11 exf5 exf4 12 ♝xf4 d5 is not appealing either. On 10 ♘b3 Black first plays 10...a5, provoking the weakening 11 a4, when the routine 11...♝e6, helped by the pair of knights, covers the sensitive central points. Depending on what White does, Black has a wide range of good options, which make the pressure on d6 innocuous.

10...♘g4 11 f5? *(D)*

11 ♘d5 could not satisfy his ambitions because 11...♘xe3 12 ♛xe3 exf4 13 ♛xf4 ♝e6 simplifies things.

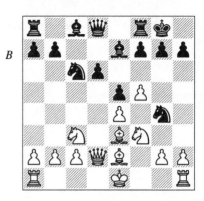

B

This is the position White was aiming for. Here we have the classical case of a backward pawn and a weak square in front of it, while the e6-square, which belongs traditionally to the queen's bishop, is denied to Black. However, despite appearances there is a flaw in White's reasoning...

11...♘b4!

A brutal reply: Black denies the c3-knight the d5-square and prepares the freeing central thrust 12...d5, which follows whatever White does.

12 ♝d3

After 12 0-0-0, 12...d5 is possible because 13 exd5 ♝xf5 frees the light-squared bishop, and 13 a3 does not work due to 13...♘xe3 14 ♛xe3 d4 15 ♛f2 ♛c7. 12 ♝g1 d5 leads to the same disagreeable results.

12...d5 13 ♘xd5

After 13 exd5 ♘xd3+ White has to play 14 cxd3 because 14 ♛xd3? ♝xf5 is fatal.

13...♘xd5 14 exd5 e4! *(D)*

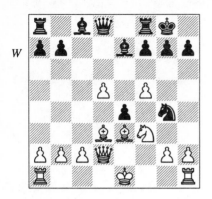

We see the final consequences of Black's vehement counter-attack. The white king has stayed in the centre too long and now White will have to pay a high material price in order to castle.

15 ♗xe4 ♖e8

The hidden decisive move.

16 0-0-0 *(D)*

16 0-0 loses to 16...♗d6 17 h3 ♘xe3 18 ♕xe3 ♗xf5 19 ♘d2 ♕e7, whereas long castling, as we shall see, fails to 16...♗f6. 16 h3 would be a solution if it were not for 16...♗h4+.

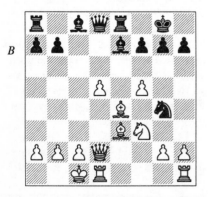

16...♗f6 17 ♗g5

After 17 ♕d3 ♘xe3 18 ♕xe3 ♗xf5 19 ♘d2 ♗g5 White's king is again in the wrong place. The text-move, of course, is resignation.

17...♖xe4 18 h3 ♘e5 19 ♗xf6 ♕xf6 20 ♘xe5 ♕xe5 21 g4 ♗d7 22 ♖he1 ♖e8 23 ♖xe4 ♕xe4 24 ♕a5 ♕e3+ 25 ♔b1 ♕xh3 26 ♕xa7 ♕xg4 27 ♖c1 ♗xf5 28 ♕xb7 h5 29 b3 ♕d4 30 a4 ♕c3 0-1

Beware of apparently innocuous backward pawns. If they can advance, and if their advance is supported by pieces, in general they represent a grave danger. That the case is rare only adds to the warning.

Some General Observations

We have analysed a series of illustrative games in order to throw light on backward pawns. Now, I hope, we can see objectively their notorious drawbacks as well as their virtues.

The problems backward pawns cause are in general due to several factors. In the first place it is their position on the board. We find them on their second or third ranks. Apart from exceptional cases, they are stuck there, where they are regularly exposed to all kind of pressures. There is often pressure from enemy major pieces on the file, frequently enhanced by active minor pieces. Their very place on the board suggests that the attacker commands a spatial advantage and freedom to manoeuvre. It suggests also the necessity of defence, which is confined to the last two ranks and, therefore, unavoidably passive. If a backward pawn appears on its second rank, it is mostly a desperate case in which not only the pawn's position tells against it, but also very notably the lack of co-ordination of the defensive forces. There is simply not enough space to organize an effective defence.

Things improve dramatically in the case of backward pawns on their third rank. Firstly, the defender is more capable of resisting, as the coordination behind the pawn can be significantly better. Moreover, being on its third rank, the pawn controls some central squares, denying them to enemy pieces and supporting its own centralized minor pieces, which in general have a significant influence on the course of the game. In a variety of modern variations, such as the King's Indian Defence, the Keres variation of the Chigorin Ruy Lopez, and several modern lines of the Sicilian, such pawns play a positive role in full harmony with other pieces, as we could verify during our analysis. Naturally, they always remain potentially weak, but as long as there is active play, as a rule, their drawbacks remain concealed. Paraphrasing Alexander Alekhine, where there is activity all the positional weaknesses are suspended. It is owing to the capability of counterpressure and counterplay that backward pawns can play their part in the general strategic plan and, as a rule, fare well in spite of their shortcomings.

In the evaluation of backward pawns, much depends on that quality: either they are sitting targets, tying other pieces to their defence, or by their central position and influence they support active piece-play. To the extent that they can do that, their role in the game is positive.

Together with a backward pawn, there comes a weakened square in front of it, which the enemy pieces can often exploit to emphasize their spatial advantage and strengthen their pressure. When that square is left at the mercy of the opponent's pieces, the pawn itself is, as a rule, in grave danger. When the square is well controlled by pieces, the pawn is, again as a rule, safe and healthy. It is not by chance that in the Scheveningen Sicilian or the Fianchetto variation of the King's Indian, for example, it is so difficult to threaten the d6-pawn: the square in front of it is under control. The pawn and square share a common destiny and it is important to stay aware of it.

To sum up our experience most concisely, we could say that backward pawns on their second rank are, as a rule, the source of fatal passivity. We could also affirm that backward pawns on their third rank are in general sounder, but mostly remain exposed and shaky, unless they participate in the general strategic plan in harmony with minor pieces and unless the square in front of them is under watchful control.

6 Pawn-Chains

In our exploration of pawn-structures we have reached an important chapter. Here we shall discuss the pawn-chain, a series of pawns on a diagonal.

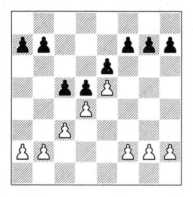

The diagram represents the well-known chain characterizing the Advance Variation of the French Defence, which was extensively studied and discussed by Aron Nimzowitsch, to whom we owe the first systematic observations about the pawn-chain. For the time being we shall conclude just what we see in the diagram. The pawn-chain divides the board in two. It starts at the base and ends as a wedge in enemy territory.

The central wedge marks out a spatial advantage, securing greater manoeuvring space and restricting the opponent's normal development. The basic questions facing both sides are how to make use of the spatial advantage and how to fight against the pawn-chain. Since, as we shall see, the pawn-chain is not a peculiarity of the French Defence, but arises in other systems as well (notably the King's Indian Defence), the answers will have a wider significance in opening theory.

Let us first acquire some practical knowledge on the subject.

Nimzowitsch – Salwe
Karlsbad 1911
French Defence

1 e4 e6 2 d4 d5 3 e5 c5 4 c3

And after a couple of moves there it is – a pawn-chain with its base on b2 and its wedge on e5. It is a position Nimzowitsch thought about, wrote about and played with relish. Let us first consider its basic features.

White's third move blocked the centre, seizing space on the kingside and directing his thoughts towards an initiative on that wing. Black reacted naturally with pressure on d4, the support for the wedge, which was reinforced by c3. We learnt from Nimzowitsch that in most cases it is on the support for the wedge we put pressure, not on the wedge itself. Salwe's moves follow his advice...

4...♘c6 5 ♘f3 ♕b6 6 ♗d3 ♗d7?!

Experience confirmed the first impression left by this game that the text-move is premature. Correct is 6...cxd4 7 cxd4 ♗d7, exposing the d4-pawn to strong pressure.

7 dxc5 ♗xc5 8 0-0 f6? *(D)*

Now that the wedge e5 has lost its support, Salwe thought it was the proper time to eliminate the blockade and free his central pawns. However, the timing was bad. 8...a5 is in order, to thwart b4; if White achieves this advance, he is able to build his influence in the centre to the maximum.

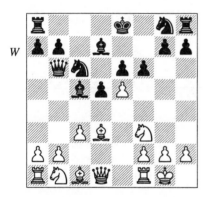

9 b4 ♗e7 10 ♗f4 fxe5 11 ♘xe5 ♘xe5 12 ♗xe5 ♘f6

12...♗f6 does not work owing to 13 ♕h5+ g6 14 ♗xg6+ hxg6 15 ♕xg6+ ♔e7 16 ♗xf6+, etc.

13 ♘d2

The inconsistent 13 ♕c2 0-0 14 ♗xf6 ♗xf6 15 ♗xh7+ wins material, but completely cedes the initiative to Black. The text-move introduces one of Nimzowitsch's favourite subjects: when the pawn-chain is broken, the

control of the centre can be held only by pieces. The knight hurries to f3 to fulfil the idea.

13...0-0 14 ♘f3 ♗d6

The attempt to exchange the light-squared bishops would accentuate the weakness of the e6-pawn. For instance: 14...♗b5 15 ♗d4 ♕a6 16 ♗xb5 ♕xb5 17 ♘g5.

15 ♕e2

If 15 ♗d4, then 15...♕c7 16 ♕e2 ♘g4 17 h3 e5 and Black is free. It is crucial to keep the lid on the central pawns.

15...♖ac8

In case of 15...♗xe5 16 ♘xe5 ♖ac8 there is the strong 17 c4.

16 ♗d4 ♕c7 17 ♘e5! *(D)*

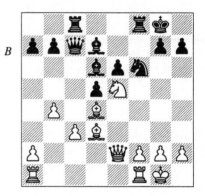

The blockade has been realized. Executed by pieces, it demonstrates some advantages in comparison with the pawn blockade carried out in the first moves of the game. The central pawn-chain squeezes Black, but the blockaders in the centre increase that feeling. The centralized pieces are mighty and they act on both wings, while the blockaded pawns have become weaker, more exposed to attack. On the basis of such positions Nimzowitsch came to one of his great truths: it is more valuable to control the centre with pieces than to occupy it by pawns. It was on that simple truth that several important theoretical openings were founded, the Nimzo-Indian Defence in the first place.

17...♗e8 18 ♖ae1 ♗xe5 19 ♗xe5 ♕c6 20 ♗d4 ♗d7

The bishop returns to its passive duty because the e6-pawn is backward and vulnerable.

21 ♕c2 ♖f7 22 ♖e3 b6 23 ♖g3 ♔h8 24 ♗xh7! *(D)*

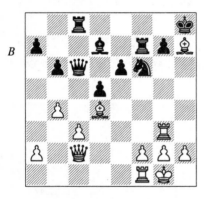

Apart from keeping Black's central pawns subdued, White's centralized minor pieces exert powerful pressure on the black kingside, which starts to crumble.

24...e5

24...♘xh7 loses to 25 ♕g6, which means that the pawn is gone.

25 ♗g6 ♖e7 26 ♖e1 ♕d6 27 ♗e3 d4 28 ♗g5 ♖xc3 29 ♖xc3 dxc3 30

♕xc3 ♔g8 31 a3 ♔f8 32 ♗h4 ♗e8 33 ♗f5 ♕d4 34 ♕xd4 exd4 35 ♖xe7 ♔xe7 36 ♗d3 ♔d6 37 ♗xf6 gxf6 38 h4 1-0

An important lesson to draw from this game: the blockade by pawns, if broken, can be turned into an even stronger blockade by pieces. Nimzowitsch showed very convincingly how effective it could be.

The question, however, remains: would it be better to attack the wedge of the pawn-chain at once? The following game gives some qualified answers.

Nimzowitsch – Levenfish
Karlsbad 1911
French Defence

1 e4 e6 2 d4 d5 3 e5 c5 4 c3 ♘c6 5 ♘f3 f6?

This early straightforward attempt to attack the pawn-wedge itself will fail. The reasons are instructive.

6 ♗b5 ♗d7 7 0-0 ♕b6

Note in passing that 7...♘xe5 does not work due to 8 ♘xe5 ♗xb5 9 ♕h5+, leaving Black without a good reply.

8 ♗xc6 bxc6 9 exf6 ♘xf6 10 ♘e5 ♗d6 11 dxc5 ♗xc5 12 ♗g5 *(D)*

The game reminds us of what we saw in the previous encounter. White has succeeded in carrying out the blockade in the centre in much the same way. His centralized knight is powerful, while the black central pawns have become sensitive. The early attack on the wedge has backfired. It was not prepared, and when the crucial piece

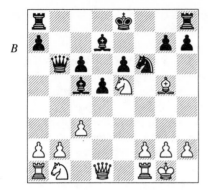

B

exercising pressure on e5, the c6-knight, was exchanged, the failure became obvious. It is equally instructive to watch how Nimzowitsch proceeds to make use of his advantage.

12...♕d8

After 12...♕xb2 13 ♘d2, White's superior development gives him excellent compensation.

13 ♗xf6 ♕xf6 14 ♕h5+ g6 15 ♕e2 ♖d8 16 ♘d2 0-0 17 ♖ae1 ♖fe8

Burdened by his passive d7-bishop and backward pawn, Black is lacking some tempi to free himself. The dominant knight on e5 has a suffocating effect on Black's position.

18 ♔h1 ♗d6 19 f4 c5 20 c4 ♗f8

In order to get some counterplay, Black decides to sacrifice a pawn.

21 cxd5 ♗c8

21...exd5, of course, loses to 22 ♘xd7.

22 ♘e4 ♕g7 23 dxe6

23 d6 is also strong.

23...♗xe6 24 ♕a6 ♔h8 25 ♖d1 ♗g8 26 b3 ♖d4 27 ♖xd4 cxd4 28 ♕a5

Played to prevent ...♖d8.

28...♖c8 29 ♖d1 ♖c2 30 h3 ♕b7 31 ♖xd4 ♗c5 32 ♕d8!

In trying to seize the initiative by giving up material, Black has seriously weakened his kingside and the reaction hits him at once.

32...♗e7

After 32...♗xd4 33 ♕xd4 ♕g7 34 ♘d6 Black cannot parry the threatened ♘e8.

33 ♕d7 ♕a6 34 ♖d3 ♗f8 35 ♘f7+ ♗xf7

Or 35...♔g7 36 ♕d4+, etc.

36 ♕xf7 ♖c8 37 ♖d7 1-0

This game and the previous one were lost after notorious mistakes, but do not underrate these pioneer attempts. They remain valuable pedagogical material due to the clear sequence of thoughts displayed by Nimzowitsch.

Bogoljubow – Alekhine
Bad Nauheim 1937
French Defence

1 d4 e6 2 e4 d5 3 ♘c3 ♗b4 4 e5 c5 5 dxc5

Who could tell the reasons which prompted Bogoljubow to choose this rare continuation? Perhaps he wanted to entice Black into 5...d4 6 a3 ♗a5 7 b4 dxc3 8 bxa5 ♕xd1+ 9 ♔xd1, a continuation that is favourable to White. Whatever his secret motives, the idea is contrary to the stability of the pawn-chain: the wedge on e5 loses its support.

5...♘c6

Since White can neutralize the influence of this knight on the centre by pinning it, it was wiser to wait with the development of the b8-knight, giving preference to 5...♕c7 6 ♘f3 ♘e7 7 ♗d3 ♘d7, followed by ...♘xc5, with a balanced position.

6 ♘f3 f6? *(D)*

By taking on c5 White weakened his wedge, but not so much as to allow Black to undermine it successfully. It is true that in case of 6...d4 there is again 7 a3 ♗a5 8 b4 when 8...♘xb4 9 axb4 ♗xb4 is refuted by 10 ♗b5+ ♗d7 11 0-0 ♗xc3 12 ♖b1. The best, therefore, was simply to develop by 6...♘ge7.

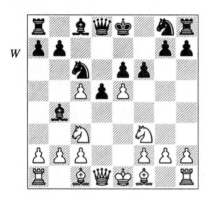

7 ♗b5

The point e5 must be upheld at all costs.

7...♗xc5 8 0-0 ♗d7 9 ♖e1

Played not only in defence of the e5-pawn, but also to be able to meet 9...f5 by 10 ♘xd5 exd5 11 e6 (and if 11...♗c8, then 12 ♘e5).

9...fxe5 10 ♘xe5 ♘xe5 11 ♖xe5 ♗xb5 12 ♘xb5 ♘f6 13 ♖xe6+ ♔f7

Black expected 14 ♖e2, in reply to which he intended 14...♕b6, when his initiative would compensate for the

pawn. However, this is not White's only option.

14 ♖xf6+! gxf6

14...♔xf6 15 ♕h5 h6 16 ♗f4 quickly introduces White's forces into play.

15 ♕h5+ ♔g8 16 ♗h6 ♕d7 17 ♘c7!

Protected by the possibility of ♕g4+, the knight starts its little walk.

17...♕f7

On 17...♖d8 White planned 18 ♖e1.

18 ♕h3 ♖b8 19 ♖e1 ♖d8 20 ♘xd5

The desperate position of the naked king admits little tactical tricks.

20...♖xd5 21 ♕g4+ ♖g5 22 ♕c8+ ♗f8 23 ♗xf8 h5 24 f4 ♔h7 1-0

Black overstepped the time-limit in a lost position.

Again there is an unequivocal lesson: breaking the pawn-chain brings little solace if your opponent succeeds in controlling the same squares with active pieces.

Smyslov – Hollis
Hastings 1962/3
French Defence

1 e4 e6 2 d4 d5 3 ♘c3 ♗b4 4 e5 c5 5 a3 ♗xc3+ 6 bxc3 ♘c6 7 ♘f3 ♕a5 8 ♕d2 ♕a4?

With this early sally by his queen Black has blocked the a3-pawn, preventing White's natural development with a4 followed by ♗a3. At the same time he has kept pressure on the pawn-chain and probably intended ...b6 followed by ...♗a6.

9 dxc5! *(D)*

Quite unconventional and strong. Again White voluntarily weakens his

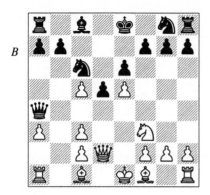

pawn-chain, but in different circumstances. Although White's e5-pawn has lost its support, and three exposed pawns have appeared on the c-file, Smyslov was correct in his judgement. What he had in mind is demonstrated clearly by the further course of the game.

9...♘ge7 10 ♗d3 0-0

If Black sought to undermine the wedge by 10...f6 at once, then 11 exf6 gxf6 12 ♕h6 is not easy to counter: 12...♔f7 loses to 13 ♕h5+ ♔g8 14 ♕e8+ ♔g7 15 ♗h6+.

11 0-0 f6 12 ♖e1 *(D)*

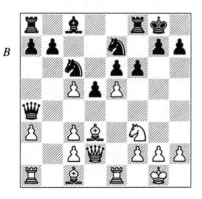

12...fxe5

If Black increases his pressure on the e5-pawn by 12...♘g6, then after 13 exf6, 13...♖xf6 14 c4 undermines Black – the doubled pawns are not useless after all, while 13...gxf6 is met by 14 ♕h6 ♘ce7 15 ♖b1, threatening ♖b4 and the rook enters the attack.

13 ♘xe5 ♕h4

Now 13...♘xe5 14 ♖xe5 ♘c6 would finally make ...e5 possible, but 15 ♖h5 all of a sudden smells the weakness of the kingside. Hence the text-move.

14 ♘f3 ♕h5 15 ♕g5 ♕f7 16 ♗e3 h6 17 ♕g3 *(D)*

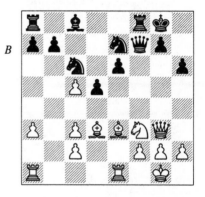

Black's central pawns have been blocked by skilled manoeuvres. White threatens ♗d4 with a full blockade; Black has been outplayed. He continued...

17...♘f5 18 ♗xf5 exf5 19 ♗f4 ♗e6 20 ♗xh6

...and resigned after a couple of useless moves.

Our instinctive reaction to 9 dxc5 may have been negative, but objective analysis wipes it out: the shattered pawns on the c-file were not a burden to White. On the contrary, at a crucial point the undermining move c4 was the key to success, while at another point the open fourth rank would have made possible the important manoeuvre ♖b4-g4. The process of the blockade leans on these side-options; without them it would not succeed.

We have so far seen the fight against the pawn-chain in its negative aspect. How to do the job correctly, then? We shall seek an answer in the following games.

Bondarevsky – Botvinnik
*'Absolute' USSR Ch,
Leningrad/Moscow 1941*
French Defence

1 e4 e6 2 d4 d5 3 e5 c5 4 ♘f3 ♘c6 5 ♗d3?! *(D)*

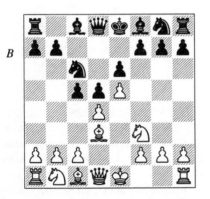

In his detailed and careful examination of all the possible consequences of the French pawn-chain, Nimzowitsch came up with the idea shown in the diagram. White does not take on

c5 and does not defend the d4-pawn. In order to save time he is ready to risk weakening his central chain – a daring idea.

5...cxd4 6 0-0 ♗c5

Logical and strong. Black develops and defends the pawn.

7 a3?

We shall see that in the further course of the game White gave up his initial idea of the pawn advance b4-b5, so the text-move remains in the air, superfluous. The immediate 7 ♘bd2 is better, as is 7 ♗f4, consistently fortifying the e5-pawn.

7...♘ge7 8 ♘bd2 ♘g6 9 ♘b3 ♗b6 10 ♖e1 ♗d7 11 g3

White has in mind taking on g6 and then on d4, when he cannot allow ...♕h4.

11...f6

Black finally decides that the time has come to break the wedge. Remember the basic lesson: when fighting against the pawn-chain, one first attacks the base, d4 in our case, and then attacks against the wedge itself.

12 ♗xg6+ hxg6 13 ♕d3

In order to diminish the pressure on e5 White had to cede his bishop-pair. It happens, however, that the intended capture on d4 does not work. On 13 ♘bxd4 commentators give two good replies: 13...♗xd4 14 ♘xd4 ♘xe5 15 f4 ♘c6 16 ♘xe6 ♗xe6 17 ♖xe6+ ♔f7 and 13...♘xd4 14 ♘xd4 fxe5 15 ♖xe5 ♕f6 16 f4 g5 17 c3 0-0-0 18 ♖xg5 ♖h3.

13...♔f7 14 h4 ♕g8!! *(D)*

Deep and beautiful! By moving his queen to h7 and threatening to open

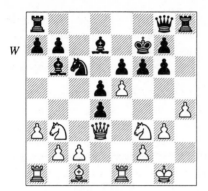

the h-file, Black will force his opponent to make a concession in the centre. If White had pinned his hopes on 15 ♗f4, propping up the centre, he must now have understood it was too late. After 15...♕h7 16 ♘bxd4 ♘xd4 17 ♘xd4 there follows 17...g5.

15 ♗d2 ♕h7 16 ♗b4 g5 17 ♕xh7 ♖xh7 18 exf6

If 18 hxg5, then 18...fxe5 19 ♘xe5+ ♘xe5 20 ♖xe5 ♗c7 with similar consequences.

18...gxf6 19 hxg5 e5!

The job has been completed. The text-move embodies one of the fundamental truths preached by Nimzowitsch. He used to say that the central pawns have a lust to expand, and that the pawn-chain thwarts it, but when it gets broken, the pawn-mass breaks loose and the pent-up energy is released. When such pawns start moving, the game is usually decided. What follows justifies Nimzowitsch fully.

20 gxf6 ♔xf6 21 ♗d6 ♖e8 22 ♘h4 ♖g8 23 ♔h2 ♗f5 24 ♖e2 d3 25 ♖d2

There is no hope in 25 cxd3 ♗xd3 26 ♖d2 ♗c4 27 ♘c1 ♘d4.

25...dxc2 26 f4 ♗e3 27 ♗xe5+ ♘xe5 28 fxe5+ ♔e7 29 ♖f1

The threat was ...♖xh4 followed by ...♗f4+.

29...c1♕ 0-1

Played with impressive consistency from the very beginning, Botvinnik's win remains one of the greatest lessons on pawn-chains in the whole of chess literature.

Timman – Korchnoi
match (game 3), Leeuwarden 1976
French Defence

1 e4 e6 2 d4 d5 3 ♘c3 ♗b4 4 e5 c5 5 a3 ♗xc3+ 6 bxc3 ♘e7 7 ♘f3 ♘bc6 8 a4

All is clear and consistent in the Winawer Variation of the French Defence. White is ready to accept lasting damage to his pawn-formation in return for a strengthened pawn-chain in the centre.

8...♕a5 9 ♗d2

Having played a4, 9 ♕d2 seems more consequential, as this would preserve the possibility of developing the dark-squared bishop on its natural a3-f8 diagonal. However, 9 ♕d2 has not fulfilled the expectations and, besides, d2 is meant as a temporary residence for the bishop in the hope it will be able to return to a3 in favourable circumstances.

9...♗d7 10 ♗e2

10 c4 would be a sort of hara-kiri leading after 10...♕c7 11 cxd5 exd5 12 dxc5 0-0 to a shattered pawn-centre. According to some analysts, the provocative 10 ♗b5 or 10 g3 0-0-0 11

♗h3, in expectation of a later ...f6, should be considered.

10...f6! *(D)*

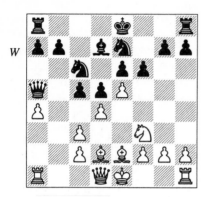

The most energetic. Before castling, Black undermines the pawn-centre by ...c5 and ...f6. Korchnoi's recipe looks healthy and challenging.

11 c4

Perhaps White adopted this risky move on the general consideration that his bishops needed more open space. 11 ♖b1 seems to me more cautious.

11...♕c7 12 cxd5 ♘xd5 13 c4?!

In Spassky-Korchnoi, Candidates match (game 4), Belgrade 1977, Spassky posed more difficulties by deviating on the previous move with the less obliging 12 exf6 gxf6 13 cxd5 ♘xd5 14 c3.

13...♘de7 14 exf6 gxf6 15 dxc5 0-0-0 16 ♗c3 e5

At the cost of an unimportant pawn Black has managed to shatter the stifling pawn-chain. It is worth noticing that White's bishop-pair did not get the desired open spaces. While limited by the enemy pawn-structure, the

bishops remain innocuous. At the same time, Black has obtained two files on which he can exert pressure: on the g-file by ...♖g8, and on the d-file by ...♘f5-d4.

17 ♕d6 ♘f5

Were it not for this effective response, the course of the game would change. However, it is a neat reply. As 18 ♕xf6 ♖df8 gives Black a powerful initiative, he is happy to enter the endgame, in which his knights will be superior to the white bishop-pair.

18 ♕xc7+ ♔xc7 19 0-0 ♘fd4 20 ♘xd4 ♘xd4 21 ♗d1

The best chance. On d1, the bishop is passive, but it limits the knight. After 21 ♗xd4 exd4 22 ♗d3 ♖he8 the passed pawn will be ready for its traditionally destructive role.

21...♔c6 22 ♗xd4?

This change of mind has no justification. 22 f4 ♔xc5 23 fxe5 fxe5 24 ♖e1, enhancing the scope of the bishops, looks solid.

22...exd4 23 ♗f3+ ♔xc5 24 ♗xb7 ♗f5

This is all that Black could hope for. The well-supported passed pawn is in its element.

25 ♗f3 ♖he8 26 ♖a2 ♖b8 27 ♖d2 ♖b1

White is forced into some unnatural manoeuvring, as an exchange of rooks will open the way to the d4-pawn. The fight is practically over.

28 g4 ♖ee1 29 ♖xe1 ♖xe1+ 30 ♔g2 ♗e4 31 ♗xe4 ♖xe4 32 ♔f3 ♖e5 33 h4 ♔xc4 34 ♖c2+ ♔b3 35 ♖c7 d3 36 ♖xh7?! ♖d5 37 ♖b7+ ♔c2 38 ♖c7+ ♔b1 39 ♖b7+ ♔a1 40 ♖b5 ♖d8 0-1

Padevsky – Berthold
Bulgaria – East Germany 1958
French Defence

1 e4 e6 2 d4 d5 3 ♘c3 ♗b4 4 e5 c5 5 a3 ♗xc3+ 6 bxc3 ♘e7 7 ♕g4 ♕c7 8 ♕xg7 ♖g8 9 ♕xh7 cxd4 10 ♘e2 ♘bc6 11 f4 ♗d7 12 ♕d3 dxc3 *(D)*

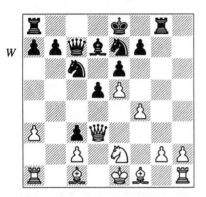

This is an important position in a long theoretical line. White has spent several tempi with his queen but has the possibility of winning a pawn. White's neglect of his development is obvious from a glance at the diagram. White's king will have to stay in the centre for a while, disrupting the normal coordination of his pieces. This fact exposes White's position to certain risks. It is not by chance that White failed to produce a secure road to an advantage after years of searching. It induces us to believe the whole line is quite risky in most of the continuations tried in recent decades.

13 ♗e3?!

13 ♘xc3 a6 followed by ...♘a5 will just broaden Black's counterchances, while 13 ♕xc3 does little for White's development. The possibility chosen by Padevsky is not a happy solution either...

13...♘f5 14 ♘d4? ♘fxd4 15 ♗xd4 0-0-0 16 g3 *(D)*

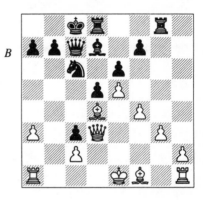

An unusual position has arisen, characterized by two crossing pawn-chains. White has just prepared to develop his bishop and castle, finishing his development in satisfactory fashion. Eventually, his passed pawn on the h-file should secure a win in any endgame. It seems that nothing could change this inevitable process. What follows must have been quite shocking for White...

16...f6!

A move of brutal strength. White's king is still on e1 and between the king and black pieces there is only the pawn-chain. Black attacks the wedge of the chain and we soon understand that the blockade cannot be sustained.

17 exf6

17 ♕e3, trying to keep the position closed, is met by 17...fxe5 18 ♗xe5

♘xe5 19 ♕xe5 ♕xe5+ 20 fxe5 ♖g5, while 17 ♕xc3 ♘xd4 18 ♕xd4 fxe5 19 ♕xe5 ♕xc2 is not appealing either.

17...e5!

Whenever the blockade is broken, the pawns advance menacingly.

18 fxe5

18 ♗xe5 looks even worse, while 18 f7 ♖gf8 does not change things.

18...♖g4 19 ♗e3 ♕xe5 20 ♗h3 ♖e4 21 ♗xd7+ ♖xd7 22 ♔f2 ♕xf6+ 23 ♔g2 ♘e5 0-1

Violent breakthroughs are not rare in grandmaster practice. The blocked pawns erupt with tremendous power, but not without some specific cause behind them. In our case it was White's failure to finish his development and coordinate his forces. When the central thrust happened, there was nobody to defend the king that was still in the middle of the board.

Reshevsky – Vaganian
Skopje 1976
French Defence

1 e4 e6 2 d4 d5 3 ♘d2 ♘f6 4 e5 ♘fd7 5 f4 c5 6 c3 ♘c6 7 ♘df3 ♕a5

White has strengthened his pawn-wedge by f4, obtaining a spatial advantage. Exploring this continuation, Black used various approaches and for a short period of time the text-move was relatively popular. The intention is obvious: by pinning the c3-pawn Black intensifies the pressure on the d4-pawn.

8 ♔f2 *(D)*

This move was much in vogue in the 1970s, but the simple 8 dxc5 ♕xc5

9 ♗d3 ♗e7 10 ♘e2 ♕b6 11 ♘ed4 gives White the advantage without the need for any extraordinary measures.

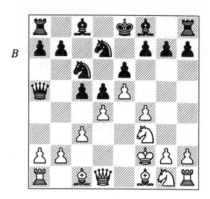

8...♗e7

Two approaches to the problems of our position characterized the games in which the variation was applied: 8...b5, with the idea of a later ...b4, attacking the support for the pawn-centre, and 8...f6, opening the f-file in order to make use of the cumbersome position of the white king. We shall analyse the former possibility later in this chapter in the game Matanović-Kovačević. In the current game, Vaganian chooses the latter, only somewhat veiled by his move-order. On 8...f6 White usually continued 9 g3 ♗e7 10 ♔g2, finding a secure refuge for his king in time. Reshevsky should have followed the prevailing cautious wisdom, but instead he decided for the seemingly logical quick development of his kingside.

9 ♗d3?! ♕b6 10 ♘e2 f6

All of a sudden, the wedge is shaky under full pressure. Making use of the pin, Black threatens to grab a pawn. In retrospect, White must have wished that he had protected his king in time.

11 exf6

After 11 ♔g3, 11...g5 opens the position unpleasantly.

11...♗xf6 12 ♔g3

This is how Reshevsky hoped to solve his difficulties.

12...cxd4 13 cxd4 0-0 14 ♖e1? *(D)*

White is still unaware how vulnerable his king really is. He should have played 14 h3, seeking some sanctuary for his king. There now comes a bolt out of the blue:

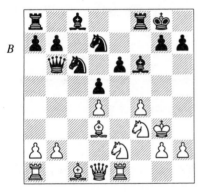

14...e5!

When the chain is broken, many a time pawns step forward with destructive energy. The badly protected white king becomes the target.

15 fxe5 ♘dxe5 16 dxe5 ♗h4+!

We must admit that it is quite easy to miss this crushing check.

17 ♔xh4 ♖xf3!

Another brutal stroke leaving White but one temporary exit. The danger lurks from f2, b4 and d8 and White

cannot parry the numerous enemy threats.

18 ♖f1

18 gxf3 loses to 18...♕f2+, and after 18 g3 Black wins by 18...♕d8+ 19 ♗g5 ♕d7.

18...♕b4+ 19 ♗f4 ♕e7+ 20 ♗g5 ♕e6 21 ♗f5 ♖xf5 22 ♘f4 ♕xe5 23 ♕g4 ♖f7 24 ♕h5 ♘e7 25 g4 ♘g6+ 26 ♔g3 ♗d7 27 ♖ae1 ♕d6 28 ♗h6 ♖af8 0-1

Not a stone has been left of the mighty pawn rampart in the centre!

Reshevsky – Lombardy
USA Ch, Oberlin 1975
Queen's Gambit

1 ♘f3 ♘f6 2 c4 e6 3 ♘c3 d5 4 d4 ♗e7 5 ♗g5 0-0 6 ♖c1 c6 7 e3 ♘bd7 8 ♗d3 a6

Black intends ...dxc4 followed by ...b5 and quick queenside expansion. White's next move prevents this.

9 c5 *(D)*

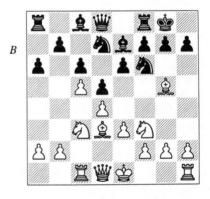

White builds a pawn-chain with its wedge on c5, seizing space on the queenside. Black is squeezed into his back two ranks and cannot wait passively: he must attack the chain. The only question is how to do so.

9...e5!

For a long time, following old analysis by Ståhlberg, Black thought that the text-move, undermining the chain by attacking the support for the wedge, did not work due to 10 ♗xf6 ♗xf6 11 dxe5 ♘xe5 12 ♘xe5 ♗xe5 13 ♗xh7+ winning a pawn. Impressed by the 'obvious', Black turned to 9...b6, attacking the wedge itself. After 10 cxb6, 10...♕xb6 11 0-0 ♕xb2 12 ♘a4 ♕b7 13 ♘e5 c5 14 ♘xd7 ♗xd7 15 ♘xc5 ♗xc5 16 ♗xf6 gxf6 17 ♕g4+ ♔h8 18 ♕h4 f5 19 ♕f6+ ♔g8 20 dxc5 left Black in serious trouble in Hort-Portisch, Madrid 1973. In Portisch-Petrosian, Candidates match (game 10), Palma de Mallorca 1974, probably remembering his unpleasant experience in Madrid, Portisch went in for the same continuation as White. On that occasion Petrosian tried to improve on Hort's play by 10...c5 11 0-0 c4 12 ♗c2 ♘xb6, but White seized the initiative by 13 ♘e5 ♗b7 14 f4 ♖b8 15 f5. Although Petrosian's play could be improved further, Black lost interest in the whole discussion until William Lombardy turned his attention to it in 1974...

10 dxe5

In Visier-Lombardy, Olympiad, Nice 1974, White followed Ståhlberg's advice, but after 10 ♗xf6 ♗xf6 11 dxe5 ♗e7 12 ♕c2 h6 13 ♘a4 ♕a5+ 14 ♔e2 ♕c7 15 ♕c3 ♖e8 16 ♖he1 ♗f8 17 ♔f1 ♘xe5 the game was level. Attacking

the support for the wedge again proved healthier than attacking the wedge itself.

10...♘e8 11 ♗f4 ♘xc5 12 ♗b1 ♗g4 *(D)*

In the game Gligorić-Marović, Yugoslav Team Ch 1977, Black achieved good play by 12...f5 13 exf6 ♘xf6. With the pawn-chain broken, Black liberated his game.

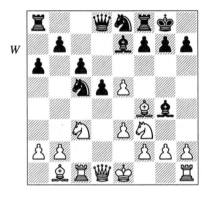

13 ♕c2 g6 14 ♘d4 ♘e6 15 ♗h6 ♘8g7 16 0-0 ♖e8 17 ♕d2 ♘xd4 18 exd4 ♗f5 19 ♗xg7 ♗xb1 20 ♖xb1 ♔xg7 21 b4 f6

There is a new wedge to fight. Black cannot wait for ♘a4-c5, for example.

22 f4 fxe5 23 dxe5

23 fxe5 ♗g5 is good for Black, while the text-move liberates the d5-pawn.

23...d4 24 ♘e4 ♕d5 25 ♕d3 ♖ad8 26 f5 gxf5 27 ♖xf5 ♔h8 28 ♖bf1 ♕e6 29 ♖f7 ♕g6 30 ♖1f3 ♖g8 31 g3 ♖g7

Skilful defence keeps the game in the balance.

32 ♖7f5 ♕e6 33 a3 ♔g8 34 ♘f6+ ♗xf6 35 exf6 ♖g4

The passive 35...♖f7 36 ♕d2 would be favourable to White.

36 f7+ ♔f8 37 ♔g2 ♕e4 38 ♕xe4 ♖xe4 39 ♖g5 ♔e7 40 ♖g7 ♖f8 41 ♖xh7 b6 42 ♖h6 ♖e6 43 ♖h4 c5 44 bxc5 bxc5 45 ♖f5 ♖xf7 46 ♖xc5 ♖e2+ 47 ♔h3 ♖ff2 48 ♖xd4 ♖xh2+ 49 ♔g4 ♖e3 50 ♔f4 ♖xa3 51 ♖e5+ ♔f7 52 g4 ♖b2 53 ♖d7+ ♔f8 54 ♖f5+ ♔e8 55 ♖g7 ♖a4+ 56 ♔g3 ♖e4 57 ♖f6 a5 58 ♖a6 ♔f8 59 ♖h7 ♔g8 60 ♖c7 ♖be2 61 ♖xa5 ♖e7 62 ♖cc5 ♖2e3+ 63 ♔h4 ♔g7 ½-½

In the games we have analysed so far, the pawn-chain was either successfully replaced by blockading minor pieces or it crumbled under strong pressure. In most cases, however, the wedge and its base survive the undermining blows and influence the play throughout the middlegame. With the centre blocked, fronts are opened on the wings.

Nimzowitsch – Tarrasch
San Sebastian 1912
French Defence

1 e4 e6 2 d4 d5 3 e5 c5 4 c3 ♘c6 5 ♘f3 ♕b6 6 ♗d3 cxd4 7 cxd4 ♗d7

As we saw earlier, Salwe played the poor 6...♗d7 against Nimzowitsch and was punished by 7 dxc5. In the move-order chosen by Tarrasch, the d4-pawn is under attack, prompting White to lose a tempo to defend it. It leads to the conclusion that 6 ♗e2 should have been played at once, all the more so because the sacrifice of the d4-pawn cannot be recommended.

8 ♗e2 ♘ge7 9 b3 ♘f5 10 ♗b2 ♗b4+ 11 ♔f1 *(D)*

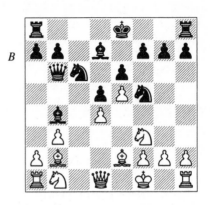

11...♗e7

This is an important position for the understanding of pawn-chains. Black has increased the pressure exerted on d4 to the maximum. He would like to maintain that pressure and withdraws the bishop in order to be able to meet g4 by ...♘h4. Studying this type of position, Nimzowitsch reached the correct conclusion that maintaining the pressure on weakened pawn-chains ties the opponent's pieces in defence. However, he also concluded that one does not have to insist on the pressure, if some other weakness can be created or provoked in the position. Then these other weaknesses become the target, while the initial weakness or potential weakness, like the d4-pawn in our case, cannot escape and can still be exploited in the endgame. For the moment the d4-pawn is simply well defended and it is useless to hope to take advantage of it soon. Nimzowitsch, therefore, analysed 11...0-0 12 g4 ♘h6 13 ♖g1 and found the unexpected, strong reply 13...f6, when 14 exf6 ♖xf6 15 g5 is met by 15...♖xf3 16 ♗xf3 ♘f5 17 ♖g4 ♗e8 (17...♖f8 also seems adequate) with excellent activity for the exchange.

12 g3 a5

This weakens the b5-square, while placing under control the b4-square. The course of the game demonstrates that b5 is more valuable and the bargain was dubious.

13 a4 ♖c8 14 ♗b5 ♘b4 15 ♘c3! *(D)*

Paulsen-Tarrasch, Nuremberg 1888 continued 15 ♗xd7+? ♔xd7 16 ♘c3 ♘c6 17 ♘b5 ♘a7 18 ♘xa7? ♕xa7 19 ♕d3 ♕a6 and Black penetrated to White's second rank. The exchange on d7 was wrong in the first place; the king feels quite well on d7, as it is protected by the pawn-mass. Taking on a7 was another, decisive mistake. Nimzowitsch found an improvement.

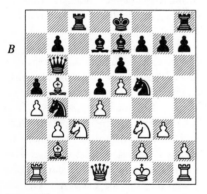

15...♘a6

15...♗xb5+ 16 ♘xb5 ♘c2 17 ♖c1 ♘ce3+ 18 fxe3 ♘xe3+ 19 ♔e2 ♘xd1

20 ♖xc8+ ♔d7 21 ♖xh8 ♘xb2 22 ♖c1 wins for White. Given that does not work, White can stop Black's activity on the queenside and turn his attention towards the other wing.

16 ♔g2 ♘c7 17 ♗e2 ♗b4 18 ♘a2 ♘a6 19 ♗d3

The bishop finally takes its natural place announcing White's action.

19...♘e7 20 ♖c1 ♘c6 21 ♘xb4 ♘axb4 22 ♗b1 h6 23 g4! *(D)*

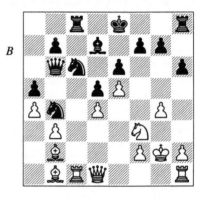

This is the fruit of a good strategy carried out with remarkable attention to positional details. Things have developed so well for White that the majority of the black force is committed to the queenside without achieving anything, while the text-move opens a new front on the kingside, seizing space and preparing further aggressive action.

23...♘e7

Perhaps 23...♔e7 was more to the point, in order to transfer the queen's rook to the defence of the king.

24 ♖xc8+ ♗xc8 25 ♘e1 ♖f8 26 ♘d3 f6

Opening the position cannot be in Black's interest.

27 ♘xb4 ♕xb4 28 exf6 ♖xf6 29 ♗c1?

29 ♗d3! is natural and strong. The impatient text-move can be answered by 29...e5! 30 g5 ♖f7! with counterplay.

29...♘c6? 30 g5 hxg5 31 ♗xg5 ♖f8 32 ♗e3 ♕e7 33 ♕g4 ♕f6 34 ♖g1 ♖h8 35 ♔h1 ♖h4 36 ♕g3 ♖xd4 37 ♗xd4 ♘xd4 38 ♕xg7 ♕f3+ 39 ♕g2 ♕xg2+ 40 ♖xg2 ♘xb3 41 h4 1-0

Matanović – V. Kovačević
Yugoslav Team Ch 1970
French Defence

1 e4 e6 2 d4 d5 3 ♘d2 ♘f6 4 e5 ♘fd7 5 f4 c5 6 c3 ♘c6 7 ♘df3 ♕a5 8 ♔f2 b5 *(D)*

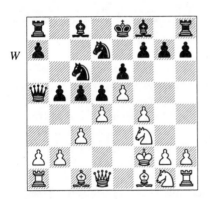

This optimistic advance of the b-pawn may look somewhat strange, but nobody can accuse Black of inconsistency. Having played f4, White will evidently try to carry out f5, attacking the base of the black chain. Black, on the contrary, strives to seize space on the queenside and to attack the base of the white pawn-chain by advancing to b4. With the centre blocked, actions take place on the wings.

9 ♗d3

Another approach is 9 ♘e2 b4 10 ♗d2 ♗a6 11 g4, as in Estrin-W.Stern, Correspondence World Ch 1965-8. Then Black's 11...h5 12 gxh5 ♖xh5 13 ♘g3 ♖h8 14 cxb4 cxb4 15 f5 was grist to White's mill. It is difficult to say what is better. The bishop is naturally placed on d3, but it costs a tempo.

9...b4 10 ♘e2 ♗a6 *(D)*

10...g6 would not stop White's efforts on the kingside: then 11 g4 h5 12 h3 is favourable for White.

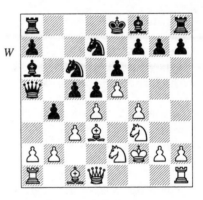

11 f5 bxc3 12 fxe6 fxe6 13 bxc3 ♗xd3

Black should have played 13...cxd4 14 cxd4 ♗e7.

14 ♕xd3 ♗e7 15 ♘f4 c4?

Closing the position on the queenside can only favour White, as he gets a free hand on the kingside.

16 ♕c2 ♘d8 17 h4! *(D)*

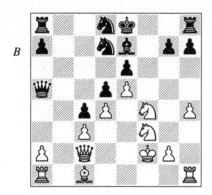

By preparing ♘g5, White wins the strategic battle. Two actions run in parallel on two wings. While Black's endeavours on the queenside are definitely stopped, White dominates on the other wing.

17...♖b8 18 ♘g5 ♗xg5

This worsens the situation. 18...♘f8 was called for.

19 hxg5 ♘f8 20 g6 h6 21 ♘h5 ♖b7 22 ♖h3 ♘c6 23 ♖b1 ♖e7 24 a4

Black has been outplayed. White will dominate both open files and by entering the battle via a3 the dark-squared bishop announces that the end is nigh.

24...♘d7 25 ♖f3 ♘b6 26 ♗a3 ♖b7 27 ♔g1 ♘d8 28 ♖b5 ♕a6 29 ♗b4 ♖c7 30 ♗d6 ♖b7 31 ♕f2 ♕xa4 32 ♖f8+ ♔d7 33 ♖xh8 ♕xb5 34 ♕f8 ♕b1+ 35 ♔h2 ♕xg6 36 ♘f4 ♕f7 37 ♕xd8+ ♔c6 38 ♖f8 1-0

The French Defence is not the only system in which the central pawn-chain influences the course of the play by channelling it to the wings. The King's Indian Defence is characterized

by parallel actions on two wings with the board divided by a pawn-chain running across the board. It is of great importance to understand the laws governing the events in similar circumstances.

Najdorf – Gligorić
Mar del Plata 1953
King's Indian Defence

1 d4 ♘f6 2 c4 g6 3 ♘c3 ♗g7 4 e4 d6 5 ♘f3 0-0 6 ♗e2 e5 7 0-0 ♘c6 8 d5 ♘e7 9 ♘e1 ♘d7 10 ♘d3 f5 11 f3 f4

The board has been divided by the two sides' pawn-chains. The intentions of both sides were clearly announced by White's manoeuvre ♘e1-d3 and Black's ...♘d7, opening the way to the f7-pawn. Now the interlaced chains condition the further course of events. A glance at the board will tell us that White will carry out c5, while Black will attack on the kingside.

12 ♗d2 g5 13 b4?!

The crucial question is whose attack will be quicker; the element of time becomes the decisive factor. It is a part of elementary wisdom to save each tempo, because in the end each tempo will have its weight. Therefore instead of the text-move White would do better to choose 13 ♖c1, trying to do without b4. For instance, in case of 13...♘f6 14 c5 ♘g6 15 cxd6 cxd6 16 ♘b5 ♖f7 17 ♕c2 ♘e8 18 a4 ♗f8 White opens the c-file having saved a tempo, which can now be invested to slow down Black's attack on the kingside by 19 ♘f2 h5 20 h3.

13...♘f6 14 c5 h5 15 ♘f2

Playing on two fronts reminds me of a fencing duel: a thrust forward and then retreat. The knight moved to d3 to support c5; now it withdraws to prevent ...g4.

15...♘g6 16 ♖c1 ♖f7

Again the same clever play of attack and defence: in expectation of ♘b5 Black must protect c7, but at the same time prepares ...♗f8 followed by ...♖g7, transferring the rook to an attacking position on the g-file.

17 cxd6 cxd6 18 a4 ♗f8 19 a5?!

In later decades, when it became apparent that offence on one wing and defence on the other must be coordinated in detail, White turned to a slightly different move-order – 19 h3 ♖g7 and then 20 ♗e1 ♘h8 21 a5 ♘f7 22 ♘b5 ♘h6 23 ♕c2. Each step deeper into the variation was examined and paid for by attempts which fell through. After 20 ♘b5 Black resorted to 20...♘h4 21 ♗e1 a6 22 ♘a3 ♗d7, provoking 23 a5 when 23...b5 either excludes the a3-knight from the play or achieves fine play after 24 axb6 ♕xb6.

19...♖g7 20 h3 ♘h8 21 ♘b5

Again paying attention to detail, later experience recommended 21 ♗e1 ♘f7 22 ♘b5 ♘h6 23 ♕c2 securing the penetration via c7.

21...g4 (D)

White was first to strike at the base of the black pawn-chain; now it is Black's turn to do likewise. In most cases one can do nothing against the wedge and must seek counterplay by undermining the base.

22 fxg4 hxg4 23 hxg4 a6

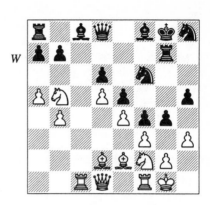

Black seizes his chance to force the knight back, slowing down White's attack. In a position characterized by pawn-chains and simultaneous attacks on both wings, such a consideration is more important than the static weakness on b6.

24 ♘a3 ♗d7!

Black is not impatient to recapture the pawn. He gives preference to exchanging his inactive rook.

25 ♘c4 ♖c8 26 ♘b6 ♖xc1 27 ♗xc1 ♗e8

Black will need his light-squared bishop on the other wing and is not willing to trade it for the wayward knight.

28 ♗a3 ♘f7 29 ♕c2 ♘h6 30 g5 ♖xg5 31 ♖c1 ♖g3

White is finally ready to use the open c-file, but Black's counterattack is quick and does not offer respite.

32 ♗b2 ♘fg4 33 ♘xg4 ♘xg4 34 ♗xg4 ♖xg4 35 ♕f2 ♗g6

The patient bishop has found its target – the base of the broken chain.

36 ♖c4 ♕e7 37 ♗c3 ♕h7 38 ♕e2 ♖h4 39 ♔f2

What we see is quite a common picture. The slower, failed attack on the queenside left behind a couple of wayward pieces, while the quicker, successful attack on the other wing will force the king into exile.

39...f3!

The brutal final act. When the two sides are attacking on opposite wings, the attack on the king threatens the more immediate danger, as this remarkable pioneer game from the 1950s shows.

40 ♕e3 ♖f4 41 gxf3 ♕h2+ 42 ♔e1 ♕h1+ 43 ♔e2 ♗h5 44 ♔d2 ♖xf3 45 ♕g5+ ♗g7 46 ♔c2 ♖f2+ 47 ♗d2 ♕d1+ 48 ♔c3 ♕a1+ 0-1

Larsen – Tal
Candidates match (game 5),
Eersel 1969
King's Indian Defence

1 d4 ♘f6 2 c4 g6 3 ♘c3 ♗g7 4 e4 0-0 5 ♘f3 d6 6 ♗e2 e5 7 0-0 ♘c6 8 d5 ♘e7 9 ♘e1 ♘d7 10 ♘d3 f5 11 ♗d2 ♘f6 12 f3 f4 13 c5 g5

By using a somewhat different move-order, Larsen has quickened his attack. Having omitted the unnecessary b4, he has attacked the base d6 a move more quickly, and is ready to open the c-file.

14 ♖c1 ♘g6 15 ♘b5

White provokes 15...a6, which looks promising for Black after 16 ♘a3 g4, but Larsen had concocted something new: 16 cxd6 axb5 17 dxc7 ♕d7 18 ♕b3, breaking the chain to his advantage.

15...♖f7 16 cxd6

Further increasing the pressure by 16 ♗a5 can be met successfully by 16...b6 17 cxb6 cxb6.

16...cxd6 17 ♕c2 g4

Disregarding the penetration by the knight, Tal strikes back. A more cautious player would play 17...♘e8 postponing the thematic ...g4.

18 ♘c7 gxf3 19 gxf3 ♗h3 (D)

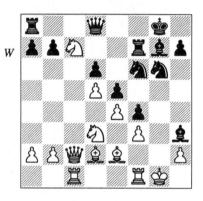

In playing for a win, Tal was ruthless, many a time overstepping the limits of caution, but his play against Larsen is logical and consistent. By advancing his g-pawn he sought counterplay on the kingside to compensate for White's queenside activity. As long as the two attacks are carried out correctly, the game is in the balance.

20 ♘xa8

Had Larsen foreseen the coming attack, he would have probably played 20 ♘e6, forgetting the material advantage, and ideas of establishing a mighty bishop at h3 (see next note).

20...♘xe4!

White was hoping for 20...♕xa8, when 21 ♘f2 ♗xf1 22 ♗xf1 switches the bishop to h3 with full domination on the light squares, but Tal struck in his typical manner.

21 fxe4

21 ♔h1 fails to protect the king after 21...♘g3+ 22 hxg3 fxg3, when there is no way to parry 23...♕h4.

21...♕g5+ 22 ♔f2 ♕g2+

Black needed a win and was not satisfied with the perpetual check by 22...♕h4+.

23 ♔e1 ♘h4 (D)

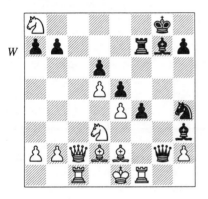

24 ♗e3?

Confused by the sudden change of fortunes, Larsen misses his chance hidden in the unexpected 24 ♘f2!. For instance, 24...♘f3+ 25 ♔d1 ♘d4 26 ♕c3.

24...♕xe4

White was reckoning on 24...fxe3 25 ♖xf7.

25 ♗f2 f3 26 ♗xh4 ♕xh4+ 27 ♘f2 fxe2 28 ♕xe2 e4 29 ♖g1

The only meaningful resistance. 29 ♖c7 loses to 29...♗xf1 30 ♔xf1 ♖f5, and 29 ♖c4 to 29...♗xf1 30 ♔xf1 ♕xh2.

29...e3 30 ♕xe3 ♖e7 31 ♖xg7+ ♔xg7 32 ♖c7 ♗d7 33 ♖xd7 ♖xd7 34 ♕xa7?

In trying to save the knight, White puts his king in jeopardy. He could still resist by 34 ♕c3+ ♕f6 35 ♕g3+ ♔f8 36 ♘d3, activating the knight.

34...♖e7+ 35 ♔d1 ♕c4 36 ♕b6 ♕f1+ 37 ♔d2 ♖e2+ 38 ♔c3 ♕c1+ 39 ♔d4 ♕e3+ 40 ♔c4 ♖c2+ 0-1

The same instructive process of counterplay against the pawn-chain brought Black success. Again attacking the king proved more dangerous in practice than queenside action – a little fact we should keep in mind.

Some General Observations

The pawn-chain is a central pawn-formation, characteristic of many variations in the French Defence and the King's Indian Defence, but arising occasionally in other opening systems as well.

Driven into the enemy camp, the central wedge seizes a spatial advantage. The wedge denies one's opponent normal development and manoeuvring space and narrows his options.

When fighting the pawn-chain, one, as a rule, attacks the base. Breaking the chain at some point weakens the wedge, which then can be put under strong pressure. Sometimes, however, a direct attack on the wedge is also possible. In order to succeed against a wedge supported by a healthy base, undermining it by pawns is not enough. They need strong support from pieces, exerting simultaneous pressure on the wedge. One should take care that the pieces generating pressure cannot be excluded by pins, and often violent measures, including material sacrifices, are indispensable.

At the critical moment, when the chain falls apart, the side possessing it will try to substitute minor pieces for the central pawns. If successful, the squeezing pressure will increase instead of being diminished. The minor pieces will target both wings, while the blocked pawns will be more exposed than earlier, when they were shielded by the enemy pawns.

On the contrary, if the blockade by pieces does not succeed, then the pawn-mass, set free in the centre, will advance with great power and, as a rule, turn the tables utterly.

In general, however, after mutually correct play, the wedge and its base will withstand the pressure and survive. If attack is equal to defence, the play is in the balance. In that case, to seek an advantage one must turn to additional motifs on the wings, where the battle is transferred naturally.

Firm pawn-chains, crossing the centre of the board, force the players to seek their chances on opposite wings. Extremely sensitive situations arise, in which positional values lose their natural importance. The game becomes characterized by simultaneous attacks. The element of time becomes the essential factor in the evaluation of these positions, which are often decided by a single tempo. Such positions require great understanding and experience. One defends on one wing and attacks on the other simultaneously. Two actions, aggressive and defensive, are intertwined. Carrying them out requires great skill and sensibility. In this tricky game of dagger and shield, grandmaster experience can recommend but one verified recipe: spare the defensive moves, in particular reducing pawn moves to the minimum, and constantly weighing the invested time against the concrete effects. One's full weight should be thrown into the attack, but with a watchful eye on the other wing. Whatever happens there can have drastic repercussions on your own attack.

In conclusion, there is little need to emphasize further how essential it is to understand pawn-chains, and the principles on which they work. Such an understanding is essential for a full comprehension of a series of important theoretical variations.

7 Pawn-Islands

After discussing at some length the elementary types of pawns, we become aware of the direct relation between the soundness of pawn-structures and the general health of the positions we play. It is a deep relation and we could say without exaggeration that we must appreciate it if we are to make objective evaluations.

However, apart from the positive or negative values of various pawn-formations, there is yet another quality of pawns which influences our judgement in significant measure. I am talking of what José Raúl Capablanca called *islas de peones* (islands of pawns).

A pawn-island is a group of pawns cut off from other pawns.

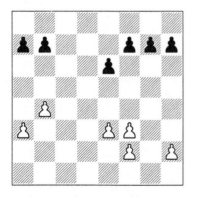

In the above diagram White's pawn-structure contains three pawn-islands,

Black's two islands. The more islands you have in your position, the more exposed they are and more difficult to defend. And vice versa: the fewer islands in the pawn-structure, the more compact and strong the structure tends to be.

We should certainly not underestimate the importance of this subject. The following instructive games will help us to understand its meaning and significance.

E. Cohn – Rubinstein
St Petersburg 1909
Queen's Gambit

1 d4 d5 2 ♘f3 c5 3 c4 dxc4 4 dxc5 ♕xd1+ 5 ♔xd1 ♘c6 6 e3 ♗g4 7 ♗xc4 e6 8 a3 ♗xc5 9 b4 ♗d6 10 ♗b2 ♘f6 11 ♘d2 ♔e7 12 ♔e2 ♗e5

Weaker than his opponent and obviously knowing it, Cohn plays for a draw from the start. Black reacts well. White's queenside pawn advance has somewhat weakened his position, and the exchange of dark-squared bishops emphasizes it in a quiet manner.

13 ♗xe5 ♘xe5 14 ♖hc1 ♖ac8 15 ♗b3 ♖hd8 16 ♘c4 ♘xc4 17 ♖xc4 ♖xc4 18 ♗xc4 ♘e4 19 ♔e1 ♗xf3 20 gxf3 ♘d6 21 ♗e2?!

Correct was 21 ♗d3, but White is completely unaware of the significance of the subtle change in his pawn-structure after the exchange on f3.

21...♖c8 22 ♔d2 ♘c4+ 23 ♗xc4 ♖xc4 24 ♖c1? *(D)*

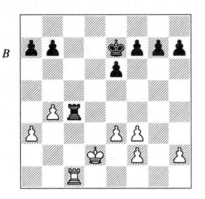

This is consistent with Cohn's previous play and his wish to make a draw, but he misses an important point: his pawn-formation, broken into three pawn-islands, is not as good as his opponent's. We shall see that this seemingly unimportant detail will be decisive.

24...♖xc1 25 ♔xc1 ♔f6 26 ♔d2 ♔g5 27 ♔e2

It is easy to calculate that if he goes for the b7-pawn, White will come too late. He must hurry to protect the weak point in his pawn-structure – the h2-pawn.

27...♔h4 28 ♔f1 ♔h3 29 ♔g1 e5 30 ♔h1

Forced to protect his little island on h2, White's choice is narrowed to passive waiting and repetition of moves. He cannot win a tempo on the queenside and he cannot play 30 e4 because of 30...g5 31 ♔h1 h5 32 ♔g1 h4 33

♔h1 g4 34 fxg4 ♔xg4 35 ♔g2 h3+, when the e4-pawn falls.

30...b5 31 ♔g1 f5 32 ♔h1 g5 33 ♔g1 h5 34 ♔h1 g4 35 e4

After 35 fxg4 fxg4! followed by ...h4 and ...g3, forcing exchanges, Black's king will capture the white e-pawn, winning easily.

35...fxe4 36 fxe4

If 36 fxg4 then 36...hxg4 37 ♔g1 e3 38 fxe3 e4 39 ♔h1 g3, etc.

36...h4 37 ♔g1 g3 38 hxg3 hxg3 0-1

39 f4 exf4 40 e5 is too slow due to 40...g2 41 e6 ♔g3 42 e7 f3 and mate next move.

Beware of too many pawn-islands; try to keep your pawn-formations compact and healthy! Rubinstein's lesson is unforgettable.

Schlechter – Rubinstein
San Sebastian 1912
French Defence

1 e4 e6 2 d4 d5 3 ♘c3 ♘f6 4 ♗g5 dxe4 5 ♘xe4 ♘bd7 6 ♘f3 ♗e7 7 ♘xf6+ ♘xf6 8 ♗d3 b6

This move looks risky at first sight, but it is well founded. White now tries to punish Black for weakening the c6-square.

9 ♘e5 ♗b7 10 ♗b5+ c6 11 ♗xc6+?!

White has got carried away. 11 ♕f3 fails to 11...♕d5, but 11 ♗e2 is the correct continuation.

11...♗xc6 12 ♘xc6 ♕d5 13 ♘e5 ♕xg2 14 ♕f3 ♕xf3 15 ♘xf3 ♖c8 *(D)*

Following the opening complications, Black has entered a favourable

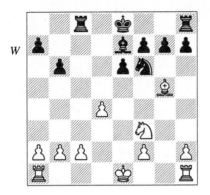

endgame. At the moment it does not look much, but it is the pawn-formation that makes the difference: White will have to worry about three pawn-islands, two of them isolated pawns, while the black structure is much more compact, divided into two natural pawn-islands.

16 0-0-0

This move was criticized and 16 c3 proposed instead, with the idea of continuing 17 a4 waging battle where the pawn-majority offers better chances. However, Black then has 16...b5, thwarting the intention at once.

16...♘d5 17 ♗xe7 ♔xe7 18 ♔b1 ♖hd8 19 ♖hg1 g6 20 ♘e5 ♘b4 21 c3 ♘c6 22 ♘xc6+?

The criticism of this move is much sounder. After the exchange of knights, White enters a rook endgame in which Black's more compact pawn-structure offers him the advantage. White should have continued 22 ♘g4 and 23 ♘e3. With the knight the defence of the weak spots is easier.

22...♖xc6 23 ♖d3 ♖d5 24 ♖h3 h5 25 ♖f3

To defend such positions is always a daunting task. The text-move covers the f-file against 25...♖f5, but allows the game continuation, 25...e5. If that is thwarted by 25 ♖e1, then 25...♖f5 26 ♖e2 ♖d6, planning ...♖f4, and the other rook penetrates via d5.

25...e5! *(D)*

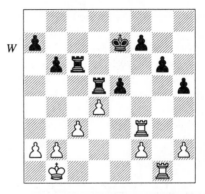

Simple and strong. White's pawn-islands on the kingside are vulnerable and in order to reach them Black must open the position.

26 dxe5

The possible pin by 26 ♖e1 is of little help after 26...♖e6.

26...♖xe5 27 ♖e3

This exchange will not bring relief. Nothing can change substantially the fact that there are two sensitive pawn-islands in White's camp. After 27 ♖d1 ♖f6 Black is again quicker.

27...♖xe3 28 fxe3 ♖e6 29 ♖e1 ♖f6 30 ♖e2 ♔e6

Now the black king penetrates. Together with the more active rook and better pawn-structure it represents an overwhelming advantage.

31 ♔c2 ♔e5 32 c4 ♔e4 33 b4 g5 34
♔c3 g4 35 c5 h4 36 ♖g2 ♖g6 37 ♔c4
g3 38 hxg3 hxg3 39 ♔b5 bxc5 40
bxc5 ♔f3 41 ♖g1 a6+ 0-1

Another classic case of weak pawn-
islands.

Chigorin – Tarrasch
Budapest 1896
Ruy Lopez

1 e4 e5 2 ♘f3 ♘c6 3 ♗b5 ♘f6 4 ♕e2

This is a good choice against the
early ...♘f6. Having defended his e-
pawn, White can carry out d4 with or
without c3.

4...d6 5 d4 exd4

Black would do better to continue
5...♗d7.

6 e5

This breakthrough is consistent with
the fourth move.

6...d3

This makes possible the later check,
which gives Black a tempo to castle,
but difficulties remain.

**7 cxd3 dxe5 8 ♘xe5 ♗b4+ 9 ♗d2
0-0 10 ♗xc6 ♗xd2+ 11 ♘xd2 bxc6
12 ♘xc6 ♕d6**

In A.Ivanov-Romanishin, Tashkent
1980, Black tried to improve on the
text-move by 12...♕d7 but he did not
manage any better than Tarrasch: 13
♘e7+ ♔h8 14 ♘xc8 ♖e8 15 ♘e4
♖axc8 16 0-0.

**13 ♘e7+ ♔h8 14 ♘xc8 ♖axc8 15
0-0 ♖fd8 16 ♘e4 ♕xd3 17 ♕xd3
♖xd3 18 ♘xf6 gxf6** *(D)*

The dust has cleared. Black has
maintained the material balance, but
his shattered pawn-formation tells

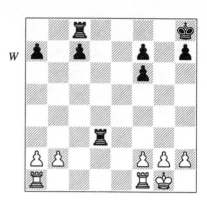

against him. White has the advantage
owing to his sounder pawn-structure
with fewer pawn-islands.

19 ♖fd1!

Considering that Black will occupy
White's second rank, it is indispensable to exchange a pair of rooks.

**19...♖cd8 20 ♖xd3 ♖xd3 21 g3
♖d2 22 ♖c1 ♖xb2 23 ♖xc7 ♖xa2**

Black should consider 23...♔g7 24
♖xa7, when the white rook is in an unfavourable position in front of its
pawn and the black rook occupies
White's sensitive second rank. However, the material balance has its special weight in our considerations even
when great players are in question.

**24 ♖xf7 ♖a6 25 ♔g2 ♔g8 26 ♖b7
♖a2**

Black has maintained the material
balance, but at a high price: his king is
cut off, his pawn-structure is broken
into three units and his passed pawn is
more an embarrassment than a useful
factor. If Black continues 26...♖a1, in
order to march his passed pawn down
the a-file, then White replies 27 h4 a5
28 h5, when after 28...a4, 29 h6,

making ♖g7+ possible, decides. If 28...h6 then the a-pawn cannot advance because the white king will take a walk to g6 and win in simple fashion.

27 h4 a6

Black plans 28...h5 and wants to prevent ♖b5.

28 ♔f3 h5 *(D)*

Not an easy decision, because by weakening the g6-square Black exposes his g-pawn and invites White's king to penetrate. However, Black's king is immobile (28...♔f8 drops the h7-pawn, while 28...♔h8 29 ♖f7 picks off the f6-pawn) and the text-move at least makes his prison walk (g8-f8 and back) possible. It is, therefore, easy to understand his decision, but in spite of the general concurrence about it Black should have considered 28...♖a4 29 ♖a7 a5 30 h5 h6 (Black obviously cannot allow h6 followed by ♖g7+) 31 g4 ♔f8 and if 32 ♖h7 then 32...♖b4 33 ♖xh6 ♔g7 34 ♖g6+ ♔f7 and the a5-pawn finally becomes valuable.

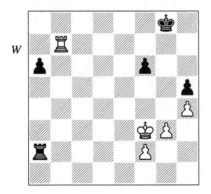

29 ♖c7 ♖a5

Otherwise there comes 30 ♖c5, demonstrating that 28...h5 had its risks.

30 ♔f4 ♔f8 31 f3

Here the commentators were right in noticing that the correct move-order was 31 ♖a7 ♔g8 32 f3, because after the text-move Black could reply 31...♖a4+ 32 ♔f5 ♖a3 33 f4 ♖xg3 34 ♔xf6 ♔g8 – an opportunity both players passed by.

31...♔g8 32 ♖a7 ♔f8 33 g4

Another drawback of 28...h5: White is presented with a chance to create a passed pawn.

33...hxg4 34 fxg4

The material is somewhat reduced, but the basic elements remain unchanged: Black's king is still cut off, his rook is still less active, and he is still burdened with two pawn-islands against White's one island.

34...♖a1?

This move opens the door to the white king into Black's camp. For the second time in this game Tarrasch thinks more of material than of the activity of his pieces, which in a rook endgame as a rule represents a fatal mistake. Black has been constantly worried about the survival of his passed pawn, which limits the possibilities of his king and rook to the minimum. Here there was a chance to get rid of it and pass into a drawn endgame by 34...♔g8 35 h5:

1) If Black decides to wait by 35...♔f8?, then 36 h6 ♔g8 37 ♖g7+ ♔f8 (or 37...♔h8 38 ♖f7) 38 ♖g6 ♔f7 39 h7 wins because 39...♖a4+ 40 ♔g3 ♖a3+ 41 ♔h4 ♖a1 fails to the clever

42 h8♘+ ♔f8 (or 42...♔e7 43 ♖g8) 43 ♖xf6+ ♔g7 44 ♔g5 ♔xh8 (alternatively, 44...♖a5+ 45 ♖f5 ♖xf5+ 46 gxf5 ♔xh8 47 ♔f6 and White is faster) 45 ♔g6 ♔g8 46 ♖b6, etc., according to old analysis by the Soviet master Fridshtein.

2) 35...♖b5 36 ♖xa6 ♔g7 37 ♖a7+ ♔g8 38 ♔g3 ♖c5 39 ♔h4 ♖b5 40 h6 ♖c5 41 ♖g7+ ♔f8 42 ♖g6 ♔f7 43 h7 ♖c8 44 ♔h5 ♖c1 45 h8♘+ ♔f8 46 ♖xf6+ ♔g7 47 ♖f7+ ♔xh8 48 ♔g6 ♖c8 with a draw.

It is true, sometimes there is not enough time to calculate long variations precisely, but experience teaches us that the problems of rook endings should be solved intuitively, thinking primarily of the activity of one's pieces. As a rule, material is a millstone pulling us to the bottom.

35 ♔f5 ♖f1+ 36 ♔g6 ♖f4 37 g5 fxg5

37...♖xh4 loses at once to 38 ♖a8+, etc.

38 hxg5 *(D)*

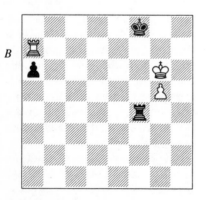

38...♖a4

After 38...♖g4 39 ♖xa6 ♖g1 40 ♖a8+ ♔e7, 41 ♔h6 ♔f7 42 ♖a7+ ♔g8 43 ♔g6 ♔f8 achieves nothing for White, but 41 ♖g8, making 42 ♔h7 possible, wins.

39 ♖a8+ ♔e7 40 ♔h6 a5 41 g6 ♖a1 42 g7 ♖h1+ 43 ♔g6 ♖g1+ 44 ♔h7 ♖h1+ 45 ♔g8 ♖a1 46 ♖a7+ ♔e8 47 ♖a6

By threatening ♖h6, White wins a pawn and achieves Lucena's position.

47...♖h1 48 ♖xa5 ♖e1 49 ♖h5 ♖g1 50 ♖e5+ 1-0

Perhaps all rook endgames are drawn, as one grandmaster said, but sometimes it is not simple to find the way to draw. If the pawn-structure is broken into several pawn-islands, the task may be daunting. Now take a look at two other memorable games!

Alekhine – Spielmann
New York 1927
French Defence

1 e4 e6 2 d4 d5 3 ♘c3 ♘f6 4 ♗g5 ♗e7 5 exd5 ♘xd5 6 ♗xe7 ♕xe7 7 ♕d2 ♕b4 8 ♘xd5 ♕xd2+ 9 ♔xd2 exd5 10 ♖e1+ ♗e6

Considering the closed character of the position, Black could calmly continue 10...♔f8, but he starts to commit a series of minor imprecisions.

11 ♘h3 ♘c6?!

11...0-0 12 ♘f4 ♘c6 13 c3 a6 works, but not the text-move. Even at this early stage of the game, Black must find 'only' moves if he wants to survive.

12 ♗b5 ♔d7 13 ♘f4 ♖ae8 14 c4 ♔d6 15 c5+ ♔d7 16 ♖e5

Alekhine pointed out that 16 ♖e3 was strong too. The rook has the third rank at its disposal and ♘h5 is a constant menace.

16...f6 17 ♖xe6 ♖xe6 18 ♘xe6 ♔xe6 19 ♗xc6 bxc6 20 ♖e1+ ♔d7 *(D)*

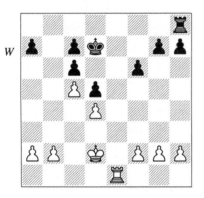

With the experience of the previous games in mind we can easily conclude that Black's problems stem from his three pawn-islands, and in particular from his little island on a7, which will sooner or later tie down either the rook or the king to passive defence. Unfortunately for Black, he cannot oppose rooks on the only open file because of his isolated a7-pawn, so White can use the third rank as it pleases him.

21 ♔c3 ♖b8

After 21...♖e8 22 ♖xe8 ♔xe8 23 ♔b4 ♔d7 24 ♔a5 ♔c8 25 ♔a6 ♔b8 26 b4, etc., Black would lose in the manner Cohn lost against Rubinstein (compare the two positions!).

22 ♖e3 ♖f8 23 ♖g3 ♖f7 24 ♔b4 ♖e7 25 ♔c3 ♖f7 26 ♖h3 h6 27 ♔d2 ♖e7

All of a sudden opening the third rank endangers the pawn. 27...♖f8 28 ♖a3 ♖a8 29 ♖a6 ♖b8 30 ♔c3 ♖b7 31 f3 and Black will run out of useful moves. 27...♔c8 is even worse: 28 ♖a3 ♔b7 29 ♖e3 and the rook penetrates.

28 ♖a3?!

Alekhine's long analysis demonstrates that 28 ♖e3 was correct. By denying Black the e4-square, White wins the pawn endgame as follows: 28...♖xe3 (28...♖f7 loses to 29 ♖a3 ♖e7 30 f3) 29 ♔xe3 ♔e6 30 ♔f4 g6 31 g4 g5+ 32 ♔e3 ♔d7 33 ♔d3 ♔c8 34 ♔c3 ♔b7 35 ♔b4 ♔a6 36 ♔a4 ♔b7 37 ♔a5 a6 38 a4 ♔a7 39 b3 (White must catch his opponent on the wrong foot) 39...♔b7 40 b4 ♔a7 41 b5 axb5 42 axb5 ♔b7 43 b6 cxb6+ 44 cxb6 ♔b8 45 ♔a6 c5 46 dxc5 d4 47 b7 d3 48 ♔b6 and White mates in time. That would be the logical end, demonstrating masterfully the weakness of the black pawn-structure. The text-move lets the win slip.

28...♖e4

Naturally, Black jumps at the opportunity.

29 ♖a4 ♔c8 30 f3 ♖h4 31 h3 ♔b7 32 ♔e3 f5 33 ♖b4+ ♔c8 34 a4 g5?!

Now it is Black's turn to err. After 34...f4+ 35 ♔f2 ♖h5 36 ♖b3 ♖f5 37 ♖c3 ♖f7 38 ♖c2 ♖e7 39 ♖e2 ♖xe2+ 40 ♔xe2 the position is blocked and no passage left. The text-move, however, is not so bad as the commentators claimed.

35 a5 g4

35...a6 closes the door to White's rook, which cannot penetrate without the support of a pawn on a6, but after 36 ♔f2 the black rook is in a trap: 36...g4 loses to 37 ♔g3 gxh3 38 gxh3 ♖h5 39 f4, while after 36...h5 37 ♔g3 f4+ 38 ♔h2 g4 39 ♖a4 the rook penetrates on the e-file.

36 hxg4 fxg4 37 a6 *(D)*

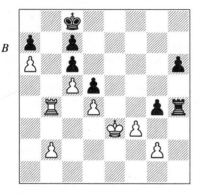

37...gxf3?

Kotov correctly pointed out that 37...g3? loses to 38 f4, but it is strange that he and Dr Euwe, as well as Alekhine himself, missed that this was a critical moment. Taking on f3 is a serious mistake, because it creates a passed pawn on the f-file, adding essentially to Black's problems due to the passed pawn White is about to obtain on the a-file. Black should continue 37...♖h2, when both 38 ♔f2 gxf3 39 ♔xf3 ♖h4 and 38 fxg4 ♖xg2 lead to a position in which the g4-pawn is held back by the h6-pawn. Notice also that the h6-pawn cannot be won unless the g4-pawn falls. White can try 38 f4 ♖xg2 39 f5 (if 39 ♖b7, then 39...♖g3+ 40 ♔e2 ♖g2+ 41 ♔f1 ♖d2), though after 39...g3 he must be careful, since

40 ♖b7? ♖f2 41 ♖xa7 leads to defeat after the unexpected 41...♔b8 42 ♖b7+ ♔a8 43 ♖xc7 ♖xf5 44 ♖g7 ♖g5. Black is safe in some other continuations, too. Spielmann probably overrated his passed pawn and underrated White's passed pawn. This is easily understandable, because what follows would not be out of place in an endgame study.

38 gxf3 ♖h1 39 ♖b7 ♖e1+ 40 ♔f4

40 ♔d2 ♖e7 41 ♖xa7 ♔b8 42 ♖b7+ ♔a8 is an obvious draw. The king must stay with his passed pawn.

40...♖d1 41 ♔e5 ♖e1+ 42 ♔f5 ♖d1 43 ♖xa7 ♖xd4 44 ♖a8+ ♔d7 45 f4 ♖a4 46 a7!

From now on the white rook is stuck on a8, but it is important to limit the movements of the black rook to its file.

46...h5

46...d4 is held by the king and after 47 ♔e4 h5 48 b3 ♖a1 49 f5 ♔e7 50 ♔xd4 h4 51 ♔e5 ♖e1+ (otherwise ♖h8 wins) 52 ♔f4 ♖a1 53 ♔g5 h3 54 ♖h8 the win is simpler than in the game.

47 b3

Necessary to free the king.

47...♖a1 48 ♔e5 ♖e1+ 49 ♔f6 ♖a1 50 ♔e5 ♖e1+ 51 ♔d4 ♖d1+ 52 ♔c3 ♖a1 53 f5 ♔e7

Black obviously cannot allow f6.

54 ♔d4!

Having won a tempo for f5, White returns to the kingside to eliminate the passed pawn.

54...h4 55 ♔e5 ♖e1+

55...h3 loses to 56 ♖h8 ♖xa7 57 ♖xh3 ♖a1 58 f6+, etc.

56 ♔f4 ♖a1 57 ♔g5 ♖g1+

57...h3 again loses in a similar manner: 58 ♖h8 ♖xa7 59 ♖xh3 ♖a1 60 f6+, etc.

58 ♔xh4 ♖a1 59 ♔g5 ♖g1+ 60 ♔f4 ♖a1 61 ♔e5 ♖e1+ 62 ♔d4 ♖a1 63 ♔c3

The rook will be further squeezed, its mobility reduced to minimum.

63...♖a3 64 ♔b2 ♖a6 65 b4 ♔f7 66 ♔b3 ♖a1 67 f6!

The final little touch to a magnificent endgame.

67...♖a6 68 b5 cxb5 69 ♔b4 1-0

Either the king penetrates via b5 or 69...c6 70 ♖h8 costs a whole rook.

We are far from the opening but do not forget that everything began with Black's compromised pawn-formation which had a weak spot in the little pawn-island on a7.

Capablanca – Kupchik
Havana 1913
Four Knights Game

1 e4 e5 2 ♘f3 ♘c6 3 ♘c3 ♘f6 4 ♗b5 ♗b4 5 0-0 0-0 6 ♗xc6 bxc6 7 ♘xe5 ♕e8 8 ♘d3 ♗xc3 9 dxc3 ♕xe4 10 ♖e1 ♕h4 11 ♕f3 ♗a6 12 ♗f4 ♖ac8 13 ♗e5 ♗xd3 14 cxd3 ♕g4 15 ♗xf6 ♕xf3 16 gxf3 gxf6 *(D)*

Black's difficulties in the opening started with 6...bxc6 instead of the natural 6...dxc6. At that moment it may have seemed unimportant to Black, but the subsequent exchanges leading to the position in the diagram accentuated the disagreeable fact that Black's pawn-structure remains broken into more islands than White's. Like in the

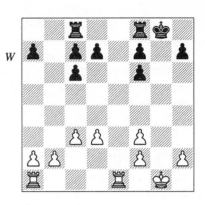

previous example, there is the weak a7-pawn, an isolated pawn which will need constant care.

17 ♖e4 ♖fe8 18 ♖ae1 ♖e6 19 ♖1e3 ♖ce8 20 ♔f1

The e4-rook is ready to move along the fourth rank and attack the a7-pawn, but before that White has to strengthen the point e3. The text-move prevents the liberating 20...f5 by 21 ♖d4 ♖xe3 22 fxe3 ♖xe3 23 ♔f2 ♖e7 24 ♖a4, while 20...d5 fails to 21 ♖g4+ ♔f8 22 ♔e2, when ♖a4 is inevitable.

20...♔f8 21 ♔e2 ♔e7 22 ♖a4 ♖a8 23 ♖a5!

Very typically, the attacking rook is mobile and the last move improves its privileged position on the a-file: from a5 it controls the fifth rank preventing freeing moves. At the same time the defending rook is forced to an ignominious post on a8.

23...d5 24 c4!

An excellent move squeezing Black further, because 24...dxc4 25 dxc4 causes more damage to Black's pawn-structure and 24...d4 25 ♖e4 ♔d6 26 b4 worsens his situation.

24...♔d6 25 c5+ ♔d7 26 d4 f5

Black did not like 26...♖g8 because of 27 ♔f1 and the text-move seemed the most natural way to force the exchange on e6 by threatening 27...♖h6.

27 ♖xe6 fxe6 28 f4

Had White continued 28 ♖a6, Black would have found himself in trouble.

28...♔c8 29 ♔d2?!

In view of the next note, in which Black can force White to close the third rank, White should have played 29 ♖a3 at once, as then 29...♖b8 can be met by 30 b3 ♔b7 31 b4 ♔a8 32 ♖b3, keeping the road to h3 open.

29...♔b7?! (D)

Both players lose concentration. 29...♖b8 would force White to close the third rank by 30 ♔c3, because after 30 ♔c2 ♖b4 White must step to c3 anyway.

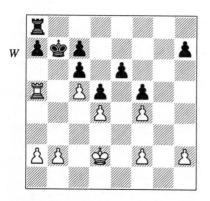

W

30 ♖a3 ♖g8 31 ♖h3 ♖g7

Now Black's rook is tied to passive defence of another isolated pawn and the mobile white rook again dominates the scene.

32 ♔e2 ♔a6 33 ♖h6 ♖e7 34 ♔d3 ♔b7 35 h4 ♔c8 36 ♖h5 ♔d7 37 ♖g5

Capturing the open file brings White a step nearer to his aim.

37...♖f7 38 ♔c3

Having won the only open file, White can create threats on both wings.

38...♔c8 39 ♔b4 ♖f6 40 ♔a5 ♔b7 41 a4 a6 42 h5 ♖h6 43 b4 ♖f6 44 b5?

Before the breakthrough is carried out, 44 ♖g7! is necessary in order to constrain Black's rook to a passive position on h6. Then 44...♖h6 45 b5 axb5 46 axb5 cxb5 47 ♔xb5 ♖xh5 48 c6+ wins for White.

44...axb5 45 axb5 ♖f8!

That makes the difference! Black activates his rook and manages to drive White's king back, thwarting the scenario from the above comment.

46 ♖g7 ♖a8+ 47 ♔b4 cxb5 48 ♔xb5 ♖a2 49 c6+ ♔b8 50 ♖xh7 ♖b2+ 51 ♔a5 ♖a2+ 52 ♔b4 ♖xf2?

The intermediary 52...♖b2+! would have made an essential difference, forcing the king further from the critical c5-square. After 53 ♔c3 ♖xf2 54 ♖e7 ♖xf4 55 h6 ♖h4 56 h7 there is 56...♔a7 57 ♖xc7+ ♔b6 58 ♖e7 ♔xc6 59 ♖xe6+ ♔b5 and the activated black king saves the draw.

53 ♖e7 ♖xf4

Now after 53...♖b2+ 54 ♔c3 ♖h2 55 ♖xe6 ♖xh5 56 ♔b4 Black is too late.

54 h6 ♖xd4+ 55 ♔b5 ♖d1

55...♖h4 56 h7 leaves Black without an answer.

56 h7 ♖b1+ 57 ♔c5 ♖c1+ 58 ♔d4 ♖d1+ 59 ♔e5 ♖e1+ 60 ♔f6 ♖h1 61 ♖e8+ ♔a7 62 h8♕ ♖xh8 63 ♖xh8

♔b6 64 ♔xe6 ♔xc6 65 ♔xf5 ♔c5 66 ♔e5 c6 67 ♖h6 ♔b5 68 ♔d4 1-0

Two isolated pawn-islands on two wings proved too difficult to defend.

Fischer – Unzicker
Zurich 1959
Ruy Lopez

1 e4 e5 2 ♘f3 ♘c6 3 ♗b5 a6 4 ♗a4 ♘f6 5 0-0 ♗e7 6 ♖e1 b5 7 ♗b3 d6 8 c3 0-0 9 h3 ♘a5 10 ♗c2 c5 11 d4 ♕c7 12 ♘bd2 ♗d7 13 ♘f1 ♖fe8

In Smyslov's variation, typified by 12...♗d7, the alternative 13...♘c4 fails to satisfy Black after 14 ♘e3 ♘xe3 15 ♗xe3 ♗e6 16 ♘d2, when White is ready for f4, as in Tal-Petrosian, USSR Ch, Riga 1958.

14 ♘e3 g6 15 dxe5 dxe5 16 ♘h2 ♖ad8 17 ♕f3 ♗e6 18 ♘hg4 ♘xg4 19 hxg4 ♕c6

The fight for the potentially strong light square d5 goes on. Black tries to cover it fully, but later experience indicated that 19...♘c4 20 ♘d5 ♗xd5 21 exd5 ♘b6 was good.

20 g5 ♘c4 21 ♘g4 ♗xg4 22 ♕xg4 f6?! *(D)*

22...♘b6 is stronger.

At this moment it may not look so important but the text-move leads to Black's pawn-formation being broken up into more islands, which is, generally speaking, unfavourable. In the course of this game Black will have to feel the consequences of his decision.

23 gxf6 ♗xf6 24 a4 ♘b6

24...♘d6 came into consideration.

25 axb5 axb5 26 ♗e3 ♖a8 27 ♖ed1 ♔h8 28 b3 ♗g7

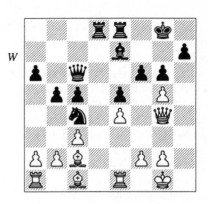

In case of 28...♖xa1 29 ♖xa1 ♖a8 Fischer intended 30 ♖xa8+ ♘xa8 31 ♕d1 to be followed by 32 ♕a1. White will keep the initiative by harassing Black's pawns.

29 ♕h4 ♗f6 30 ♗g5 ♗xg5 31 ♕xg5 ♖xa1 32 ♖xa1 ♘d7 33 ♗d1!

Great players see nuances which might otherwise pass unnoticed. The idea of exchanging the dark-squared bishops becomes clearer now. Since 33...♕xe4 does not work due to 34 ♗f3, White manages to transfer his bishop to a much more active position. With a superior bishop and healthier pawn-structure, there is no doubting White's advantage.

33...♘f6 34 ♖a7 ♕d6 35 ♗e2 ♖e7

Black must accept the punishment. 35...b4 36 cxb4 cxb4 loses to 37 ♖f7. 35...♖b8 also fails to 36 ♖f7 ♘g8 37 ♖d7. It is difficult to defend pawns on different wings, especially when you have a lame knight against a long-range bishop.

36 ♖xe7 ♕xe7 37 ♗xb5 ♔g7 38 ♗e2 ♕c7 39 ♕e3 ♕a5 40 g3 ♕a3 41 ♔g2

A quicker solution is 41 b4 cxb4 42
♕c5, but the result will be the same in
any case.

**41...♕a5 42 ♕d3 ♕b6 43 ♕c4 ♕c6
44 ♗d3 ♕b6 45 b4 cxb4 46 cxb4
♘g4 47 ♕c5 ♕xc5 48 bxc5 ♔f7 49 f4
♔e7 50 ♔f3 ♘f6 51 ♗b5 ♔e6 52
♗c4+ ♔e7 53 c6 ♘e8 54 fxe5 h6 55
♔e3 ♘c7 56 ♔d4 h5 57 ♔e3 g5 58
♗e2 h4 59 gxh4 gxh4 60 ♗c4 ♘e8 61
♔f4 ♔d8 62 ♔g4 ♔c7 63 ♗f7 ♘g7
64 ♔xh4 ♔xc6 65 ♔g5 1-0**

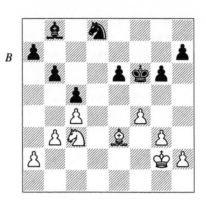

B

Smyslov – Golombek
USSR – England, London 1947
Sicilian Defence

**1 e4 c5 2 ♘c3 ♘c6 3 g3 g6 4 ♗g2
♗g7 5 d3 e6**

In this quiet variation of the Sicilian, 5...d6 is a better choice.

6 ♗e3 ♘d4 7 ♘ce2

Black's particular move-order has
allowed White this useful option.

**7...♘e7 8 c3 ♘xe2 9 ♘xe2 d6 10
0-0 0-0 11 ♕d2 ♖e8 12 d4 ♕c7 13
dxc5 dxc5 14 ♖fd1**

As a consequence of Black's inac-
curate play, White has been able to
seize the open file, although that is not
much owing to the closed nature of the
position.

**14...b6 15 ♕d6 ♕xd6 16 ♖xd6
♗a6 17 ♗f1 ♗e5 18 ♖d2 ♖ad8 19
♖ad1 ♘c6 20 f4 ♗b8 21 e5 ♖xd2 22
♖xd2 ♖d8 23 ♖xd8+ ♘xd8 24 b3
♔g7 25 c4 f6 26 exf6+ ♔xf6 27 ♘c3
♗b7 28 ♗g2 ♗xg2 29 ♔xg2** *(D)*

Passing into an endgame after a
series of exchanges, Black was able
to simplify the position, accepting a

somewhat weaker pawn-structure, broken into three units. In the following
moves he had a chance to advance the
e6-pawn and get rid of the isolated
pawn at once, but he hesitated.

**29...♘c6 30 ♔f3 ♘b4?! 31 ♗d2
♔e7?! 32 ♔e4 ♘c6**

Black's waiting moves have wors-
ened his situation. With his powerful
centralized king, more active dark-
squared bishop and superior pawn-
formation, White starts to hope he will
be able to increase his advantage.

33 ♘d1!

Since now 33...e5 can be met by 34
f5, creating a pawn-majority on the
kingside, it is the right time to transfer
the bishop to c3, from where it firmly
controls e5 as well as b4. At the same
time the knight is bound for g4 and f6
in order to provoke the advance of the
h7-pawn and further weaken Black's
pawn-formation.

33...♗d6 34 ♘f2 ♘d8

The knight is bound for f7, where it
will perform a useful role defending
the weak spots e5 and g5.

35 ♗c3 ♘f7 36 ♘g4 h5

Not bad, but not necessary either.

37 ♗f6+

This is a good intermediary move, played in order to control the g5-square.

37...♔d7 38 ♘f2 ♗c7?!

The bishop is quite a nuisance at f6 and Black would do better to chase it away by 38...♗e7. By doing so, he would control the h4-square, where the white knight shortly moves.

39 ♘d3 ♔c6 40 ♘e1!

If Black had in mind to play ...b5, he had to give up the idea, as ♘f3-h4 threatens to decide the game quickly. In comparison with some of Black's aimless moves, Smyslov's game is characterized by determination and logic.

40...♘d6+ 41 ♔d3 ♘f5 42 ♘f3 ♔d7

Black must take care of the e6-pawn now that ♘g5 is available. The weakened pawns on e6 and g6 influence his decisions more and more.

43 ♔e4

White has in mind 44 ♘e5+ ♗xe5 45 ♔xe5, when the king would penetrate via f6.

43...♘d6+ 44 ♔e3 ♘f5+ 45 ♔f2

The king is needed here to prepare a kingside advance by h3 and g4.

45...♗d6 46 h3 ♗c7 47 g4 hxg4 48 hxg4 ♘h6 49 ♔g3 *(D)*

49...♘f7?!

According to Smyslov Black could put up more resistance by 49...♔e8 50 ♗e5 ♗d8 51 ♗b8 a6 52 ♘e5 g5 although 53 ♘c6 ♗f6 54 ♗e5 keeps the advantage.

50 g5

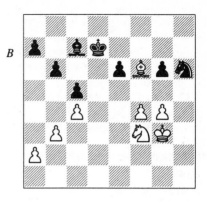

The g6-pawn is doomed and the game is lost.

50...♗d8 51 ♔g4 ♗xf6 52 gxf6 ♔d6 53 ♘e5 1-0

A memorable endgame. White was able to squeeze victory out of the minimal advantages based on his better pawn-structure and somewhat more active minor pieces.

This ending reminds me of the fact that positions with an isolated pawn in the centre can lead to difficult endings with three pawn-islands versus two. Even in the typical endgame of knight versus bishop it very often proves difficult to keep the balance, although most of these positions are drawn with correct play.

Averbakh – Matanović
USSR – Yugoslavia, Belgrade 1961
English Opening

1 c4 ♘f6 2 ♘c3 e6 3 ♘f3 c5 4 e3 d5 5 cxd5 exd5 6 d4 ♘c6 7 ♗e2 ♗e7?!

A sheer loss of time. 7...cxd4 8 ♘xd4 ♗d6 is correct, with an equal position.

8 dxc5 ♗xc5 9 0-0 0-0 10 b3 a6 11 ♘a4 ♗e7 12 ♗b2

White stands better because Black does not have enough compensation for his weak d-pawn.

12...♘e4 13 ♖c1 ♗f6 14 ♗xf6 ♘xf6 15 ♘d4 ♘e5 16 ♘c5 ♕e7 17 ♘d3 ♘xd3 18 ♕xd3 ♗e6 19 ♖c2 ♖ac8 20 ♖fc1 ♕d7 21 f3

Played in order to control the e4-square, but also, later in the endgame, g4 will be available.

21...♖xc2 22 ♕xc2 ♖c8 23 ♕xc8+ ♕xc8 24 ♖xc8+ ♗xc8 (D)

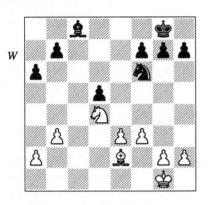

The exchange of pieces forms part of the consistent plan in such positions. White hopes that the isolated pawn will be more exposed when the material is reduced. Of course, the game still remains within the bounds of a draw, but with his weaker pawn-formation Black must work hard to prove it.

25 ♔f2 ♔f8 26 ♔e1 ♔e7 27 ♔d2 ♔d6 28 b4 ♘e8?!

Black is attracted by the possibility of transferring the knight to c7 and then to e6. He should do better to restrict White's queenside possibilities by 28...♗d7.

29 ♗d3 g6

Black's desire to deny the enemy minor pieces the f5-square is natural, but again 29...♗d7 was a better choice.

30 ♔c3 ♘c7 31 a4 b6?!

After this the a6-pawn will remain a lasting weakness in Black's pawn-structure, adding to the d5-pawn a new target.

32 a5 bxa5 33 bxa5

The weakness is fixed, and from now on one of the black pieces will be tied to the defence of it – a small but important positional victory. One should learn to enjoy these little victories, by which one accumulates small advantages in the process of realizing an advantage.

33...♔c5 34 ♘b3+ ♔d6 35 ♔b4 ♘e6 36 g3 ♘d8

The knight stands well at e6 for the moment. There is no need to remove it.

37 ♘d4 ♘c6+

With all the pawns on the squares of the white bishop, one should refrain from this exchange. It can only make things worse.

38 ♘xc6 ♔xc6 39 f4 (D)

39...f5?

The critical moment. Instead of fixing all his pawns on light squares, Black should try to put them on dark squares, avoiding a situation in which his bishop will be burdened with the impossible task of defending two or more fixed weaknesses. 39...h6 was essential, aiming at the first opportunity

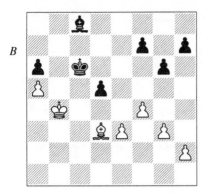

to move the kingside pawns onto dark squares. By preparing ...g5, Black could hope for salvation following a reduction of material.

40 h4 ♔d6

Black's bad luck lies in the little detail that he cannot block the position. After 40...h5 there follows 41 ♗c2 ♔d6 42 ♗a4, threatening 43 ♗e8, which decides.

41 h5 gxh5

Or 41...♗b7 42 h6 ♗c8 43 ♔c3 ♔c5 44 ♗e2 ♗b7 45 g4 fxg4 (45...♗c8 46 g5 ♗b7 47 ♗h5, etc.) 46 ♗xg4, etc.

42 ♔c3 1-0

After 42...♔c5 43 ♗f1 ♗b7 44 ♗e2 ♗c8 45 ♗d3 Black is in zugzwang and in order to prevent the penetration of the white king his best chance is 45...h6 46 ♗f1 ♗b7 47 ♗e2 ♗c8 48 ♗d3 (another inevitable zugzwang) 48...d4+ 49 exd4+ ♔d5, but 50 ♗c4+ ♔d6 51 d5 ♔c5 52 d6 ♔xd6 53 ♔d4 ♗b7 54 ♗e2 ♗c8 55 ♗d3 decides the issue. Whatever you do with your pawns is of a lasting nature. If your pawn-formation is broken into several islands, you may find it difficult to

defend such a structure, especially if there is some other disadvantageous element in the position. This time the pawns happened to be on the wrong squares and it was decisive.

We have analysed different types of endgames characterized by a broken pawn-formation. In each of them, in the circumstances of reduced material, the side having the compact pawn-structure had an advantage over the side whose pawn-formation was damaged and broken into a greater number of pawn-islands. Naturally, it took some additional elements to prevail, but the basic pawn weakness was invariably there. However, chess is not that simple. It is on many elements that we must base our judgement. Take a look at the following game.

Fischer – Euwe
Olympiad, Leipzig 1960
Caro-Kann Defence

1 e4 c6 2 d4 d5 3 exd5 cxd5 4 c4 ♘f6 5 ♘c3 ♘c6 6 ♘f3 ♗g4 7 cxd5 ♘xd5 8 ♕b3 ♗xf3 9 gxf3 e6

We now enter a forced line. Instead, 9...♘xd4? loses to 10 ♗b5+, while after the main alternative, 9...♘b6, White has ideas of d5.

10 ♕xb7 ♘xd4 11 ♗b5+ ♘xb5 12 ♕c6+ ♔e7 13 ♕xb5 ♘xc3?!

After this game we know that Black should play 13...♕d7 14 ♘xd5+ ♕xd5 15 ♕xd5 exd5, when White's advantage remains small.

14 bxc3 ♕d7 15 ♖b1! *(D)*

A glance at White's horrible pawn-structure suggests difficulties for him.

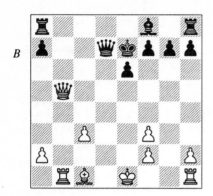

However, in spite of his four pawn-islands, the text-move seizes the initiative. White's better development and more active pieces will prove more relevant elements on which to assess this position.

15...♖d8

Better is 15...♕xb5 16 ♖xb5 ♔d6, but this is still not easy for Black because there is 17 ♖b7 f6 18 ♔e2 ♔c6 19 ♖f7 a5 20 ♗e3.

16 ♗e3 ♕xb5 17 ♖xb5 ♖d7 18 ♔e2 f6 19 ♖d1

As simple as possible: by exchanging his opponent's active pieces, White increases his advantage.

19...♖xd1

19...♖c7 does not help due to 20 ♖c5.

20 ♔xd1 ♔d7 21 ♖b8 ♔c6 22 ♗xa7 g5 23 a4 ♗g7 24 ♖b6+ ♔d5 25 ♖b7 ♗f8 26 ♖b8 ♗g7 27 ♖b5+ ♔c6 28 ♖b6+ ♔d5 29 a5 f5 (D)

29...♖a8 is not sufficient in view of 30 ♖b7 ♗f8 31 ♖xh7 ♗c5 32 ♗b6, etc.

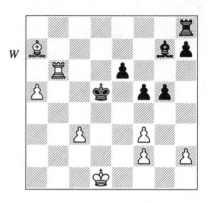

30 ♗b8 ♖c8 31 a6 ♖xc3 32 ♖b5+ ♔c4

32...♔c6 does not change the outcome due to 33 ♖a5 ♗d4 34 ♔e2, etc.

33 ♖b7 ♗d4 34 ♖c7+ ♔d3 35 ♖xc3+ ♔xc3 36 ♗e5 1-0

A short, simple game which hardly needs explanation. I include it at the end of our considerations as a warning that no rules are sacred and no maxims without exceptions.

We have been trying to learn lessons and draw logical conclusions not in order to respect them to the letter, but in order to understand them so well that we can see beyond the rules and disregard general advice. Only he who commands the laws of the chessboard to perfection can do that.

Index of Players

When a page number appears in **bold**, the named player had White.

Index of Openings